The Art of Collabora

STUDIES IN INCLUSIVE EDUCATION

Volume 32

Scope

This series addresses the many different forms of exclusion that occur in schooling across a range of international contexts and considers strategies for increasing the inclusion and success of all students. In many school jurisdictions the most reliable predictors of educational failure include poverty, Aboriginality and disability. Traditionally schools have not been pressed to deal with exclusion and failure. Failing students were blamed for their lack of attainment and were either placed in segregated educational settings or encouraged to leave and enter the unskilled labour market. The crisis in the labor market and the call by parents for the inclusion of their children in their neighborhood school has made visible the failure of schools to include all children.

Drawing from a range of researchers and educators from around the world, Studies in Inclusive Education will demonstrate the ways in which schools contribute to the failure of different student identities on the basis of gender, race, language, sexuality, disability, socio-economic status and geographic isolation. This series differs from existing work in inclusive education by expanding the focus from a narrow consideration of what has been traditionally referred to as special educational needs to understand school failure and exclusion in all its forms. Moreover, the series will consider exclusion and inclusion across all sectors of education: early years, elementary and secondary schooling, and higher education.

The Art of Collaboration

Lessons from Families of Children with Disabilities

Katharine G. Shepherd, Colby T. Kervick and Djenne-amal N. Morris

SENSE PUBLISHERS
ROTTERDAM/BOSTON/TAIPEI

A C.I.P. record for this book is available from the Library of Congress.

ISBN: 978-94-6300-822-8 (paperback)
ISBN: 978-94-6300-823-5 (hardback)
ISBN: 978-94-6300-824-2 (e-book)

Published by: Sense Publishers,
P.O. Box 21858,
3001 AW Rotterdam,
The Netherlands
https://www.sensepublishers.com/

Printed on acid-free paper

TABLE OF CONTENTS

Acknowledgements   vii

Chapter 1: Introduction and Overview   1
   Who We Are   1

Chapter 2: Exploring the Research: Historical and Legal Roots of
   Family-Professional Collaboration   9
   Parent Involvement in General Education   10
   Historical, Legal, and Theoretical Underpinnings of Parent Participation
      in Special Education   12
   From Theory and Law to Practice: Studies of Parent Involvement   18
   Chapter Summary   25

Chapter 3: Identifying a Disability   33
   Conceptualizing Disability: Naming the Process   34
   Parents' Journeys to Diagnosis   38
   Possibilities for Collaboration   47
   Chapter Summary   55

Chapter 4: Understanding Parents as Actors and Experts   61
   Becoming Experts and Actors: Key Roles of Parents   62
   Back to the Cliche: Understanding Parents as Experts   70
   Chapter Summary   79

Chapter 5: Joining Parent and Professional Knowledge   83
   The Nature of Professional Knowledge   83
   Parent Expectations of Professionals and the Program   86
   Strategies for Joining Parent and Professional Knowledge   90
   Chapter Summary   97

Chapter 6: Enhancing Collaboration   103
   What Makes It Work? Definitions and Characteristics of Collaboration
      as Identified in the Literature   103
   What Makes It Difficult? Barriers to Collaboration as Identified in the
      Literature   107
   Why Is It So Difficult? Family Perspectives on Barriers to Collaboration   108
   Chapter Summary   123

Chapter 7: Finding Voice: Promoting Advocacy, Choice, and Leadership   129

Resources and Tools for Promoting Knowledge and Advocacy   130
Tools for Promoting Choice and Family Engagement   132
Tools for Promoting Leadership and Advocacy   142
Chapter Summary   151

Chapter 8: Building Capacity for Collaboration: Nurturing Self-Efficacy,
Resiliency and Hope   159

Resiliency   160
Growth Mindset   161
Advice for the Journey to Collaboration: From Parents, for Parents   163
Advice for Professionals   167
Looking within and Beyond   171
Chapter Summary   177

Chapter 9: Conclusion   181

Clarifying the Purpose of Collaboration   182
Focusing on Human Dimensions and Relationships   183
Recognizing the Power of Formal and Informal Knowledge   183
Advocating for Improved Conditions for Collaboration   184
Incorporating Strategies and Tools Focused on Collaboration as a
Developmental and Growth-Oriented Process   185
Encouraging Families to Participate in Activities That Link Them to Others   187
Acknowledging the Need for Broader Social Change   188
Final Thoughts   188

About the Authors   189

ACKNOWLEDGEMENTS

We have many people to thank for their support in the writing of this book. First and foremost, we wish to thank the many parents and family members who took time to tell us their stories. Their words are at the center of our work and what we hope to convey. We value all that these family members have given us, including their time, recollections, energy, emotions, and willingness to share both painful and happy stories. Their contributions create the collective wisdom that we have tried to capture and share in these pages. We acknowledge the financial support we have received for our work, including funding received from the Office of Special Education in the U. S. Department of Education, the Department of Health and Human Services, the College of Education and Social Services at the University of Vermont, and the Center on Disability and Community Inclusion at the University of Vermont. Our findings are our own and should not be construed to reflect the perspectives of these organizations, but our work would not have been possible without the resources they provided in support of the multiple research studies represented in the book. Key friends and colleagues associated with a number of parent organizations have also supported this project by engaging in research efforts, adopting materials, allowing us to interview workshop and conference participants and sharing their thoughts on what we were learning along the way. Though we risk overlooking some individuals, we would especially like to thank Paula Goldberg, Executive Director of the PACER Center in Minneapolis, MN and her co-director Sharman Barrett-Davis; Anne Smith, former U. S. Department of Education employee and project director of the Parents as Collaborative Leaders Project; Tracy Luiselli of the New England Consortium of Deaf-Blind Projects; Susan LaVenture of the National Association of Parents of Children with Visual Impairments (NAPVI); the wonderful directors and staff at the Vermont Family Network; and members of the I-Team at the University of Vermont. Thanks also to our UVM colleagues who understand why this work is so important, including Michael Giangreco, Shana Haines, and George Salembier.

On a more personal note, we would like to thank the many friends and family members who have supported our combined efforts to complete this project.

Djenne wishes to thank her family of educators and activists who taught her to value the life, education, potential and diversity of all peoples. To my husband Michael: you're my rock and have held my hand on this journey. To Imani and Zakiya, who have listened endlessly to my ideas and have defined sibling resilience. And to Malik, my King, through whom I learned the true meaning of unconditional love and laughter. To Malik's village, for pushing me in front of the podium and giving me the vision to see things as they should be and doing something about it.

Colby is grateful for her sons Turner and Declan who inspire her advocacy. She wishes to acknowledge her husband Garth for his steadfast support and for modeling how to partner with families and youth to make communities stronger. Many thanks to extended family and friends who understand the importance of this ongoing work. Lastly, Colby recognizes her grandmother Shirley for believing that all people deserve a purposeful life regardless of ability.

Katie's thanks extend to her husband Bern, for his love and unwavering support and belief in her work; to daughters Hannah and Liza for their love and understanding and the many gifts they bring to their own journeys through this world; and all family, friends and colleagues who have been waiting patiently for this project to come to completion.

A debt of gratitude that cannot be fully expressed goes to Dr. Susan Brody Hasazi, Professor Emeritus at the University of Vermont and a mentor and friend who has inspired us and so many in the field who are concerned about the lives of children and adults with disabilities and their families. Susan's vision for an equitable, accessible and caring educational system that embraces parents as collaborators and leaders underlies much of what is written here. Her constant support and desire to see others succeed and carry on this work is beyond words.

INTRODUCTION AND OVERVIEW

WHO WE ARE

Three of us are writing this book: two university professors who are former special educators and one parent of a child with a disability whose profession it is to support other parents in developing their skills in leadership, advocacy and parenting a child with a disability. The idea for the book began with a question that we have encountered often throughout our collective careers: namely, *Why is it that meaningful collaboration among families and school professionals is so difficult to achieve, and what can we do to make it better?* The EHA (Education of All Handicapped Children's Act of 1975, P.L. 94-142), now known as the Individuals with Disabilities Education Act (IDEA), requires parents to participate as educational decision-makers in the processes of assessing children to determine eligibility for special education and developing Individualized Education Programs (IEPs), and guarantees parents a set of due process rights that are meant to ensure implementation of the IDEA and its associated regulations (Turnbull, Turnbull, Shank, & Smith, 2004; Yell, 2012; Yell, Rodgers, & Rodgers, 1998). Standards and ethical principles established by the Council for Exceptional Children (CEC, 2012) include a focus on parent participation and parent and professional collaboration, and special education teacher and leadership preparation programs are expected to include curriculum that aligns with these standards as well as relevant laws and regulations. The framework for collaboration among families and school professionals is thus clearly established in the law and in standards for professional practice, but, as the research presented in chapter two indicates, the rhetoric of collaboration far exceeds its reality in practice. As professionals and a parent dedicated to improving education for children with disabilities, we remain committed to exploring ways to enhance and improve family and professional collaboration in school and community settings. This book is one way of contributing to this effort.

Our Purpose

Our focus is not a new one: other authors address the issue of parent and professional collaboration, asserting that effective collaboration can result in the development of meaningful family-professional partnerships (e.g., Blue-Banning, Summers, Frankland, Nelson, & Beegle, 2004; Fialka, Feldman, & Mikus, 2012; Friend & Cook, 2013; Haines, McCart, & Turnbull, 2014; Sheehey & Sheehey, 2007;

Sileo & Prater, 2012; Staples & Diliberto, 2010; Turnbull, Turnbull, Erwin, Soodak, & Shogren, 2015). Works by these authors and others provide a solid conceptual framework for collaboration and extensive information regarding the skills and competencies that professionals need to establish and maintain effective partnership with family members. The United States Department of Education funds over 100 centers dedicated to parents of children with disabilities, and many of these organizations have taken on the work of promoting positive partnerships between families and school professionals through the development and dissemination of information and creation of multiple opportunities for parents to come together with other parents to engage in knowledge and skill development.

These and other efforts to promote collaboration persist—and yet so do stories of relationships between families and school professionals that fall far short of the intent of the law and the ideals of collaboration. Our purpose in adding to existing conversations about collaboration is to do so in a way that puts the voices of family members at the front and center of this discussion and suggests some new directions for collaboration between families and school professionals. Over the past 10 years, we have been engaged in numerous research projects focused on family-school collaboration and leadership development that have included over 100 parents of children with disabilities. These include a federally funded research project on leadership development that included data from over 60 parents of children with disabilities (Shepherd & Hasazi, 2008; Shepherd & Kervick, 2016); an intensive study of 12 families' experiences with collaboration (Kervick, 2013); two research projects focused on the use of person-centered planning processes with a total of 10 families of children with disabilities (Haines, Francis, Shepherd, Ziegler, & Mabika, in review; Shepherd, Kervick, & Salembier, 2015); and interviews with 20 parents conducted specifically for the current project. In addition to formal research, our collective experience on this topic includes engagement with hundreds of families, teachers, and education leaders through university course work, parent and professional development opportunities, direct support and advocacy for families, informal conversations, and our lived experiences as parents and teachers.

In this book, we include findings from our research and stories from Djenne's experiences as a parent, as well as quotes and lessons learned from parents and other family members whom we have listened to, worked next to, and learned from over time about what it takes to develop effective collaboration and family-professional partnership. In doing so, we seek to answer questions and provide new information about school and family collaboration from an angle that emphasizes parents' understanding of their engagement with school and other professionals, over time and across settings. We weave in relevant literature on collaboration and include ideas for special educators and other professionals to consider, but our primary purpose is to give voice to parents' perspectives in order to inform and improve collaboration. We take a strengths-based perspective in our work, focusing on the ways in which parents' stories and strategies inform our understanding about collaboration and can serve to make this a more successful, positive, mutually satisfying and productive enterprise.

Overview of the Book

Our work is organized around the themes that have emerged from our collective experience as well as our formal research on family-school collaboration. In chapter two, *Exploring the Research: Historical and Legal Roots of Family-Professional Collaboration*, we begin with a more traditional (and academic) review of the current literature on parent and family participation and collaboration, highlighting the historical and legal roots of collaboration, as well as research on what we do and do not know about this complex phenomenon and related processes. Chapters 3–8 undertake to describe the nature of parent and professional relationships and collaborative processes as they are understood by family members. Throughout these chapters, we review relevant literature and, based on the input of families, propose some new ways that parents and professionals might understand their relationship in order to promote more effective collaboration and partnership. In chapter three, *Identifying a Disability*, we discuss parents' experiences as they have learned about and come to understand that one or more of their children has a documented disability, noting that the process of diagnosis often sets the stage (in both positive and negative ways) for future relationships and interactions between families and professionals. Chapter 4, *Understanding Parents as Actors and Experts,* explores the multiple roles that parents may take on when they have a child with a disability, and the ways in which these roles contribute to their knowledge of disability and expertise as parents. In chapter five, *Joining Parent and Professional Knowledge,* we delve into the nature of professional knowledge and explore the benefits and challenges of merging parent and professional knowledge for the benefit of creating positive outcomes for children. Chapter 6, *Enhancing Collaboration,* explores the structure and interpersonal conditions that appear to foster collaboration, drawing on the parents' views of and visions for effective collaboration.

Having established the basic framework for collaboration, we then explore tools and resources that can support families in finding their voice through opportunities for increased advocacy and leadership. To this end, chapter seven, *Finding Voice: Promoting Choice, Advocacy and Leadership,* describes tools that can be used to support parents in expressing their voices, becoming advocates, and finding opportunities for leadership. These include use of the Making Action Plans, or MAPS strategy (Forest & Lusthaus, 1987; Shepherd, Kervick, & Salembier, 2015; Vandercook, York, & Forest, 1989) and a project known as Parents as Collaborative Leaders (Morris & Shepherd, 2011; Shepherd & Hasazi, 2008; Shepherd & Kervick, 2016). Chapter 8, *Building Capacity: Nurturing Self-Efficacy, Resiliency and Hope* focuses on frameworks and approaches that can support families and professionals in building increased capacity for collaboration. We highlight family's stories of their journeys over time and the factors that have supported them in maintaining a sense of hope and resilience. Finally, we propose new directions in chapter nine, *Re-defining and Re-envisioning Collaboration,* in the hopes of offering new ways of thinking and acting to promote effective collaboration among families, professionals, and community members.

Guiding Assumptions and Frameworks

Over time, our collective research and experiences with families has helped us to clarify our assumptions and beliefs and to identify frameworks supporting these assumptions. We offer these here, both as a way to clarify our personal beliefs about collaboration and to suggest guiding principles that may be helpful to others. Chapter 9 elaborates on these assumptions in light of what we have learned from parents, but we present them here in the interest of being explicit about the perspectives that guide our work.

1. *The skills and processes that contribute to successful collaboration and family-school partnerships need to be learned and practiced.* We assume that both parents and professionals need opportunities to be engaged in developing their individual skills and bringing those to the "collaborative table." Recognition of collaboration as a learned skill emphasizes the need for both parents and professionals to be intentional about understanding what it is and engaging in opportunities for skill development. At the same time, we acknowledge that mastery of these skills will come more easily for some than others, and that supports may need to be put into place for those who have had fewer opportunities for skill development.

2. *Collaboration is a developmental process requiring a strengths-based and growth-oriented view on the part of both parents and professionals.* If we assume that collaborative skills need to be learned by individuals, then it follows that groups of people engaged in collaboration will need time to develop as a team. They will also need to see the possibility for collaboration, even during difficult times. The literature on stages of group development (e.g., Wheelan, 2016), growth mindset (Dweck, 2006), and the principle of "least dangerous assumption" (Jorgenson, 2005) provide useful frameworks for helping families and professionals to adopt strengths-based and growth-oriented views of one another and the collaborative process.

3. *Effective collaboration places a family's voice and values at the center of the process, balancing them with the need to consider clinical judgment, research-based practices, and legal and institutional constraints that are part of the fabric of school life.* As described in chapters four and five, we see a need for parents and professionals to develop a deeper understanding of the knowledge and beliefs that each brings to the table and to use the collaborative process as

a way to express their ideas, identify common perspectives, and work through potential differences of opinion. Parents' voices need to be the drivers of the conversation, but effective collaboration requires both sides to practice empathy, deep listening, and openness.

4. *The lives of families of children with disabilities extend well beyond school and may be quite complex.* Time and time again, we have heard families talk about the complex demands and multi-faceted nature of their lives. Most express a strong desire to have school professionals understand that although they value education, school is not at the center of their worlds. In addition, we acknowledge that the capacity for collaboration may vary among families and professionals and that certain conditions in school and society may make it more difficult to achieve in some situations than others. A number of our participating families remind us that collaboration may be an idealized state; when defined as a set of skills and practices that are learned over time and mediated by various relationships and contexts, collaboration may be best viewed as something we strive for but may not always achieve.

Given these assumptions, our audience for the book includes family members as well as in-place and aspiring professionals. We view the book as a tool for giving voice to family perspectives and for sharing ideas and approaches that can be discussed by parents and other family members, school professionals, pre-service education professionals: possibly separately, but, more ideally, in settings that include all of the aforementioned. We conclude each chapter with a set of discussion questions and activities that can aid parents, aspiring teachers and leaders, support personnel and other professionals in cultivating their own collaborative approaches and skills. Throughout, our intent is to expand our collective ideas about collaboration, to understand what holds us back from collaborating with one another, and to identify ways to improve upon our skills for realizing the vision of working together to create more positive outcomes for all of us.

A Note on Language

Throughout the book, we use pseudonyms to refer to individual parents and family members. In some of our research projects, parents chose their own pseudonyms; in others, pseudonyms were assigned as part of the data analysis process. Pseudonyms are also used when we refer to parents who are known to us but were not official research participants, with the exception of Djenne and her husband Michael, who speak in their own voices in the book about their experiences as parents of Malik, and Clara Berg, a well-known leader in the parent advocacy world. By using pseudonyms, we intend to maintain the confidentiality of participants who describe a range of experiences, including some that were painful or difficult. We use "person-first" language to demonstrate our focus on people, rather than the conditions of disability that they experience, and, to the greatest extent possible, utilize language that maintains gender neutrality. We break this rule when the person's gender is relevant to their experience (e.g., fathers talking about their experiences as compared to the experiences of their wives or partners). Finally, we use the terms "parent" and "family" (and their plural forms) somewhat interchangeably. There are times when the use of the term "parent" is the appropriate reference point for the topic being discussed or the story being told; at other times, we use the term "family" to reflect the diversity that exists in families. We recognize that caregivers and advocates of children and youth with disabilities may not always be biological parents and/or may be members of an extended family structure, and that the composition of families varies widely.

Research Methods and Limitations

We have chosen not to go into great detail regarding the research methods used to gather data presented in this book, as the methods used to obtain information are described elsewhere in individual articles and chapters associated with each of the projects included in this collective work (i.e., Salembier & Furney, 1994; Salembier & Furney, 1997; Shepherd & Hasazi, 2008; Shepherd & Kervick, 2016; Shepherd, Kervick, & Salembier, 2015). Taken together, however, it can be said that each of the studies has used qualitative and/or mixed methods approaches to data collection and analysis (e.g., Creswell, 2009; Glesne, 2015), including individual interviews with parents, focus groups, surveys, and document reviews. In a few instances (i.e., Morris & Shepherd, 2011; Shepherd & Hasazi, 2008; Shepherd & Kervick, 2016), data were collected as part of professional development opportunities for parents that included follow-up research activities; in most other cases, data were collected through formal research studies, including studies of the experiences of individual parents and case studies of various approaches used to promote family and professional collaboration. Analyses of the data collected across projects included coding of qualitative data, summaries of quantitative data collected through surveys, and thematic analyses of all data. The majority of the data were analyzed by at least two people, with coding and theme development undergoing checks for inter-rater reliability. The exception to this is the data obtained through the Kervick (2013) study, which were coded and analyzed by the author in consultation with persons serving as "critical friends." Data obtained through interviews and focus groups were, in most cases, subjected to checks for accuracy by participants.

Exceptions to use of these research procedures include Djenne's personal story, which is presented in a narrative format, and the collective points of view we offer as a result of our personal and professional experiences. Use of the pronoun "we" signals our collective ideas as authors. Throughout, we take care to distinguish between ideas gleaned from the literature, ideas and experiences as expressed by parents in our own research, Djenne's personal story, and our collective thoughts on various issues.

Participants.   The over 100 parents who participated in the research leading up to this book represent diverse factors including participants' ages, socioeconomic and cultural backgrounds, and age and disability categories of their child/children with a disability. Additionally, participants represent diversity with respect to their previous experience with collaboration and engagement with special education processes (ranging from little to a great deal), their perceived skills in collaboration (ranging from emerging to well-defined skill sets), and perceptions of the collaborative processes (including both positive and negative experiences). It is important to note that sampling for each of the individual research studies generally included snowball and/or convenience sampling techniques (Glesne, 2015) in which we reached out to schools, community and parent organizations and other networks to locate parents who might be interested in participating in our work. Across all of the studies, we attempted to recruit as diverse a sample as possible, and in our most recent group of 20 parents, we oversampled parents from diverse cultural, ethnic and socioeconomic backgrounds so as to further diversify our pool of participants.

Limitations.   The primary limitation of our work lies with our sampling procedures. We believe that our sample of parents represents a wide range of views, backgrounds, and experiences, but it is not a representative sample. As such, while the findings and conclusions we present represent a rather large and diverse set of voices, they cannot be generalized or claimed to represent the voices of all parents and families of children with disabilities. In particular, we acknowledge that our sample contains only a handful of parents whose primary language was other than English and/or were recent arrivals to this country. Other underrepresented voices include parents who have been generally reluctant to share their stories, and those who may have been very inexperienced with collaboration and/or the most disenfranchised from schools. This group of parents is one we hope to reach out to in future studies.

REFERENCES

Blue-Banning, M., Summers, J. A., Franklin, H. C., Nelson, L. L., & Beegle, G. (2004). Dimensions of family and professional partnerships: Constructive guidelines for collaboration. *Exceptional Children, 70*, 167–184.

Council for Exceptional Children. (2012). *Council for exceptional children standards for evidence-based practices in special education.* Arlington, VA: Council for Exceptional Children.

Creswell, J. W. (2009). *Research design: Qualitative, quantitative and mixed methods approaches.* Los Angeles, CA: Sage.

Dweck, C. S. (2006). *Mindset: The new psychology of success.* New York, NY: Random House.

Education for all Handicapped Children's Act of 1979 § 1401 *et seq.*

Fialka, J. M., Feldman, A. K., & Mikus, K. C. (2012). *Parents and professionals partnering for children with disabilities: A dance that matters.* Thousand Oaks, CA: Corwin.

Forest, M., & Lusthaus, E. (1987). The kaleidoscope: Challenge to the cascade. In M. Forest (Ed.), *More education/integration* (pp. 1–16). Downsview, Ontario, CA: G. Allan Roeher Institute.

Friend, M., & Cook, L. (2013). *Interactions: Collaboration skills for school professionals* (7th ed.). Boston, MA: Pearson.

Glesne, C. (2015). *Becoming qualitative researchers: An introduction* (4th ed.,). Boston, MA: Pearson.

Haines, S. J., McCart, A., & Turnbull, A. P. (2013). Family engagement within early childhood response to intervention. In V. Buysse & E. Peisner-Feinberg (Eds.), *Handbook on Response to Intervention (RTI) in early childhood* (pp. 313–324). New York, NY: Brookes.

Haines, S. J., Francis, G. L., Shepherd, K. G., Zeigler, M., & Mabika, G. (in review). *MAPS for the future: Using person-centered planning with students from refugee families.* Manuscript in review.

Jorgenson, C. (2005). The least dangerous assumption: A challenge to create a new paradigm. *Disability Solutions, 6*(3), 1–15.

Kervick, C. T. (2013). *Constructing a seat at the table: Parents' perceptions of collaboration with schools* (Unpublished doctoral dissertation). University of Vermont, Burlington, VT.

Morris, D. A., & Shepherd, K. G. (2011). *Parent leadership institute.* Boston, MA: Unpublished Curriculum.

Salembier, G., & Furney, K. S. (1994). Promoting self-advocacy and family participation in IEP and transition planning. *Journal for Vocational Special Needs Education, 17*(1), 12–17.

Salembier, G., & Furney, K. S. (1997). Facilitating participation: Parents' perceptions of their involvement in the IEP/transition planning process. *Career Development for Exceptional Individuals, 20*(1), 29–42.

Sheehey, P. H., & Sheehey, P. E. (2007). Elements for successful parent-professional collaboration: The fundamental things apply as time goes by. *TEACHING Exceptional Children Plus, 4*(2). Retrieved from http://escholarship.bc.edu/education/tecplus/vol4/iss2/art3

Shepherd, K., & Hasazi, S. (2008). *Parents as collaborative leaders: Ten modules for supporting the development of leadership skills.* Web-based curriculum modules. Retrieved from http://www.uvm.edu/~pcl/index.php

Shepherd, K. G., & Kervick, C. T. (2016). Enhancing collaborative leadership among parents of children with disabilities: New directions for policy and practice. *Journal of Disability Policy Studies, 27*(1), 32–42. doi:10.1177/1044207315576081

Shepherd, K. G., Kervick, C. T., & Salembier, G. (2015). Person-centered planning: Tools for promoting employment, self-direction and independence among persons with intellectual disabilities. In American Association on Intellectual and Developmental Disabilities (Ed.), *Way leads on to way: Employment of people with intellectual and developmental disabilities* (pp. 299–320). Washington, DC: American Association on Intellectual and Developmental Disabilities.

Shepherd, K., Hasazi, S. B., Kucij, D., Brick, B., & Goldberg, P. (2007). *Parents as collaborative leaders: Improving outcomes for children with disabilities. Participant manual.* Minneapolis, MN: PACER Center.

Sileo, N. M., & Prater, M. A. (2012). *Working with families of children with special needs: Family and professional partnerships and roles.* Boston, MA: Pearson.

Staples, K. E., & Diliberto, J. A. (2010). Guidelines for successful parent involvement: Working wtih parents of students with disabilities. *TEACHING Exceptional Children, 42*(6), 58–63.

Turnbull, A., Turnbull, R., Erwin, E. J., Soodak, L. C., & Shogren, K. A. (2015). *Families, professionals, and exceptionality: Positive outcomes through partnerships and trust* (7th ed.). Boston, MA: Pearson.

Turnbull, R., Turnbull, A., Shank, M., & Smith, S. J. (2004). *Exceptional lives: Special education in today's schools* (4th ed.). Upper Saddle River, NJ: Merrill Prentice Hall.

Vandercook, T., York, J., & Forest, M. (1989). The McGill Action Planning System (MAPS): A strategy for building the vision. *Journal of the Association for Persons with Severe Handicaps, 14,* 205–215.

Wheelan, S. (2016). *Creating effective teams: A guide for members and leaders* (5th ed.). Thousand Oaks, CA: Sage.

Yell, M. L. (2012). *The law and special education* (3rd ed.). Upper Saddle River, NJ: Pearson.

Yell, M. L., Rogers, D., & Lodge Rodgers, E. (1998). The legal history of special education: What a long strange trip it's been. *Remedial and Special Education, 19*(4), 219–229.

EXPLORING THE RESEARCH

Historical and Legal Roots of Family-Professional Collaboration

Almost 30 years of research and experience has demonstrated that the education of children with disabilities can be made more effective by... strengthening the role and responsibility or parents and ensuring that families... have meaningful opportunities to participate in the education of their children at school and at home.

(IDEIA, 2004)

The general idea that parents and school professionals should work together to improve the education of children has a great deal of history and can be thought of as a broad topic that applies to both general and special education. In special education, however, this important concept can be traced to a distinct set of events and legal precedents. Parent involvement is a key principle of special education with roots in the field's development, laws, practices, and overall goal to meet the needs of all children and youth with disabilities. Following years of advocacy by parents and key Supreme Court cases affirming the right of children and youth with disabilities to receive a free and appropriate public education (Yell, 2012; Yell, Rodgers, & Rodgers, 1998), the United States Congress asserted its belief in the importance of parent participation in the passage of the Education of All Handicapped Children's Act of 1975 (EHA, P.L. 94-142), the original federal law that established the right of children with disabilities to attend public schools at no cost. Over the years, the law has been re-authorized, expanded, and re-named as the Individuals with Disabilities Education Act (IDEA, 1990) and Individuals with Disabilities Education Improvement Act (IDEIA, 2004) and has grown to include new provisions; however, these changes have not significantly altered the overall intent of the law with respect to parent participation. In fact, many authors claim that re-authorization of the law and its alignment in 2001 with the No Child Left Behind Act (NCBLA, 2001) has re-affirmed the federal government's commitment to the importance of parents as educational partners and decision-makers in improving outcomes for students with disabilities (Turnbull, 2005; Turnbull, Turnbull, Erwin, Soodak, & Shogren, 2011; Yell, 2012).

Although the literature has identified numerous benefits of parent participation in various aspects of the special education process—including special education assessment and the development of Individualized Education Programs (IEP) (Smith, 1990; Turnbull, Turnbull, & Wheat, 1982) – theoretical analyses and applied research suggest that the realities of participation generally fall far short of the IDEA's vision of parents as true partners in planning (Furney & Salembier, 2000; Harry, 1992a, 1992b, 2008; Shepherd, Giangreco, & Cook, 2013; Turnbull et al., 2011). In other words, although the law implies that collaboration will lead to more effective family-professional partnerships and our underlying assumptions about the benefits of collaboration remain essentially unchanged, there are many parents and family members who have not found their experiences with schools to be collaborative or positive. Teachers, too, continue to identify challenges within the special education process, including their ability to create and sustain meaningful relationships with all families. Throughout, the need continues to explore and improve upon practices that support positive interactions and collaboration between parents and school professionals.

In this chapter, we first review the legal and theoretical justification for parental involvement in their children's schooling. We examine this both in education in general and more specifically, in the context of special education identification and IEP development. We define how the terms "parent-professional collaboration" and "family-professional partnership" both relate to and extend the legal definitions of involvement as expressed through the IDEA. Second, we review the literature on observed levels of parent involvement and the roadblocks that stand in the way of higher levels of engagement and collaboration, particularly for families from diverse cultural and linguistic backgrounds. We conclude with a review of the literature that describes how collaboration might and ought to occur among families and professionals and some of the strategies that have been used to create enhanced partnerships.

PARENT INVOLVEMENT IN GENERAL EDUCATION

Although it is beyond the scope of this book to give full attention to the issue of parent involvement in both general and special education, it may be helpful to consider the ways in which the participation of parents of children with disabilities in special education processes links to broader discussions about parent involvement in general education. Thus, we begin our discussion with a brief overview of parent involvement in education as a whole, noting the ways in which this history relates to developments in special education. Education historians remind us that education in the United States was initially a family matter, with responsibility eventually shifting from families in an agrarian society (Kaestle, 2001) to schools and professionals by the middle of the 20th century (Cutler, 2000). As we moved from a society that educated children in the home to one that educated children in "the schoolhouse," questions emerged about whose role it was to ensure a high quality education for all.

In many ways, the increasingly bureaucratic and professionalized nature of schools initially acted as a force that discouraged family involvement in schooling (Henry, 1996). From about 1950 to 1990, public schools became more institutionalized and structured. Small, local schools were often replaced by larger consolidated schools. Teacher preparation programs expanded, and the profession of teaching became more specialized as schools added special education teachers, mathematics specialists, literacy specialists, school counselors, etc. (Epstein, 2010). Increasingly, many parents viewed themselves as having a lesser role in the task of educating their children. However, by the 1990s, researchers and practitioners began to promote parent involvement as a strategy for improving public schools and increasing student achievement, attendance, and attitudes (Epstein, 2010; Henderson & Mapp, 2002). The importance of parent involvement began to be addressed more explicitly in general education policy and practice, with advocates for school reform calling for the need to ensure that parents engage in leadership opportunities at the school, community, and policy levels (Epstein, 2010; Henderson, Jacob, Kernan-Schloss, & Raimondo, 2004). For example, the NCLBA requires schools to work with parents to develop policies for parental involvement (National Coalition for Parent Involvement in Education (NCPIE), 2004), and schools receiving federal Title I funds at the school wide level are required to expend 1% of those funds to promote parent-teacher collaboration around student performance (Henderson et al., 2004).

As efforts to increase parent involvement increased, research on the relationship between increased family involvement in general education and improved student outcomes also began to emerge, with somewhat mixed results. A relatively large body of literature supports a connection between parent involvement and student performance, with some studies showing that students whose parents are more engaged with school show higher academic and behavioral achievement (Ferguson, 2008; Hattie, 2009; Henderson & Mapp, 2002; Leithwood, 2010), improved attendance rates, and higher aspirations for post-secondary education (Jeynes, 2007). Some scholars in fact began to see engagement with families and the community as a key role of principals and other school leaders, noting that leaders who pay more attention to supporting families and increasing family involvement in school activities are more likely to see increased student achievement and outcomes than leaders who ignore this important aspect of education (Leithwood, 2010; Leithwood, Patten, & Janzi, 2010).

Other researchers, however, have cautioned that differences in the definition of parent participation and challenges related to study designs limit the degree to which a clear link between parent involvement and student achievement can be firmly established (Mattingly, Prislin, McKenzie, Rodriguez, & Kayzar, 2002; White, Taylor, & Moss, 1992). Few studies, for example, have been fully representative of families from diverse cultural and linguistic backgrounds; as such, it is important to be cautious about assuming that the claims we make about parent participation apply to all families. Similarly, the term "parent participation" means different things to different people and may well be affected by the varied needs and circumstances of families. For example, some researchers note that families' socioeconomic status and employment conditions may make it difficult for them to fully engage with schools (Salembier & Furney, 1997; Overton, 2005). Definitions of parent participation that focus on only a few factors (e.g., attendance at school functions, amount of time spent on homework with children) assume a level of access, education, and feasibility that may exclude certain families. As such, we may be at risk of setting a standard for participation that is not inclusive of all families, and in turn, may not be able to accurately assess the relationship between participation and increased student achievement. Still, in spite of the fact that there is not full agreement that increased parent involvement leads to higher achievement for all students, most researchers agree that efforts to promote increased parent involvement are important and necessitate that schools become intentional and creative about providing multiple opportunities for parents of all backgrounds to engage with their schools (Epstein, 2010; Henderson et al., 2004).

Interestingly, the body of literature describing the importance of encouraging family involvement in school does not tend to distinguish between involving parents of children with disabilities from parents of typically developing children. On the one hand, the lack of explicit discussion of parents of children with disabilities in the general literature may be considered to be a non-issue, in the sense that it implies that involvement benefits all families and children. On the other hand, it may also be considered as an omission, in that those who are more acquainted with the general education literature may overlook the additional considerations and barriers that are faced by many parents of children with disabilities. Going forward, it seems important to examine the ways in which research on parent involvement in the context of general education and research on parent involvement in the context of special education can be joined together to inform one another and to create a more inclusive and holistic approach to the topic.

HISTORICAL, LEGAL, AND THEORETICAL UNDERPINNINGS OF PARENT PARTICIPATION IN SPECIAL EDUCATION

Parent Participation Prior to the EHA

As described in the introduction, the concept of family and professional collaboration has been defined over time and embraced in policy and practice in the United States. Historically, the roles of parents of children and adults with disabilities have been viewed in a variety of ways, each of which has influenced expectations for parent participation in educational planning. In times when we have viewed people with disabilities in a more negative light, families have tended to be blamed for their children's disabilities and their participation has not been seen to be valuable. The eugenics movement of the late 1800s and early 1900s, for example, contributed to a socially constructed notion of individuals with disabilities as deviant and potentially dangerous individuals (Turnbull et al., 2011). Societal responses to the perceived "problem" of disability, such as widespread institutionalization of children with disabilities, typically removed parents from decision-making roles and reinforced the notion that professionals were more knowledgeable and better able to determine the futures of children with disabilities than were their parents.

Beliefs about the roles of parents of children with disabilities began to shift during the 1940s to 1970s as a growing number of parents expressed their dissatisfaction and advocated for changes in the residential and educational services available at the time (Yell et al.,1998). During this time, the voices of parents of children with disabilities were expressed at the local, regional, and national levels and gained new attention from policymakers and educational leaders. Parents began to form national level advocacy groups, typically organized around the needs of children with specific disabilities and their families (Turnbull et al., 2011). These included the National Association for Retarded Citizens (now known as the ARC), formed in 1950 by a small group of families with children with intellectual disabilities (www.thearc.org); the National Society for Autistic Children, founded in 1965 on behalf of children and families with autism and now known as the Autism Society (www.autism-society.org); and the Association for Children with Learning Disabilities, established in 1964 by parents to serve the needs of children with learning disabilities and now known as the Learning Disabilities Association of America (www.ldaamerica.org). Along with others, each of these organizations served as networks of support for families through which they could share ideas and assist each other in raising a child with a disability, as well as advocate at state and national levels for needed changes in schools and communities (Turnbull et al., 2011).

By the 1960s, the work of these individual organizations became more organized and aligned with the principles of the national Civil Rights movement, including the principles of de-segregation and equal opportunity in education and other arenas. Parents and advocates drew on the outcomes of the landmark Supreme Court decision in the *Brown v. Board of Education* (1954) case (i.e., that schools segregated on the basis of race did not afford an equal educational opportunity for all students) to argue that students with disabilities who were not being included in public schools were also being denied an equal opportunity under the U.S. Constitution (Yell, 2012). Several high profile cases applied the legal reasoning used in *Brown v. Board of Education* to establish the rights of children with disabilities in educational settings (Kativannis, Yell, & Bradley, 2001; Yell et al., 1998). These included the *Pennsylvania Association for Retarded Citizens v. Commonwealth of Pennsylvania* (1972) case argued at the U.S. District court level and resulting in a consent decree establishing the right of children with mental retardation to receive a free and appropriate public education, and the subsequent Supreme Court case, *Mills v. District of Columbia* case (1972), a class action suit that further established the rights of children with a variety of disabilities to receive a public education at no cost.

Provisions for Parent Participation in the EHA/IDEA

In fact, the efforts of parents, disability advocacy organizations, legislators, and the courts to bring attention to exclusionary and discriminatory practices in public schools led to changes in federal policies and funding, culminating in passage in

13

1975 of the Education of All Handicapped Children's Act (EHCA or EHA), now known as the Individuals with Disabilities Education Act or IDEA (Kativannis et al., 2001; Yell et al., 1998). No longer were children with disabilities denied access to public schooling. Parent advocacy and legal pressure had yielded a groundbreaking piece of legislation, which bestowed the right to a free appropriate public education for their children (Martin, 2013).

The EHA outlined a basic structure for the provision of special education services to children with disabilities. In practice, this meant that children with disabilities were entitled to special education and related services at no cost to the family. Educational goals and services were delivered through an IEP for children from birth through age 21 (Kativannis et al., 2001), with a strong preference given to education provided in general education settings including same-aged students with and without disabilities. Six principles articulated through the basic structure of the law laid the framework that established the ethos and legal requirements of special education that remain intact today. As outlined by Turnbull, Turnbull and Wehmeyer (2010), these principles included:

Zero Reject: All children have a right to attend public school.
Non-Discriminatory Evaluation: All testing for special education should be done using valid and non-discriminatory instruments that are administered in the child's native language so as to prevent discrimination or bias.
Appropriate Public Education: All children will have an Individualized Education Program (IEP) that serves as a legal document outlining the special education and related services that will be provided to meet their annual goals.
Least Restrictive Environment: All children have the right to be educated to the maximum extent possible with non-disabled peers in the general education setting, with justification required for all services delivered outside of the classroom.
Parent and Student Participation: Parents have the right to participate in educational decision-making through the IEP process and provide consent for evaluation leading to the initial identification of a disability and provision of services. Beginning at the age of 16, students are also considered members of IEP teams.
Due Process: All parents have the right to mediation or due process to resolve disputes with schools regarding decisions made about their child's IEP, evaluation outcomes, and other decision points covered under provisions of the IDEA (pp. 12–19).

The EHA's principles of parent and student participation and due process were critical in framing the nature of parent participation. The law required that parents participate as members of the decision-making team responsible for each child's educational program. These protections included the right to access all educational records, provision of informed consent for any educational testing, prior written notice for proposed changes in educational placements, a right to attend all meetings about their child and the right to a hearing to resolve disputes (Fischer & Schimmel, 1978; NICHCY, 2009). Accordingly, not only were parents given the right to make educational decisions regarding their child's program, but they also had the legal right to provide oversight on its implementation (Turnbull et al., 2011). These rights are critical to the provision of special education; without them, it is difficult to imagine how parents of children with disabilities can achieve meaningful participation in education decision-making and experience realization of the intent of IDEA. In fact, Bateman and Linden (2006) underscore the critical nature of the parent participation principle of IDEA, noting that failure to allow full and equal parent participation can lead to a legal determination that schools have denied a student's right to a free and appropriate public education (FAPE).

Subsequent reauthorizations. The three reauthorizations of EHA occurring in 1990, 1997, and 2004 have brought several changes to the original law but have maintained the principles of parent participation and due process, particularly at different developmental milestones in a child's life. In 1990, the EHA was reauthorized as the Individuals with Disabilities Education Act (IDEA), changing its name to reflect "person first" language and ethos (Yell et al., 1998). Part C of IDEA, enacted in 1986, mandated that services for children from birth to three be delivered through an Individual Family Services Plan (IFSP) that relies heavily on family input to identify the type and extent of special education and related services to be provided to the child (Turnbull et al., 2011). IFSP services may be delivered in a variety of settings, including families' homes and community settings; by definition, the design and delivery of these types of service require a great deal of parent participation and input.

IDEA 1990 reaffirmed the importance of parent and student participation by mandating transition planning for students leaving PK – 12 education and entering into adult life (Furney & Salembier, 2000; Hasazi, DeStefano, & Furney, 1999). The transition mandates required students' IEPs to include statements regarding transition planning by (at least) the time of the student's 16th birthday, stipulating that transition goals needed to be developed based on a student's needs, preferences, and interests. The assumption was that although some students would be able to direct the development of their transition plans, family input would remain critical in many instances. For example, students with limited expressive communication skills might need their parents to assist in articulating preferences and interests. Students who are more easily included in transition planning need to be encouraged to express their hopes and dreams; however, for students with limited skills in communication and language, conversations about their futures often require the input of parents and other family members (Salembier & Furney, 1997; Shepherd, Giangreco, & Cook, 2013). As discussed later in this chapter, considerations of families' cultural and linguistic backgrounds are critical to successful school and family partnerships, throughout a child's school career and especially in the context of transition planning (Blue-Banning et al., 2004; Harry, 2008).

Elementary and Secondary School Act (ESEA). Finally, it is important to note that the ESEA, originally passed in 1965 under President Lyndon B. Johnson as a way of improving educational opportunities for students in grades K-12, has become increasingly intertwined with the provisions of IDEA. Title I of the ESEA includes funding for programs serving students from lower socioeconomic backgrounds and while Title I funds were separate from funds for students with disabilities, the general intent to provide more opportunities for underserved children was similar in both laws. Over its 50-year history and various reauthorizations, the ESEA has become increasingly focused not only on increased opportunities, but higher standards and increased accountability for students' performance in the general education curriculum.

An official link to students with disabilities occurred with ESEA's reauthorization in 2001 as the No Child Left Behind Act (NCLBA), which required students with disabilities to be included in annual testing in reading, writing, and mathematics in grades 3–8 and once in high school (Leko, Brownell, Sindelar, & Kiely, 2015; Turnbull, 2005). The alignment of NCLBA and IDEA, along with NCLBA's requirement for schools to disaggregate and report testing results in a number of categories, including students with disabilities, has turned the IDEA's original focus on access to education for students with disabilities to a focus on increased accountability for the educational outcomes of these students. Turnbull (2005) asserts that the focus on improved performance implies an increased sense of personal responsibility among students with disabilities and their parents; as such, it raises the ante on parent and student participation in IEP planning. The most recent reauthorization of ESEA in 2015—the Every Student Succeeds Act (ESSA, S.1177, 2015) – retains the NCLBA's focus on accountability, while transferring authority for decision-making about testing to the states (White House Report, 2015). Students with disabilities will still be included in annual testing, but states now have greater authority in determining what percentages of students will be involved in alternate testing. These and related changes in state policy may in turn necessitate increased involvement on the part of parents with respect to decisions about their child's participation in annual testing or alternate forms of testing.

Theoretical underpinnings. Along with these historical events and developments within federal legislation, it is important to recognize the theoretical and attitudinal underpinnings of parent involvement and participation over time. The original definition of parent involvement as specified in the EHA drew on sociological theories present in the 1970s that attributed differences in achievement and social success to differences in opportunity (Foster, Berger, & McLean, 1991). This view proposed that parents who were empowered to take an active role in educational decision-making would be more likely to obtain services for their children than parents who were not similarly involved. Moreover, the parent participation principle of the EHA attempted to correct previous practices—such as the exclusion of children with disabilities and discriminatory assessment procedures—by giving parents a role that would hold professionals accountable for implementing IEP services (Turnbull, Turnbull, & Wheat, 1982). The purported benefits of parent participation were also connected to the underlying assumption that parents who were active participants in IEP planning would contribute to the development of educational plans with a high likelihood of success (Smith, 1990). The IEP planning process has been characterized as a constructive way for parents to gain knowledge of the school setting, for teachers to gain knowledge of students and their home environments, and for the IEP team to create a mutual understanding that will lead to mutually agreed upon goals.

Subtle shifts in thinking about the definition and meaning of parent participation emerged in the 1980s, as parents, researchers, and practitioners became more convinced that what had previously been described as parent "involvement" needed to be expanded to include a focus on parent choices and voices. Researchers and professionals began to place more emphasis on the need for IEP and transition planning to result in an increased sense of empowerment for parents and a related increase in skills in self-advocacy and self-determination for students with disabilities (Meadan, Shelden, Appel, & DeGrazia, 2010; Turnbull, Zuna, Hong, Hu, & Kyzar, 2010; Wells & Sheehey, 2012).

Self- advocacy, defined as the ability to express one's needs and preferences, is promoted for students when they are given opportunities to articulate their wishes and needs during the IEP and transition planning processes. Self-determination, defined as the ability to identify desired outcomes for one's own future, is furthered when a student's IEP goals, objectives, and related activities are built upon students' expressed needs and wishes (Miller, Lombard, & Corbey, 2007; Wehmeyer & Webb, 2011). Similarly, more focus was placed on the need for parents to gain a sense of empowerment through educational planning and decision-making. The term "person-centered planning" (also known to some as personal futures planning) was also introduced at this time, describing processes and strategies that allow persons with a disability, family members, and friends to participate in an opportunity to share information about the individual with disabilities for the purpose of creating a profile of the person's strengths, dreams, challenges, goals and needs that will result in a long-term vision (Wells & Sheehey, 2012). Person centered planning was conceptualized as a reaction to traditional planning meetings that tended to be dominated by professionals (Meadan et al., 2010; Mount & Zwernik, 1988). In creating a student and family focus, person centered planning shifted the balance of power away from professionals and created an environment more conducive to building trust, respect, communication, and positive and collaborative relationships among students, parents, teachers, service providers, and others (Furney & Salembier, 2000; Geenan, Powers, & Lopez-Vasquez, 2001; Shepherd et al., 2015).

These more expanded notions of participation included recognition that parents' perspectives are critical for systems level change (Barenok & Wieck, 1998; Henderson et al., 2004; Jeppson & Thomas, 1995; Koroloff, Hunter, & Gordon, 1995; Searcy, Lee-Lawson, & Trombino, 1995). Jeppson and Thomas noted that families can advocate for system and programmatic changes in ways that professionals cannot. Parents and family members bring "hard won" expertise to the table: wisdom gained from experience, creative problem solving abilities, and their passion for improvement (Barenok & Wieck, 1998; Libertoff, Maynard, Pandina, & Yuan, 1998). Further, their participation is essential to the development of effective policies and practice. As noted by Jeppson and Thomas, family participation in policy and program development and evaluation is a necessary condition of an effective system of care, because without it, systems cannot respond to actual needs of those it intends to serve. Popper (1994) described another benefit as the opportunity for parents to develop a public identity. "(Parents) become known not just as 'John's or Jane's parents,' but as parents knowledgeable about representing a particular disability or health condition or service needed" (Popper, 1994, p. 1). In this role, parents contribute their knowledge and skills and may often serve in advocacy roles for other families.

FROM THEORY AND LAW TO PRACTICE:
STUDIES OF PARENT INVOLVEMENT

Early Studies of Parent Participation

The historical and theoretical underpinnings of parent participation seem almost self-evident at this time; however, the research is clear about the fact that the IDEA's legal provisions did not translate into immediate changes in educational practices or the actual roles of parents. The literature on parent participation may be best viewed through two time periods: an early set of studies following passage of the EHA that tended to paint a negative picture of parents and their participation, and a later set of studies that re-examined and challenged some of the findings and assumptions asserted through the early research (Furney & Salembier, 2000).

In the first fifteen years following passage of the EHA, researchers focused on examining the roles of parents in the IEP process and identifying factors that appeared to promote or inhibit their participation (Foster, Berger, & McLean, 1981). Studies were designed to take an objective view of participation measured primarily in the context of meetings dedicated to IEP development. For the most part, these studies reported that during IEP meetings, parents engaged in less verbal participation than educators, asked fewer questions, and demonstrated behaviors (e.g., nodding, verbal indications of agreement, etc.) that suggested they largely agreed with the judgments of professionals (Cone, Delawyer, & Wolfe, 1985; Goldstein, Strickland, Turnbull, & Curry, 1980; Lusthaus, Lusthaus, & Gibbs, 1981; Vacc et al., 1985; Vaughn, Bos, Harrell, & Lasky, 1988). A finding that was initially perplexing was that most parents reported overall satisfaction with the planning process, contradicting the assumption that they would be dissatisfied with IEP meetings in which professionals maintained control over the conversation and educational planning and decision-making.

Studies focused on teachers' perceptions and behaviors also produced mixed results. On the one hand, some studies found that many educators found lower levels of parent participation to be acceptable, with many in fact defining "appropriate" parent roles in a passive rather than an active sense. Analyses of teacher self-reports on parent and professional interactions indicated that the majority felt it was more appropriate for parents to gather and present information than to participate in educational decision-making (Yoshida, Fenton, Kaufman, & Maxwell, 1978), with some reporting that parents should be allowed to waive their right to participation and place educational decision-making solely in the hands of professionals (Gerber, Banbury, Miller, & Griffin, 1986). Another set of studies focused less on teachers' perceptions of parent participation than on their actual behaviors. Findings from these studies suggested that the context of most IEP meetings was less than favorable towards parents of children with disabilities. Studies identified barriers such as teachers' use of unexplained and technical educational jargon in the reporting of test results and insufficient allocation of time for IEP meetings (Hughes & Ruhl, 1987), as well as presentation of completed or nearly completed IEPs that lacked parent input (Gerber et al., 1986; Goldstein et al., 1980). Taken as a whole, these early studies seemed to suggest that the EHA's provisions for parent participation were not being fully realized by either teachers or parents.

Re-conceptualizing parent participation. As the 1980s drew to a close, findings from the research that characterized parents as passive participants who were generally satisfied with the IEP process were re-visited and called into question. For example, because most participants in the majority of the early studies were Caucasian mothers from middle class backgrounds, the field eventually concluded that these findings could not be generalized to all parents, including fathers and families from diverse backgrounds (Turnbull et al., 1982; Turnbull et al., 2011).

The 1980s also witnessed a paradigm shift in which proponents of parent participation and early intervention began to focus on family systems theory and family support models that conceptualized families as social systems with unique characteristics and needs (Blue-Banning et al., 2004). These models posited that professionals should focus their work on identifying families' needs and choices, encouraging family control in decision-making, and creating effective and collaborative partnerships that went beyond the IEP planning context. Family-centered approaches also encouraged parents to establish their own expectations for involvement, acknowledging that some families would be more interested in playing greater roles in their children's educational programs than others (Bruder, 2000; MacMillan & Turnbull, 1983). Application of family systems theory to understand the complexity of partnering with families offered new lenses for professionals to navigate parent/professional partnerships (Turnbull et al., 2011). Important to this work were the ideas of Bronfenbrenner (1986) about the ecology of the family. Situating parents in the context of the external environment, professionals sought to understand the ways in which families were influenced by those environments

19

and contexts. By including a broader understanding of factors that might influence a family's relationship and interactions with schools, Bronfenbrenner's ecological perspective allowed teams to move away from simply trying to "fix" the child and towards improving quality of life through providing services and interventions that were compatible with the different environments in which the child and family operated (MacMillan & Turnbull, 1983).

The literature also reflected a shift in language during the 1980s. Whereas the IDEA continued to refer to "parent" participation, researchers and practitioners began to refer to the participation of "families" (Blue-Banning et al., 2004). This change was indicative of the fact that although the IEP process continued to focus on the legal authority of one or more parents, expanded definitions of participation reflected a need to collaborate with the individuals in a student's broader family constellation, both within and outside of the IEP and IFSP processes.

Re-Conceptualizing Barriers to Parent Involvement

As the research on parent participation moved away from a singular focus on the behavior of parents and teachers during IEP meetings, it evolved to include a deeper exploration of cultural and contextual barriers to meaningful participation and the development of collaborative relationships and partnerships between families and professionals.

Culture and context. In the 1980s and 1990s, researchers began to explore issues of diversity and their relationship to parent participation in the IEP process (Greene, 1996; Lynch & Stein, 1983; Sileo, Sileo, & Prater, 1996; Sontag & Schacht, 1994). These studies generally described parents from diverse backgrounds as playing passive roles in the IEP process, but they provided alternative explanations for previous deficit views of this dynamic. They identified issues of power and differences in cultural values and beliefs that were often subtle, yet defined many of the relationships between professionals and parents (Harry, 1992a, 1992b, 2008; Geenan, Powers, & Lopez-Vasquez, 2001; Rao, 2000; Sileo et al., 1996). Many of these researchers talked about the fact that responses to disability are culturally situated such that the very concept of disability and what it means to be a person with a disability is linked to one's culture in such a deep way that members of that culture may not be even be aware that other definitions exist (Kalyanpur & Harry, 2012).

The challenge then, is to understand the ways in which disability is viewed differently across cultures and time, so that we may be in a better position to understand the challenges that emerge when a school's perspective on disability varies from a family's perspective (Harry, Allen, & McLaughlin, 1995). For example, western perspectives of disability as a phenomenon that is intrinsic to an individual and has distinct medical, biological, and physical origins (Kalyanpur & Harry, 2012) are quite different from cultural and religious beliefs that may define disability from a more spiritual perspective (Lamory, 2002). Qualitative studies conducted with Latino mothers of children with developmental disabilities (Skinner, Correa, Skinner, & Bailey, 2001) and families of children with autism (Jegatheesan, Miller, & Fowler, 2010) identified spiritual and religious lenses on disability that are not generally acknowledged by white, middle class educators and may result in misunderstandings and frustration in the IEP process (Harry, 2008). Additionally, Sileo et al. (1996) noted the ways in which ideals such as efficiency, independence, self-determination, and equity are valued by Americans of European descent, but may clash with the values held by families whose cultures prize family associations and the extended family structure.

These very different ways of defining disability may lead to disagreements over how to determine the "best" educational and life outcomes for children and youth with disabilities. For example, those ascribing to the western "medical model" of disability may be focused on diagnosing a disability and figuring out how to remediate or treat it, while those viewing disability as having more spiritual origins may see disability as something to be accepted or even celebrated (Harry, 2008; Fadiman, 2012). Teachers from the U.S. who value the ideal of independence and believe that young adults with disabilities should live outside of their parents' home may feel frustrated by families who hold a more collective view of the world and see life within an extended family as a valued and typical outcome. Differences in perspectives such as these may appear to be differences of opinion or "best practice," when in fact they are tied to deeper cultural values and beliefs. Kalyanpur and Harry (2012) argue that relationships between families and school professionals need to strive for a mutual understanding that they describe as "cultural reciprocity." To them, the notion of cultural reciprocity necessitates that both family members and professionals spend time reflecting on and communicating their views about the nature of disability in relation to their personal and cultural contexts, as well as the context of school culture. By articulating these fundamental and culturally defined ideas about disability, conversations about a child's goals and supports can be contextualized and better understood by all, resulting in a higher likelihood of identifying common ground for goal-setting and planning.

Language, relationships, and collaboration. The more recent research has also identified the ways in which differences in language may create challenges within family-professional collaboration. Barriers related to language have been identified among parents from diverse linguistic backgrounds, as well as among parents who are fluent in English but do not understand the vocabulary and terms used in the IEP process (Dabkowski, 2004). Some parents report feeling excluded based on subtle messages and nonverbal communication conveyed by professionals. They may find it difficult to participate when they lack information regarding special education processes, terminology, and parental rights (Lytle & Bordin, 2001), and when they encounter IEPs that have been written prior to meetings (Spann, Kohler, & Soenksen, 2003). Families experiencing these challenges continue to report that the IEP process is characterized by a lack of trust, poor communication, and failure

21

to develop positive, collaborative relationships that could support effective planning and service delivery (Rao, 2000; Whitbread, Bruder, Fleming, & Park, 2007). This appears to be the case for families of children of all ages, including young children receiving early intervention services (McWilliam, Tocci, & Harbin, 1998) as well as older students preparing for the transition from school to adult life (deFur, 2012; McNair & Rusch, 1991; Salembier & Furney, 1997). Clearly, differences in language are also connected to the previous discussion of cultural differences. Language and culture are deeply connected and one's ability to understand a second spoken language does not necessarily result in the ability to make meaning of that language in a cultural sense.

Inequality in the development and use of collaborative skills. Finally, another set of studies focused on the specific skills and behaviors needed for collaboration within the IEP process, particularly among parents from culturally and linguistically diverse backgrounds, and the degree to which use of these skills varies among parents (e.g., Harry & Klingner, 2006; Minke & Scott, 1993; Trainor, 2008, 2010; Wilson, 2015). Across these studies, it appears that parents who are culturally and linguistically diverse may lack the social and cultural capital needed to develop and use skills such as questioning persons in authoritative roles and advocating successfully for their children that have been identified as key components of parent involvement (Trainor, 2010). Wilson (2015) asserts that a lack of social capital (i.e., resources gained through a parent's connection to social networks) and/or a lack of cultural capital (i.e., knowledge, skills, and behaviors that demonstrate understanding or alignment with the dominant cultural viewpoint) may contribute to the challenges faced by parents from diverse backgrounds and lower socioeconomic status within school planning context. These challenges are compounded by the fact that families from diverse backgrounds may face school contexts with structural and attitudinal barriers that further complicate their ability to advocate for their children (Harry & Klingner). Thus, even when parents gain skills in questioning, effective advocacy, and other collaborative skills, their input may be ignored if those within the dominant culture do not value what it is they have to say. Recommendations for supporting parents from diverse backgrounds include direct teaching and support for the development of skills in communication, decision-making, and advocacy, as well as improved preparation of teachers to ensure that they can engage in culturally responsive and reciprocal practices (Kalyanpur & Harry, 2012), and are sensitive to and skilled in responding to the challenges faced by many families (Wilson, 2015).

Current Thinking around Collaboration

Although we argue in this book that collaboration has largely been defined through the lens of school professionals and researchers in academic settings—often without adequate input from parents and family members—it is important to acknowledge that there is a solid existing research base that helps lay the groundwork for understanding family-school collaboration. It is also important to acknowledge that there are multiple definitions of collaboration that focus on different elements of the construct. Some authors define collaboration from the vantage point of the types of relationship building and interactions that occur in the collaborative process, while others view collaboration as a larger construct and a building block for the development of family school partnerships. Friend and Cook (2013), well-known authors within the field of special education, begin with a definition of interpersonal collaboration as "a style for direct interaction between at least two co-equal parties voluntarily engaged in shared decision making as they work toward a common goal" (p. 7). Within this definition, they identify several assumptions:

- Collaboration is a voluntary process
- Decision-making is shared equally
- There is a defined and mutually understood goal

Friend and Cook (2013) further identify five elements of collaboration that provide an important context for analyzing the nature of special education teams. These components include: "personal commitment, communication skills, interaction processes, programs or services and context" (p. 23).

Mostert (1996) define collaboration similarly, acknowledging elements of shared decision-making and reciprocal effort. He advises, "Indeed school professionals have a legal and ethical obligation to include families wherever possible in the entire decision-making process for effective intervention with their child" (Mostert, p. 135). Thousand and Villa (1992) underscore the importance of relationships within the collaborative process, but also focus on the structures, routines, and behaviors that are typical among effective collaborative teams. Drawing on the literature around cooperative group learning for K-12 students (Johnson & Johnson, 1989), Thousand and Villa describe underlying principles of adult collaboration as well as five observable characteristics considered to be an essential component of effective collaboration. These include: (1) face-to-face interaction (i.e., regular opportunities for teams to meet and carry out relevant tasks); (2) positive interdependence (i.e., identification of shared goals and decision-making processes); (3) positive group interactions (i.e., effective use of social skills, communication, and conflict resolution strategies); (4) individual accountability (i.e., a commitment on the part of individual team members to carry out identified individual responsibilities); and (5) group monitoring and processing (i.e., opportunities for team members to reflect on their team's strengths, challenges, and opportunities for growth).

A number of researchers (e.g., Thousand & Villa, 1992; Wheelan, 2016) also discuss collaboration in relation to the literature around psychology and group dynamics (Tuckman & Jenson, 1977) asserting that group development occurs over time and through an identifiable set of stages. The notion of stages of group development can be helpful when teams take time to reflect on where they stand in relation to emergence of effective collaboration. Though the particular terms used to described group development may differ across authors, most agree that there are four stages common to many groups: (1) forming (i.e., the initial stage in which team members establish their routines and begin to work together as individuals); (2) storming (i.e., a typical phase in which team members experience some degree of conflict and jockeying for power; (3) norming (i.e., the stage in which team members re-visit group norms and adjust their processes so as to more effectively engage in problem-solving and conflict resolution; and (4) performing (i.e., the most advanced stage of development in which team members find their work to be creative, productive, and energizing).

Other researchers have moved beyond a focus on collaboration as it occurs between individuals or within teams to think about the ways in which effective collaboration can lead to the development of a broader family school partnership (Blue-Banning et al., 2004; Haines, McCart, & Turnbull, 2013).

Turnbull and colleagues (2010, 2011) have written extensively about the importance of family school partnership in special education. They articulate seven principles of partnership that they refer to as a "doctrine" to guide practice: communication, professional competence, respect, trust, commitment, equality and advocacy. Within each of these identified principles they define concrete practices and interpersonal skills – such as sharing power, honoring diversity and honesty – that operationalize the values behind the principle. The authors assert that when the family-school partnership is present, school personnel and families experience higher levels of trust, students have more positive outcomes, and the quality of families' lives is improved (Turnbull et al., 2010).

Ultimately, the goal of family school partnership is to build trusting relationships between professionals and parents so that children with disabilities benefit from their education. In the family school partnership framework, collaboration within the context of IFSP, IEP and transition planning is seen as important; however, the focus on partnership suggests that the values of trust, equity, and shared decision-making need to transcend individuals and teams to become a defining characteristic of schools and communities.

Finally, a number of researchers have focused on the contextual and organizational features that appear to foster collaboration in school. Some note the role that effective leaders play in setting the stage for effective collaboration (Shepherd & Hasazi, 2008; Shepherd, Hasazi, & Aiken, 2008; Rubin, 2002), while others note the ways in which organizations establish cultures that may be more or less conducive to collaboration (Fullan, 2007; Spillane, 2007, 2012) and supportive of students and families with disabilities (McLeskey, Waldron, Spooner, & Algozzine, 2014). In addition, the literature describes collaboration as it occurs across organizations and disciplines (Dryfoos & Maguire, 2002; Friend & Cook, 2013), noting the ways in which interdisciplinary collaboration presents its own challenges with respect to the need for participants to understand and negotiate differences that may exist between them (e.g., differences in role definition, terminology, practices, organization and attitudes, use of resources, etc.).

CHAPTER SUMMARY

Taken as a whole, the vantage points on collaboration offered by these authors and others suggest that collaboration is a complex and interactive process occurring at the individual, team, organizational, and cross-organizational/disciplinary levels. Views on parent and professional collaboration have changed over time: the focus has shifted from simply getting parents "to the table" to understanding how family and professional partnership can reflect the principles of collaboration, value the diverse perspectives of families and professionals, and result in equity in decision-making. Although not always fully embraced, the literature suggests that over time, early views of "passive parents" who were the recipients of information have been replaced by the call for more active participation and advocacy among parents.

Our work embraces the contributions of these various perspectives and related research, in the sense that we too, see family participation and collaboration as a key ingredient of the more recent call for the development of family school partnership. We concur that collaboration can be defined as both a style of interaction and a process that starts with the individual (whether that person be a family member or professional) and embraced at the team level (e.g., IFSP, IEP, and transition teams). Successful team level collaboration requires school leaders to provide adequate time and structures for collaboration, as well as support for individuals to develop collaborative skills and to understand the diverse perspectives and skills that exist among team members. In order to serve as a building block of family professional partnership, collaboration must be encouraged by leaders and reflected in the overall culture of schools and communities. As part of this culture, families need to be viewed as leaders who contribute to all levels of decision-making, including policy level decisions.

We acknowledge that this evolving view of collaboration is more inclusive and family-focused than it once was (at least in theory); still the fact that so many stories of failed collaboration exist suggests that even this expanded perspective does not tell the whole story. In particular, the frameworks, theories and existing research may not fully capture collaborative attitudes and processes as they are experienced by family members who may or may not have had formal training or experience with collaborative teams, and/or families who lack the social and cultural capital resources needed to negotiate the collaborative process. Existing frameworks reveal the challenges of collaboration, but they typically do so from the vantage point of professionals who may be in a position to prevent, remediate, or embrace these challenges. We applaud the efforts of professionals who choose to take on the task of establishing and sustaining collaborative approaches and processes—and we see the need to consider these in light of the voices of parents who can illuminate the particular strengths and challenges of teams they have experienced and whose "seat at the table" may be under-appreciated, under-valued, misunderstood, off to the side, or simply not desired. This is not to say that collaboration never works or that family members are not skilled in collaboration; in fact, we argue that family members are oftentimes more skillful and more dedicated to the ideals of collaboration than are professionals. We do, however, believe that the voices of families have not been present enough in identifying what contributes to (or detracts from) the establishment of effective collaboration and family school partnership. In subsequent chapters, we focus on what families have told us about their experiences, in the hopes that their lessons and words will shape a more collaborative future.

SUGGESTED QUESTIONS FOR REFLECTION AND DISCUSSION

For parents and professionals:

1. This chapter provides evidence of changes over time in the ways that parent participation has been defined, researched, and understood. Which of the research findings align best with your own experience? Why do you think this is the case?
2. How do you define the following terms: parent participation, parent-professional collaboration, family-school partnership? In what ways do your definitions align with or seem different from how the terms are used in the literature?

SUGGESTED ACTIVITIES

For parents and professionals:

3. Consider the historical evolution of the concept of parent participation as it relates to special education processes. Under IDEA states are required to collect data on implementation of key tenets of the law including parent participation. Research how your state collects data on parent satisfaction with their level of participation in special education processes. Based on what the data show, what recommendations do you have for how to improve implementation of the parent and student participation principle?
4. What organizations exist in your community to provide support for families of children with disabilities in navigating special education processes? What resources exist for professionals to support building effective and collaborative partnerships with families?
5. Investigate further one of the models for collaboration briefly outlined in this chapter. Does the definition of collaboration align with your personal experiences of collaboration within the context of special education?

REFERENCES

Barenock, T., & Wieck, C. (1998). Partners in policymaking: Far more than the object of policy. In L. Ward (Ed.), *Innovations in advocacy and empowerment for people with intellectual disabilities* (pp. 233–244). Chorley, UK: Lisieux Hall.
Bateman, B. D., & Linden, M. A. (2006). *Writing measurable goals and objectives* (5th ed.). Verona, WI: IEP Resources, Attainment Company.

Blue-Banning, M., Summers, J. A., Frankland, H. C., Nelson, L. L., & Beegle, G. (2004). Dimensions of family and professional partnerships: Constructive guidelines for collaboration. *Exceptional Children, 70*(2), 167–184.

Bronfenbrenner, U. (1986). Ecology of the family as a context for human development: Research perspectives. *Developmental Psychology, 22*(6), 723–742.

Bruder, M. B. (2000). Family-centered early intervention: Clarifying our values for the new millennium. *Topics in Early Childhood Special Education, 20,* 105–115.

Cone, J. D., Delawyer, D. D., & Wolfe, V. V. (1985). Assessing parent participation: The parent/family involvement index. *Exceptional Children, 51*(5), 417–424.

Cutler, W. W. (2000). *Parents and schools: The 150-year struggle for control in American education.* Chicago, IL: University of Chicago Press.

Dabkowski, D. M. (2004). Encouraging active parent participation in IEP team meetings. *TEACHING Exceptional Children, 36*(3), 34–39.

deFur, S. (2012). Parents as collaborators: Building partnerships with school and community-based providers. *TEACHING Exceptional Children, 44*(3), 58–67.

Dryfoos, J., & McGuire, S. (2002). *Inside full-service community schools.* Thousand Oaks, CA: Corwin Press.

Education of All Handicapped Children's Act § 1401 *et seq.*

Epstein, J. L. (2010). School/family/community partnerships: Caring for the children we share. *Phi Delta Kappan, 92*(3), 81–96.

Fadiman, A. (2012). *The spirit catches you and you fall down.* New York, NY: Farrar, Straus and Giroux.

Ferguson, C. (2008). *The school-family connection: Looking at the larger picture.* Austin, TX: Southwest Educational Development Laboratories.

Fialka, J. M., Feldman, A. K., & Mikus, K. C. (2012). *Parents and professionals partnering for children with disabilities: A dance that matters.* Thousand Oaks, CA: Corwin.

Fischer, L., & Schimmel, D. (1978). The rights of parents. *Theory Into Practice, 17*(4), 321–329.

Foster, M., Berger, M., & McLean, M. (1981). Re-thinking a good idea: A reassessment of parent involvement. *Topics in Early Childhood Special Education, 1,* 55–65.

Friend, M., & Cook, L. (2013). *Interactions: Collaboration skills for school professionals* (7th ed.). Boston, MA: Pearson.

Fullan, M. (2007). *The new meaning of educational change* (4th ed.). New York, NY: Teachers College Press.

Furney, K. S., & Salembier, G. (2000). Rhetoric and reality: A review of the literature on parent and student participation in the IEP and transition planning process. *Issues influencing the future of transition programs and services in the United States* (pp. 111–126). Minneapolis, MN: National Transition Network at the Institute on Community Integration.

Geenan, S., Powers, L. E., & Lopez-Vasquez, A. (2001). Multicultural aspects of parent involvement in transition planning. *Exceptional Children, 67,* 265–282.

Gerber, P. J., Banbury, M. M., Miller, J. H., & Griffin, H. C. (1986). Special educators' perceptions of parental participation in the individual education plan process. *Psychology in the Schools, 23,* 158–163.

Goldstein, S., Strickland, B., Turnbull, A. P., & Curry, L. (1980). An observational analysis of the IEP conference. *Exceptional Children, 46*(4), 278–286.

Greene, G. (1996). Empowering culturally and linguistically diverse families in the transition planning process. *Journal for Vocational Special Needs Education, 19*(1), 2630.

Haines, S. J., McCart, A., & Turnbull, A. P. (2013). Family engagement within early childhood response to intervention. In V. Buysse & E. Peisner-Feinberg (Eds.), *Handbook on Response to Intervention (RTI) in early childhood* (pp. 313–324). New York, NY: Brookes.

Harry, B. (1992a). An ethnographic study of cross-cultural communication with Puerto Rican-American families in the special education system. *American Educational Research Journal, 29*(3), 471–494.

Harry, B. (1992b). Making sense of disability: Low-income, Puerto Rican parents' theories of the problem. *Exceptional Children, 59*(1), 27–40.

Harry, B. (2008). Collaboration with culturally and linguistically diverse families: Ideal versus reality. *Exceptional Children, 74*(3), 372–388.

Harry, B., & Klingner, J. K. (2006). *Why are there so many minority students in special education?: Understanding race and disability in schools.* New York, NY: Teachers College Press.

Harry, B., Allen, N., & McLaughlin, M. (1995). Communication versus compliance: African-American parents' involvement in special education. *Exceptional Children, 61*, 364–377.

Harry, B., Kalyanpur, M., & Day, M. (2005). *Building cultural reciprocity with families: Case studies in special education.* Baltimore, MD: Paul H. Brookes Publishing.

Hasazi, S. B., DeStefano, L., & Furney, K. S. (1999). Progress in implementing the transition requirements of IDEA: Promising strategies and future directions. *To assure the free appropriate public education of all children with disabilities* (pp. 53–72). Education Publications Center: U.S. Department of Education.

Hattie, J. (2009). *Visible learning: A synthesis of meta-analyses related to achievement.* New York, NY: Routledge.

Henderson, A. T., & Mapp, K. L. (2002). *A new wave of evidence: The impact of school, family, and community connection on student achievement.* Austin, TX: Southwest Education Development Laboratory.

Henderson, A., Jacob, B., Kernan-Schloss, A., & Raimondo, B. (2004). *The case for parent leadership.* Arlington, VA: KSA Plus Communications.

Henry, M. (1996). *Parent-school collaboration: Feminist organizational structures and school leadership.* Albany, NY: State University of New York Press.

Heward, W. L. (2012). *Exceptional children: An introduction to special education* (10th ed.). Los Angeles, CA: Pearson.

Hughes, C. A., & Ruhl, K. L. (1987). The nature and extent of special educator contacts with students' parents. *Teacher Education and Special Education, 10*(4), 180–184.

Individuals with Disabilities Education Act of 1990, Pub. L. No. 101-476, 104 Stat. 587.

Individuals with Disabilities Education Improvement Act of 2004, Pub. L. No. 108-446, 118 Stat. 2647.

Jegatheesan, B., Miller, P., & Fowler, S. (2010). Autism from a religious perspective: A study of parental beliefs in South Asian Muslim immigrant families. *Focus on Autism and Other Developmental Disabilities, 25*(2), 98–109.

Jeppson, E. S., & Thomas, J. (1995). *Essential allies: Families as advisors.* Bethesda, MD: Institute for Family-Centered Care.

Jeynes, W. H. (2007). The relationship between parental involvement and urban secondary school student academic achievement: A meta-analysis. *Urban Education, 42*, 82–110.

Johnson D. W., & Johnson, R. (1989). *Cooperation and competition: Theory and research.* Edina, MN: Interaction Book Company.

Kaestle, C. F. (2001). The common school. In S. Mondale & S. B. Patton (Eds.), *School: The story of American public education* (pp. 11–17). Boston, MA: Beacon Press.

Kalyanpur, M., & Harry, B. (2012). *Cultural reciprocity in special education: Building family-professional relationships.* Baltimore, MD: Paul H. Brookes Publishing.

Kativannis, A., Yell, M. L., & Bradley, R. (2001). Reflections on the 25th anniversary of the individuals with disabilities education act. *Remedial and Special Education, 22*(6), 324–334.

Koroloff, N., Hunter, R., & Gordon, L. (1995). *Family involvement in policy making: A final report on the families in action project.* Research and Training Center on Family Support and Children's Mental Health, Portland State University.

Lamory, S. (2002). The effects of culture on special education services: Evil eyes, prayer meetings, and IEPs. *TEACHING Exceptional Children, 34*(5), 67–71.

Leithwood, K. (2010). Four key policy questions about parent engagement: Recommendations from the evidence. In R. Deslandes (Ed.), *International perspectives on contexts, communities and evaluated innovative practice* (pp. 8–20). London, England: Routledge.

Leithwood, K., Patten, S., & Jantzi, D. (2010). Testing a connection of how school leadership influences student learning. *Educational Administration Quarterly, 46*, 671–706. doi:10.1177/00136161X10377347

Leko, M. M., Brownell, M. T., Sindelar, P. T., & Kiely, M. T. (2015). Envisioning the future of special education personnel preparation in a standards-based era. *Exceptional Children, 82*(1), 25–43. doi:10.1177/0014402915598782

Libertoff, K., Maynard, A., Pandina, N., & Yuan, S. (1998). Family member involvement in policymaking in Vermont. *Focal Point, 12*(1), 20–23.

Lusthaus, C. S., Lusthaus, E. W., & Gibbs, H. (1981). Parents' role in the decision process. *Exceptional Children, 48*, 256–257.

Lynch, E. W., & Stein, R. (1983). Perspectives on parent participation in special education. *Exceptional Education Quarterly, 3*, 56–63.

Lytle, R. K., & Bordin, J. (2001). Enhancing the IEP team: Strategies for teachers and professionals. *TEACHING Exceptional Children, 33*(5), 40–44.

MacMillan, D. L., & Turnbull, A. P. (1983). Parent involvement with special education: Respecting individual preferences. *Education and Training of the Mentally Retarded, 18*(1), 5–9.

Martin, E. W. (2013). *Breakthrough: Federal special education legislation 1965–1981.* Sarasota, FL: Bardolf and Company.

Mattingly, D. J., Prislin, R., McKenzie, T. L., Rodriguez, J. L., & Kayzar, B. (2002). Evaluating evaluations: The case of parent involvement programs. *Review of Educational Research, 72*, 549–576.

McLeskey, J., Waldron, N. L., Spooner, F., & Algozzine, B. (2014). What are effective inclusive schools and why are they important? In J. McLeskey, N. L. Waldron, F. Spooner, & B. Algozzine (Eds.), *Handbook of effective inclusive schools: Research and practice* (pp. 3–16). New York, NY: Routledge.

McNair, J., & Rusch, F. R. (1991). Parent involvement in transition programs. *Mental Retardation, 29*, 93–101.

McWilliam, R. A., Tocci, L., & Harbin, G. L. (1998). Family-centered services: Service providers' discourse and behavior. *Topics in Early Childhood Special Education, 18*, 206–221.

Meadan, H., Shelden, D. L., Appel, K., & DeGrazia, R. L. (2010). Developing a long-term vision: A road map for students' futures. *TEACHING Exceptional Children, 43*(2), 8–14.

Miller, R. J., Lombard, R. C., & Corbey, S. A. (2007). *Transition assessment: Planning transition and IEP development for youth with mild to moderate disabilities.* Boston, MA: Pearson.

Minke, M. K., & Scott, M. M. (1993). The development of family service plans: Roles for parents and staff. *The Journal of Special Education, 22*(1), 82–106.

Mostert, M. P. (1996). Interprofessional collaboration in schools: Benefits and barriers in practice. *Preventing School Failure, 40*(3), 135–139.

Mount, B., & Zwernik, K. (1988). *It's never too early, it's never too late: A booklet about personal futures planning.* St. Paul, MN: Minnesota Governor's Planning Council on Developmental Disabilities.

NICHCY (2009). Questions and answers about IDEA: Parent participation. In N. D. C. f. C. w. Disabilities (Ed.), Washington, DC.

No Child Left Behind Act of 2001, Pub. L. No. 107-110, 115 Stat. 1425, 20 U.S.C.A. §§ 6301 et seq. (2002 Supp.).

Overton, S. (2005). *Collaborating with families: A case study approach.* Upper Saddle River, NJ: Pearson.

Popper, B. K. (1994). Who you gonna call? *Early Childhood Bulletin*, pp. 1–3.

Rao, S. (2000). Perspectives of an African American mother on parent-professional relationships in special education. *Mental Retardation, 38*(6), 475–488.

Rubin, H. (2002). *Collaborative leadership: Developing effective partnerships in communities and schools.* Thousand Oaks, CA: Corwin Press.

Salembier, G., & Furney, K. S. (1997). Facilitating participation: Parents' perceptions of their involvement in the IEP/transition planning process. *Career Development for Exceptional Individuals, 20*(1), 29–42.

Searcy, S., Lee-Lawson, C., & Trombino, B. (1995). Mentoring new leadership roles for parents of children with disabilities. *Remedial and Special Education, 16*, 307–314.

Shepherd, K., & Hasazi, S. B. (2007). Leading for social justice and inclusion: The role of school leaders. In L. Florian (Ed.), *Sage handbook of special education* (pp. 475–485), Chapel Hill, NC: Sage Publications.

Shepherd, K. G., Hasazi, S. B., & Aiken, J. (2008). Preparing school leaders to build and sustain engagement with families and communities. In R. Papa (Ed.), *Leadership on the frontlines: changes in preparation and leadership* (pp. 145–158). Lancaster, PA: ProActive Publications.

Shepherd, K. G., Giangreco, M. F., & Cook, B. G. (2013). Parent participation in assessment and in development of Individualized Education Programs. In B. G. Cook & M. Tankersley (Eds.), *Research-based practices in special education* (pp. 260–271). Boston, MA: Pearson.

Shepherd, K. G., Kervick, C. T., & Salembier, G. (2015). Person-centered planning: Tools for promoting employment, self-direction and independence among persons with intellectual disabilities. In American Association on Intellectual and Developmental Disabilities (Eds.), *Way leads on to way: Paths to employment for people with intellectual and disability* (pp. 299–320). Washington, DC: American Association on Intellectual and Developmental Disabilities.

Sileo, T. W., Sileo, A. P., & Prater, M. A. (1996). Parent and professional partnerships in special education: Multicultural considerations. *Intervention in School and Clinic, 31*(3), 145–153. doi:10.1177/105345129603100303

Skinner, D., Correa, V., Skinner, M., & Bailey, D. (2001). The role of religion in the lives of Latino families of young children with developmental delays. *American Journal of Mental Retardation, 106*(4), 297–313.

Smith, S. W. (1990). Individualized education programs (IEPs) in special education – From intent to acquiescence. *Exceptional Children, 57*, 6–14.

Sontag, J. C., & Schacht, R. (1994). An ethnic comparison of parent participation and information needs in early intervention. *Exceptional Children, 60*, 422433.

Spann, S. J., Kohler, F. W, & Soenksen. D. (2003). Examining parents' involvement in and perceptions of special education services: An interview with families in a parent support group. *FOCUS on Autism and Other Developmental Disabilities, 18*, 228–237.

Spillane, J. P. (2007). *Distributed leadership in practice.* New York, NY: Teachers College Press.

Spillane, J. P. (2012). Conceptualizing the data-based decision-making phenomena. *American Journal of Education, 118*(2), 113–141.

Thousand, J., & Villa, R. (1992). Collaborative teams: A powerful tool in school restructuring. In R. Villa, J. Thousand, W. Stainback, & S. Stainback (Eds.), *Restructuring for caring and effective education: An administrative guide to creating heterogeneous schools.* Baltimore, MD: Paul H. Brookes.

Trainor, A. A. (2008). Diverse approaches to parent advocacy during special education home-school interactions: Identification and use of cultural and social capital. *Remedial and Special Education, 42*(3), 148–162. doi:10.1177/0741932508324401.

Trainor, A. A. (2010) Reexamining the promise of parent participation in special education: An analysis of cultural and social capital. *Anthropology & Education, 41,* 245–263. doi:10.1111/j.1548-1492.2010.01086.x

Tuckman, B. W., & Jenson, M. A. C. (1977). Stages in group development revisited. *Group and Organizational Studies, 2,* 419–427.

Turnbull, H. R. (2005). Individuals with Disabilities Education Act reauthorization: Accountability and personal responsibility. *Remedial and Special Education, 26,* 320–326.

Turnbull, H. R., Turnbull, A., & Wheat, M. (1982). Assumptions about parent participation: A legislative history. *Exceptional Education Quarterly, 3*(2), 1–8.

Turnbull, R., Turnbull, A., & Wehmeyer, M. (2010). *Exceptional lives: Special education in today's schools* (6th ed.). Upper Saddle River, NJ: Pearson.

Turnbull, A., Zuna, N., Hong, J. Y., Hu, X., & Kyzar, K. (2010). Knowledge-to-action guides: Preparing families to be partners in making educational decisions. *TEACHING Exceptional Children, 42*(3), 42–53.

Turnbull, A., Turnbull, R., Erwin, E. J., Soodak, L. C., & Shogren, K. A. (2011). *Families, professionals, and exceptionality: Positive outcomes through partnerships and trust* (6th ed.). Boston, MA: Pearson.

Vacc, N. A., Vallercorsa, A. L., Parker, A., Bonner, S., Lester, C., Richardson, S., & Yates, C. (1985). Parents' and educators' participation in IEP conferences. *Education and Treatment of Children, 8*(2), 153–162.

Vaughn, S., Bos, C. S., Harrell, J. E., & Lasky, B. (1988). Parent participation in the initial placement/ IEP conference ten years after mandated involvement. *Journal of Learning Disabilities, 21*(2), 82–89.

Villa, R. A., & Thousand, J. S. (1999). *Restructuring for caring and effective education* (2nd ed.). Baltimore, MD: Paul H. Brookes.

Wehmeyer, M. L., & Webb, K. W. (2011). *Handbook of adolescent transition education for youth with disabilities.* Florence, KY: Routledge, Taylor, & Francis Group

Wells, J. C., & Sheehey, P. H. (2012). Person-centered planning: Strategies to encourage participation and facilitate communication. *TEACHING Exceptional Children, 44*(3), 32–39.

Wheelan, S. (2016). *Creating effective teams: A guide for members and leaders* (5th ed.). Thousand Oaks, CA: Sage.

Whitbread, K. M., Bruder, M. B., Fleming, G., & Park, H. J. (2007). Collaboration in special education: Parent-professional training. *TEACHING Exceptional Children, 39*(4), 6–14.

White House Report (2015, December). *White House report: The every student succeeds act.* Retrieved from https://www.whitehouse.gov/the-press-office/2015/12/10/white-house-report-every-student-succeeds-act

White, K. R., Taylor, M. J., & Moss, V. D. (1992). Does research support claims about the benefits of involving parents in early intervention programs? *Review of Educational Research, 62*, 91–125.

Wilson, N. (2015). Question-asking and advocacy by African American parents at individualized education program meetings: A social and cultural capital perspective. *Multiple Voices for Ethnically Diverse Exceptional Learners, 15*(2), 36–49.

Yell, M. L. (2012). *The law and special education* (3rd ed.). Upper Saddle River, NJ: Pearson.

Yell, M. L., Rogers, D., & Lodge Rodgers, E. (1998). The legal history of special education: What a long strange trip it's been. *Remedial and Special Education, 19*(4), 219–229.

Yoshida, R. K., Fenton, K. S., Kaufman, M. J., & Maxwell, J. (1978). Parental involvement in the special education pupil planning process: The school's perspective. *Exceptional Children, 44*, 531534.

IDENTIFYING A DISABILITY

The road to diagnosis was a long one for us. At first we just wanted to know "What is it and when and where does it end?" Every expert had their own theory, and we were constantly waiting for the other shoe to drop. It was such a difficult time.

(Djenne)

The ways in which families learn that their child has a disability are incredibly varied, and for many families, the process by which disabilities are identified or diagnosed has a significant bearing on their understanding of and early experiences regarding collaboration with professionals. Each family has a unique journey. For some the process begins immediately at birth and for others it unfolds over time. For some, diagnosis of a disability involves multiple professionals, including professionals from multiple disciplines (e.g., education, medicine, social work); for others, the process takes place primarily in the context of school. Some parents feel that professionals who have specific expertise related to their child's suspected disability should guide the identification process, while others find themselves taking a lead role in diagnosis—regardless of whether or not they prefer it that way. But for nearly all parents, the complex process that ends with a determination that their child has a disability as defined by one or more categories or conditions is a journey that can feel overwhelming, emotional, and unexpected.

In this chapter, we explore the nature of the identification process and the ways in which it relates to the larger process of collaboration. We begin by posing some possible ways of conceptualizing the process of identification (or diagnosis), focusing on the ways in which this process is situated within the educational system. In particular, we discuss how legal definitions of disability play into the process and the cultural and normative assumptions that shape how disability is defined in education. We then turn to a discussion of parents' perspectives on what it means to discover that their child has an identified disability, emphasizing the complex and often emotional nature of the process. Finally, we explore how the multiple roles parents and professionals play in recognizing, evaluating, and identifying disability may or may not lead to greater collaboration. We offer the perspective that professionals who make it a point to fully understand what families may be going through during this process are better positioned to establish a positive and empathic relationship with parents that over time, can lead to a deeper and more collaborative partnership. Parents' stories remind us that the way to true collaboration begins at the beginning—the time during which families come to understand that their path to parenthood is not going to be exactly what they expected, and that they will make this journey with people they may not have thought they would come to know.

CONCEPTUALIZING DISABILITY: NAMING THE PROCESS

In our research and work with families, we have heard multiple definitions of and reactions to the process of arriving at the identification of a disability label. Often, parents use the term "diagnosis" to describe the process that begins at the point in time they understand their child to be different in some way, continues through a more formal process of evaluation, and concludes with application of a particular label (or set of labels) that best describes the child's particular disability. For many families, the process of diagnosis is important in helping them to understand what their child is experiencing and will need at home, in school, and in the community, and how the family as a whole is going to proceed to define and manage circumstances that may have been unexpected.

The term "diagnosis" may, however, be misleading. To many, it denotes a fixed moment in time when a specific label is applied, when in fact, for most parents, diagnosis occurs over time, often through a long and messy process that may result in multiple labels or a combination of terms to describe a child's difference or disability. Additionally, "diagnosis" is laden with meanings that may not be the ideal way to describe what happens when families learn that a child's difference is defined—at least in part—by the presence of a disability. The term has a medical orientation linking the process of discovery to the identification of an illness or disease. Although some disabilities have a medical basis, we prefer to avoid viewing disability as an illness or deficit; rather, we take the view that disability may be more correctly defined as a social construction that reflects our basic assumptions and cultural values. To some, the term disability may reflect and define characteristics that are considered to be outside of the realm of "normal," while to others, the term speaks to differences in characteristics that reflect the full range of diversity within the human condition. As authors, we ascribe to the latter view. Still, we acknowledge that disability creates certain kinds of realities for families that are not experienced by families who do not have children labeled as having a disability, including the realities associated with the process of diagnosis.

The majority of the parents we have encountered speak about the process of diagnosis as a search for an explanation of their child's difference as well as identification of supports and services that will help their child reach his or her full potential. Reaching that understanding may be painful, but it is also important for most families; thus, for some, the term diagnosis captures the time when answers emerge to describe the strengths and challenges of their child. In this way, diagnosis may also be seen as a positive event or term. As such, although we acknowledge the shortcomings and potentially negative connotations of the term diagnosis, we continue to use it as a way of speaking about the process that parents go through in their search to understand and better support their child.

Disability in an Educational Context: Legal Provisions and Processes

In education, terms such as "assessment," "referral for a comprehensive evaluation," "disability determination" and "disability category" are commonplace and refer to various stages of the formal and legally driven process in which families and school teams hypothesize that a child is learning differently and determine through multiple forms of assessment that the child's difference is due to a recognized disability. According to the IDEA, special education services must be provided to students who meet the guidelines associated with determination of a disability. These specify that (a) the child must meet the criteria for at least one of the 13 disability categories recognized by the federal government (or a similar set of categories defined at the state level and approved by the federal government); (b) the disability must be determined to result in an adverse effect on the child's performance in school; and (c) the child must be in need of specialized services such as those offered through special education and related services (Heward, 2012; http://www.parentcenterhub.org/repository/categories). A multidisciplinary team, including parents, conducts a comprehensive assessment following guidelines delineated in the law, for the purpose of determining whether or not a child meets eligibility requirements under a particular category of disability. The legal parameters of making a disability determination may in fact exclude the provision of special education services for some students with disabilities. For example, a child with average to above average cognitive abilities who shows the presence of a disability (e.g., a learning disability, orthopedic impairment, other health impairment, autism spectrum disorder, etc.) who is performing academically in a way that is commensurate with peers is not likely to be eligible for special education services, in spite of the fact that the child faces certain obstacles in life and learning. A child with this profile may be eligible to receive supports and accommodations through Section 504 of the Rehabilitation Act, but the provisions of 504 do not include the full set of entitlements associated with special education as defined by the IDEA. Thus, it is possible for children to receive a diagnosis of a disability but not to be eligible for additional services through special education: a fact can be a source of misunderstanding and conflict among schools and families.

Normative and Cultural Assumptions

Along with the legal parameters discussed above, disability in the context of education in the United States is also guided by certain normative and cultural assumptions (Kalyanpur & Harry, 2012). Normative assumptions are present in the legal definitions of disability as well as in many (though not all) people's conceptualization of the nature of disability. That is, while the construct of disability may be considered in a wider context to be an element of difference or diversity, the criteria implicit in the 13 categories of disability recognized by the federal government presume that any particular disability category can be explained in part by the degree to which the characteristics associated with that disability are manifested in an individual in ways that are significantly different from the ways in which those characteristics are recognized in the general population. Implicit in this approach is a belief that certain characteristics can be considered to be "normal" and others can be considered to be outside of the realm of normal, or what we expect to see in the general population. For example, most people exhibit strengths and weaknesses in their learning profile, but a person categorized as having a specific learning disability would be expected to have a profile indicating "unexpected low achievement" in specific areas of academic performance that are significantly below that of same age peers. The disability categories recognized by the federal government articulate to at least some degree criteria that serve as "cut off points" or markers that indicate when particular differences can be thought of as being sufficiently different from "normal" so as to be considered a disability.

Although recognized by many professionals in the field, these normative assumptions and their role in the disability determination process may be unknown to parents, difficult to comprehend, or in conflict with one's personal, cultural, or religious beliefs (Kalyanpur & Harry, 2012; Harry, 2008). Some categories appear to have more objective criteria than others; for example, the criteria established for the category of visual impairment give specific guidelines for vision that can be measured by medical professionals, whereas the criteria for establishing the presence of emotional disturbance appear to some to be more subjective and contextually based. Additionally, although most parents find it somewhat helpful to learn about the label given to their child's difference, most are equally interested in understanding what will happen once a diagnosis has been made. For example, the parent of a child who exhibits characteristics associated with autism spectrum disorder (ASD) is likely to be far more concerned about the supports and services available to the child than about the extent to which those characteristics are present in such a way as to align with federal or state criteria regarding provision of special educations services to children with ASD. The view that disability can be defined and responded to through objective measures may also discount the emotional and contextual factors that families face in the identification process.

The normative assumptions that contribute to prevailing constructs of disability are also accompanied by cultural assumptions and expectations. A number of researchers (e.g., Kalyanpur & Harry, 2012; Blue-Banning et al., 2004) have explored the degree to which special education in the U.S. is layered with cultural assumptions about the nature of disability, including assumptions grounded in western beliefs about disability as a characteristic that is intrinsic to the individual, disability as something to be "overcome," and disability as a barrier to personal independence and freedom. Families from diverse cultural and linguistic backgrounds may or may not share those perspectives on disability, introducing further complexity in the eligibility determination process. For example, some cultures interpret disability through a variety of spiritual or religious beliefs that espouse varying views on the nature of disability. Jegatheesan and colleagues (2010) have written about the ways in which many Muslim families view their children with disabilities as a gift from Allah, and Fadiman (2012) writes about ways in which Hmong families may view certain types of disability as an "illness of distinction" (p. 21). In contrast, studies of families from China and South Korea (McCabe, 2007) note the stigma that families of children with disabilities experience. In these cultures, having a child with a disability implies failure for the whole family, with the source of the disability often ascribed to a previous wrongdoing by ancestors.

An additional area of concern relates to the subjectivity inherent in categories pertaining to children with mild disabilities, including learning disabilities, emotional disturbance, mild intellectual disabilities, and certain health impairments, including ADD and ADHD. Not only are these categories somewhat difficult to define, but some researchers have argued that they may be applied differentially to families from different backgrounds in ways that appear to privilege some categories over others (Blanchett, 2010). Sleeter (1987), for example found that at the time of her research, the category of learning disabilities was much more often used in diagnoses of children who were white, whereas children of color with similar profiles were more likely to be labeled as having a mild intellectual disability or emotional disturbance. Her concerns about this related to the fact that the label of learning disability seemed to carry less of a negative connotation than labels such as intellectual disability or emotional disturbance; moreover, the labels used in the diagnosis of children with color also tended to result in more segregated placements. Although labels have been applied differently over time (i.e., African-American students are now more likely to be labeled learning disabled than they were in Sleeter's time), concerns about differential use of labels, classroom placement, and delivery of special education services persist (Blanchett, 2010; Harry & Klingner, 2006).

It is beyond the scope of this work to fully explore alternatives to the normative approaches and western views of disability or the challenges of ensuring that diagnosis and decision-making remain fair and free of bias. Still, these concepts are critical to understanding some of the misunderstandings and conflicts that may arise between families and professionals in the processes associated with identifying and defining disability. This discussion is of particular importance because of the changing demographics of schools in the United States. Recent studies indicate that the percentage of learners from families with cultural and linguistic diversity has increased nearly 10% over the last decade (Aceves & Orosco, 2014) and that the population of English learners (ELs) has doubled over the same time period (Fernandez & Inserra, 2013). In spite of this increased diversity in the classroom, recent studies indicate that 80–90% of public school teachers are from white, middle class backgrounds (Aceves & Orosco, 2014; Herrara, Perez, & Escalmilla, 2015). Assuming that the majority of these teachers ascribe to the dominant and Western views of disability, it becomes clear that there is a potentially large gap between how families and school professionals interpret the origins and effects of disability on both the child and the family. For this reason, it is incumbent upon all professionals to take stock of their own assumptions and to consider the ways in which their interpretations of disability may differ from the views of the families with whom they work. Our belief is that professionals who remain aware of institutional constraints, their own assumptions, and the emotions that accompany the process of diagnosis may be in a better position to understand the perspectives of families who are experiencing the identification process through their own personal and cultural lenses.

PARENTS' JOURNEYS TO DIAGNOSIS

In this section, we explore parents' stories and emerging themes that capture some of the profound moments and challenges inherent in the process of diagnosis. Across each of these themes, it is clear that while determination of a disability brings some sense of relief and understanding for many families, the terminology and multiple steps that accompany identification or diagnosis may be complicated and confusing, especially to parents who have not encountered it before or for whom the normative and cultural assumptions described above are not explicit or consistent with their own world views. Across our interviews and experiences with parents, five issues stand out as being particularly salient in this regard: (a) lack of clarity in the processes of evaluation and disability determination; (b) lack of sensitivity in initial presentations of diagnosis; (c) the role of emotion in discovery; (d) differences in cultural interpretations and understanding disability; and (e) the proliferation of information.

The "Secret Handshake": Lack of Clarity in the Process

Many of the parents we interviewed and talked to over the years find the journey to diagnosis and eligibility determination to be fraught with a lack of clarity; many described the special education eligibility process as being "like learning a foreign language." In addition, many parents encounter confusion regarding the school's position on eligibility and disability determination, with some feeling unsure about the degree to which school professionals are invested in helping them and their child. The legal underpinnings of special education, as well as its emphasis on objectivity and measurement throughout the evaluation process seem to some parents to stand in opposition to what they care about most: accessing services and supports for their children who are struggling in life and/or in school.

The story of Lindsay's journey is illustrative. After a fairly positive preschool experience, Lindsay and her husband were surprised by the difficulties that surfaced when their son transitioned to kindergarten. As her son's behaviors became increasingly challenging to manage, Lindsay began asking for answers from the school. She recalled sitting in meetings asking for help, but feeling that she was not finding it. She described feeling that she was not asking the right questions, noting that "To this day what remains my biggest frustration is the feeling that you are going to a country where everyone knows the rules and everyone knows the language and everyone knows the secret handshakes and they don't tell you anything about it." She spoke often about a lack of transparency within the evaluation process that needed to be followed to acquire help for her son, and her sense that the school professionals she was dealing with were somehow standing in the way of a disability determination for her son. She recalled how emotionally draining it was to try to navigate the process:

> You could see the agendas of everyone in the room The special educator was sitting there with the principal, you could just see everything, but it didn't make sense. I left every single meeting crying. I cried in every meeting and I have zero problems with conflict. I have zero problem with getting in people's faces and I absolutely just lost it in every meeting.

After feeling her son's kindergarten year had not resulted in positive changes for him or in a decision by school professionals to conduct a comprehensive evaluation, Lindsay and her husband removed their son from school and began home-schooling him. Wanting to "fast track" a potential diagnosis and plan, they eventually hired an independent evaluator who determined that their son's learning and behavioral profile was consistent with the characteristics associated with Autism Spectrum Disorder (ASD), and in particular, Asperger's Syndrome. Lindsay and her husband brought this information back to the school. Ultimately, the school team reversed its position and evaluated Lindsay's son, using information from the independent evaluation to determine eligibility for special education under the category of ASD. Although grateful for the supports that ensued from the diagnosis, Lindsay described feeling frustrated that the school had put up so many roadblocks to get to that point. As she noted:

> I still can't wrap my head around it… I just find it completely intriguing that at first no one could help us, but then we got answers from other people and now everyone's going to help us. Did we get the secret handshake right? It kind of felt like that.

Furthermore, the process that Lindsay and her husband experienced involved their having to pay money out of pocket for a diagnosis. Although IDEA mandates that schools identify children with disabilities and offers parents the right (under certain conditions that did not apply in Lindsay's case) to pursue an independent evaluation at no cost, some parents feel compelled to get the answers they are seeking through their own resources. Lindsay acknowledged her frustration with the fact that although school professionals seemed to be convinced by the evaluator's findings, her family's ability to pay for an independent evaluation might not be an option for all families. She recalled sitting at the eligibility meeting with the outside evaluator she and her husband had hired, thinking that although she and her husband had been able to afford the $1700 price tag for the evaluation, not all families would have been able to resolve a similar situation in this way. "Part of me was just so enraged that not all families could do what we had to do," she commented. "This makes me so angry about the system."

Georgia shared a similar story regarding the road to diagnosis that she and her husband travelled as three of their four children were diagnosed with disabilities, including their oldest daughter's diagnosis on the autism spectrum, their second daughter's diagnosis of ASD and anxiety disorder, and their youngest son's diagnosis of pervasive developmental delay. She reflected on the fact that her experiences with the process felt more circular than linear and were linked to a number of factors both within and outside of her family:

> We were homeschooling until our oldest was in 4th grade and that's when we noticed her development was different than her peers. We're pretty quiet, quirky bookish people in general, so that just raised questions and we were having conversations with the school about what that could mean. And from their end they didn't make a big deal about it. They just thought well "we'll do this test or that test that we asked for" but they weren't really putting anything together for us. I think in their view, they were being helpful and kind of suggesting parenting books and things like that. From our view it felt like "wow, that was pretty crappy," not really helpful at all.... I think for our third child, her diagnosis was much more dramatic because we noticed this huge shift in her demeanor where she had been a toddler who was pretty engaged and talked. ...All of a sudden she kind of plateaued and then started regressing so she stopped making eye contact, she stopped when we would go outside, like the textures started to bother her physically. She wouldn't try new foods. She'd have tantrums that were pretty intense, like every day, for at least 20 minutes. We could never figure out what would happen. We couldn't put it together.... we hadn't heard anything about Autism yet ... so then as we got to talking to the folks from the school district and they came in with those assessments and that was kind of mind blowing. Like what, this is called something? This is a procedure to figure this out? We were just kind of floored by the whole process.

Eventually, Georgia's daughters were both diagnosed with Autism Spectrum Disorder. Although the initial process of diagnosis for both had been overwhelming, Georgia became more and more interested in the special education process and eventually took a job as a paraeducator in her daughter's school. Soon afterwards, her youngest child was diagnosed with pervasive developmental delay, but by then, Georgia had been accepted into an early childhood special education program and felt much better educated about the evaluation process. Her experience with her son's diagnosis felt markedly different to her, and raised questions about the relationship between the process and professionals' view of her and her family. She talked about how the knowledge she gained through the early childhood education program and later, a doctoral program, shifted her involvement with the evaluation process and caused professionals to see her and her husband in a different light. She described having mixed feelings about these changes:

On the one hand it felt really empowering to be able to advocate really well for the kids and to be more knowledgeable about our son's evaluation process. On the other hand, it felt like wow, there are so many parents who don't have access to this information. Like do you have to get a degree in special ed to really advocate for your child in this process? What does that say? And I noticed how I was treated differently when the teachers realized I wasn't just a stay at home mom but actually becoming a teacher. And even now that I'm in the doctoral program, I don't know how I feel about that. It seems like our word has more weight and gets more attention based on that. I don't know, I feel weird about that.

Like Lindsay, Georgia was troubled by the fact that the quality and outcomes of the evaluation process seemed to correlate with how she was being perceived by school professionals. Their experiences point to the need to ensure that the processes of evaluation and diagnosis are conducted equitably and consistently, no matter what a family's background and educational experiences are or appear to be.

Helpful or Disempowering? Lack of Sensitivity in Initial Presentations

For many parents, the initial presentation of their child's disability determination is a powerful moment that shapes the course of their early interactions and relationships with professionals. Although some families experience a fairly logical and transparent process leading to a determination of a disability, many parents feel that the ways in which they receive information lacks sensitivity on the part of professionals. In Jane's case, for example, evidence that her son might have a disability presented itself through complications at delivery as well as through additional medical difficulties that he encountered at only six months of age. She described a particularly difficult experience with a false diagnosis that occurred following two years of testing aimed at trying to understand why her son, who seemed to have no signs of a disability at birth, was not achieving developmental milestones. She recalled receiving a phone call from a hospital laboratory during which she was told her son had tested positively for a rare and progressive disease known as Canavan's disease. Jane was understandably upset to receive this information, but became angry when she received a second call noting that the laboratory had mixed up his blood with that of another child. At that point she nearly gave upon testing, only to finally learn from her neurologist that he had another extremely rare condition known as Leukodystrophy.

Djenne recalled a similar experience. At birth, her son Malik presented a number of complex and interrelated medical conditions, and it took many doctor's visits and failed diagnoses to arrive at a determination that he had CHARGE Syndrome, a diagnosis that includes deafness and comorbid conditions, including cognitive delays. Djenne related that:

When Malik was diagnosed with profound deafness, I said to the audiologist, "Well, at least he won't die from being deaf!" This comment came on the heels of an array of one life threatening medical diagnosis after another. The real grief set in when I realized that Malik and I would never "hear" each other say "I love you." That was devastating at that time.

Jane and Djenne's stories of false diagnoses may not be common, but many parents find it extremely frustrating to spend months and years receiving varied and conflicting disability diagnoses. Although they may be grateful to arrive at eventual clarity in the process, the "back and forth" nature of disability identification for children with complex needs can exact an emotional toll on parents.

Other family members make a clear connection between specific conversations about diagnosis and their initial response to school and medical professionals. Katie, for example, felt the professionals who first initiated a conversation about her son's language challenges did so in a manner that was not grounded in a realistic or informed understanding of her child. Unlike the experiences of parents who waited years to arrive at a diagnosis, Katie learned about her child's challenge following a brief kindergarten screening. Although the professionals may have been following protocols in place to identify students at risk, for Katie, the lack of sensitivity that she felt the professionals demonstrated in their eagerness to describe her son's challenges was enraging. She recollected this early experience:

> So we went to the kindergarten screening …and this woman wrote up this whole thing of "he's not this, he's not that and he can't do this and dah dah dah and she sent it to me." I opened this letter and I went over to the school and I was like, I said, "Are you f***ing kidding me? How dare you make these judgments about my child that you saw for an hour and a half? Who are you?" And I was like berserk. I went completely insane…Like "What are you doing? How dare you like peg my child and how many other children are you pegging based on some nothing?"

Monica, whose child was diagnosed at an early age with dual sensory loss, also relayed a story of confusion, anger, and sadness following a brief conversation with a specialist who informed her and her husband that their son had CHARGE Syndrome. The description provided to Monica and her husband was full of medical terminology, a bleak prognosis and few offers of support. Monica described how:

> We left the office and my husband just sat on the sidewalk and cried. All at once he realized that our son would not be playing baseball with him, that he would not ever be able to be a professional firefighter like he was. He was completely heartbroken about the fact that his relationship with our son would be so different from what he had imagined.

Monica and her husband went on to have more positive experiences with their child and to become advocates for other parents, but Monica recalled that her husband's devastation was profound and took him years to overcome. Meanwhile, she felt that the circumstances necessitated that she jump immediately into the role of primary caregiver for their son.

Denise, the mother of a child with learning disabilities, recalled a similarly devastating situation in which the special educator who had coordinated her daughter's comprehensive evaluation called her briefly at work to give her a "heads up" before the eligibility determination meeting to tell her that her daughter did indeed qualify for services. Although Denise was happy to learn that her daughter would receive services, she had not appreciated the brevity of the conversation or the lack of privacy she felt in receiving this phone call in her office cubicle. Years later, this interaction remained a vivid memory: Denise simply could not understand why the special educator had not thought to ask if the time was a good one to talk or if she needed time to process the information. Her story reinforces the importance of thinking carefully about family culture and context and how that needs to be considered in delivering sensitive information to families.

Additionally, Djenne reminds us that it is crucial for professionals to understand and honor the preferred learning and communication styles of parents as they provide information and recommendations of the child's disability. Some parents may not be ready for an onslaught of technical/medical information and need time to process what they have been told. Others may want to hear everything and to know as soon as possible about the range of options available to their child and family. It is important that professionals recognize this and act accordingly. Djenne's personal experiences have led her to offer this advice:

> Ask parents how they would like to receive information about diagnoses and other sensitive matters, and whether they prefer a written or verbal format. Let them know that you may have a lot of information to convey and your desire is for them to understand it thoroughly so they can make informed decisions regarding their child. Ask them the best way to aid them in this understanding.

The Role of Emotion in Discovery

Regardless of whether the process of arriving at a disability determination is short or long, complicated or straightforward, or accompanied with support or not, many parents speak about experiencing multiple emotions leading up to and at the time of identification of their child's disability. Family members learning of their child's diagnosis at birth or shortly thereafter sometimes describe how the process of diagnosis engenders a sense of loss or even injustice as they come to grips with the realities of a situation they did not expect to be involved with. Kelly, for example, relayed the story of how she and her partner came into an unplanned adoption when a family member was unable to care for their child with a disability. Kelly remembered how overwhelmed and confused the two of them felt at the time, noting that "It was a kinship adoption situation so it was very sad and not in our plan, so not only were we not prepared to be parents of a kid with challenges, we just really weren't prepared at all."

Other parents experienced a mix of emotions, with some noting that although news of a diagnosis confirmed their worries or fears about their child's development and led to a sense of closure, it was also a sad time that quickly generated lots of questions about what would happen next. Andrew, whose son was diagnosed with autism spectrum disorder at an early age, recalled experiencing an array of emotions at the time of diagnosis, including grief, isolation, and a feeling that he and his wife should focus on their son's future:

> I think that's a really natural thing for any parent to go through is at first you get this overwhelming sense of grief. ...We didn't really have anybody who was in that same situation. At the same time, we also understood early on that the autism spectrum is a very vast situation and that we were vulnerable and tender. We did not want to explore the darkest side of the concerns and so we were careful and cautious about what we wanted to expose ourselves to because just as I was saying, the natural reaction for parents of any kind, for any kind of defect is how do you optimize the life of your child? How can you make this journey as bump free for them as you possibly can?

Melissa described a very mixed journey to diagnosis. She had been concerned about her son's ability to express himself when he was in kindergarten, but the teachers she spoke with early on tried to convince her that he was just a bit behind other kids developmentally and that he would catch up. After a series of "starts and stops," including retaining him in kindergarten and moving him to another school, she finally found a special educator who shared her concerns and agreed to evaluate her son. Upon receiving a diagnosis of a learning disability for him, she experienced a full range of emotions. She recalled the day when she learned of the diagnosis and told her son and older daughter about the disability determination:

> So then when the findings came back, it was, I broke down. I started bawling....
> When I went home that night and told him, and my daughter was there, and I said, well I have some news. Can we all sit down. My daughter blurts out, he's got dyslexia just like I said. I knew that was true. And I said well, there are some learning disabilities and Cody went into panic mode because of the word disabilities so I called my support person from the university and we talked through it and so he seemed better with the terms dyslexia, dysgraphia, then disability. It's really hard. And was there any sense of relief that now you had a diagnosis or was it, it sounds like it could have been sort of a mixed bag. Like finally the testing is done, but also it's difficult.

Other parents experienced the road to diagnosis as a very isolating and lonely one, particularly if the process dragged out or they did not have a strong support system. Some reached out to other parents, only to find that they felt tenuous about sharing their stories. Djenne recalled this story about a woman named Lisa whom she met at a conference:

I met Lisa at a retreat for parents with hearing loss. We were sitting next to each other at a mom's group. At some point during the conversation, I realized that Lisa seemed very uncomfortable. When I asked her about it, Lisa admitted that she was feeling that she could not relate to the conversation the other parents were having that was about devices and equipment that would allow their children to participate in sports or swimming. She didn't know if her 2-year-old son, Sam, would ever swim, much less play sports. She was waiting on a diagnosis (which eventually was CHARGE Syndrome) for Sam, who had multiple health issues. Lisa expressed the isolation she felt even around other parents because of his additional disabilities and the lack of understanding or recognition for her situation, even in these circles. This had also been the case with medical and therapeutic professionals. Lisa felt that they were so focused on their own area of expertise, that they were unable to see her child from a holistic point of view.

For other parents, the process of reaching a diagnosis brought relief and a sense of new understanding of their child, even when it came with mixed emotions. One mother, B. B., noted how the reactions that she and her partner had when they received their daughter Marjorie's diagnosis brought feelings of wonder and understanding, as well as concern:

At six months you're supposed to be crawling and seven months you're supposed to be crawling more and we noticed she wasn't meeting her developmental milestones and so like right before her first birthday, we took her to the pediatrician and said she's not doing the things she should be doing and they gave us a referral to the developmental pediatrician and it was a very, kind of a fascinating experience. He was with us for two hours and the whole first hour all he did was play with her. And then the second hour he did his developmental testing, he told us basically that she had what he called scatter shot development which means that in some area, the way I think about it is like a patchwork quilt. Some of those patches are strong and you can stand on them, then you go to the edge of that strong patch, and you look down into the abyss.

Djenne's story recalls a longer and more complicated road to diagnosis, but it also speaks to the sense of relief she experienced after a long process leading to the correct diagnosis for her son's condition:

It took three years for Malik to be diagnosed with CHARGE Syndrome, a rare genetic condition. Due to his fragile health and chronic illnesses early in his life, we were primarily focused on keeping him alive and treating each life threatening illness in isolation. Although we had very competent and excellent medical professionals taking care of Malik, they too were primarily addressing the part of his body that was in their realm of care. It wasn't until an educational professional asked me if I ever heard of this syndrome, that things became clearer.

45

She continued, recalling a distinct sequence of events:

"Have you ever heard of CHARGE Syndrome?", asked one of the psychologists at Malik's school. Of course I had no idea what she was referring to. We sat in her office and she explained what each letter meant and things began to finally make sense to me. We were then able to put the piece of Malik's medical history together and present his geneticist with "our" findings. The doctor, who was not very familiar with CHARGE Syndrome, as it was in its infancy in being diagnosed, agreed and signed off. Finally!!! We had a name for his condition. It was a relief for me as a mother to get validation and begin to piece his complicated puzzle together. It didn't make his symptoms go away, but gave us an explanation of sorts. We were finally able to begin making more informed decisions about his educational and medical needs. The fact that we had a name for Malik's condition didn't change the condition, it gave us access to tools to enhance his life as well as a new community – albeit very small at the time – to belong to where we spoke a similar language and shared experiences. We finally belonged somewhere!

Each of these stories reminds us of the need for professionals to be cognizant of the role that emotion plays in the events and processes leading to a diagnosis. Grief is real and may be experienced in a variety of ways. Although not all parents feel a sense of grief upon learning of their child's disability diagnosis, it is probably safe to say that most parents feel some sense of loss regarding what they expected or desired upon the birth of their child. Whether or not parents' initial reactions are accompanied with sadness, anger, relief, acceptance, or any other emotion or combination of feelings, emotion is a part of this process. Diagnosis in a clinical or educational sense suggests a level of objectivity and certainty that may be quite different from the lived experiences of families, and it is important for professionals to be aware of parents' emotions and to make time and space for them to process them. That said, many families talk about how the process of diagnosis often seems to move too quickly to allow for feelings to emerge and to be observed. It is also important to recognize that emotions accompanying an initial diagnosis are likely to change over time, sometimes as a series of ups and downs, and other times, in the direction of increased strength, advocacy, hope and resilience for families.

Information Overload

For many parents, the emotional journey they experience at the time of diagnosis is accompanied by an almost immediate desire to learn more about their child's disability and the supports that might be needed going forward. A distinct difference between this generation of parents and parents of 20 or 30 years relates to how families obtain information about their child's disability and the special education process. The prevailing notion in the 1970s and 1980s was that parents would receive information from professionals; the advent of the internet and the proliferation of available resources, however, has changed that situation for many families. The majority of the parents we interviewed appreciate the information they receive from professionals, but also see themselves playing far more active roles in gathering and relaying information to others. At the same time, increased access is often accompanied with a sense of feeling overwhelmed by the volume and degree of credibility of that information.

Andrew talked about these challenges at some length, noting the ways in which he and his wife tried to piece together and determine the reliability of information on ASD that they encountered from a variety of sources. As he noted:

> The resources at the time were very confined. The Internet was full of bad pointers. There's a lot of information as well as misinformation and it's difficult, as an uneducated person in the subject, to discern the facts from fiction. So we used the resources, professional resources that we had available, and that was, our pediatrician, and the local program for families of infants and toddlers. We also used some resources that my wife pulled in from school because she works in a school district and has the resources of special ed people and speech and language pathologists and physical therapy people so we got some people to pay attention to his disabilities, to our concerns. At the same time, we were trying to get some information about what they knew about kids on the spectrum and what, from their experience, what they could see in my son as challenge or promise for the future.

For many families, information gathering is a very laborious process that involves multiple and sometimes conflicting professional opinions. Parents' personal experiences play a role too, as some discover that their understanding of diagnosis changes in relation to their own growth in knowledge and skills. School professionals can play a role in supporting families in locating information and helping them to wade through it to determine which sources are most reliable and applicable to their child.

POSSIBILITIES FOR COLLABORATION

Along with the challenges that parents meet on the road to diagnosis, many tell stories of strength that center on their roles as advocates and funds of information. Specifically, they provide examples of how their own advocacy and knowledge contributes to the process of diagnosis and the planning processes that follow it. Some families also note the importance of professional advocacy and knowledge, particularly during times of transition for children and families. They note that professionals who convey a sense of competence positively influence families' feelings about the process as a whole. Although many of the parents' stories reveal challenges and missteps, they also contain examples of possibilities for greater collaboration in the important journey that families and professionals take on the road to identifying and understanding a child's disability. We relay several of those stories here, with an eye to imagining the potential for increased communication, transparency and shared responsibility among families and professionals in the early stages of diagnosing a child's disability and understanding what that means for the child and family.

Parent Advocacy and Knowledge

As indicated in the preceding section, many of the parents we interviewed initiated the process of diagnosing a disability. Given this dynamic it seems important not to assume that professionals hold all of the cards when it comes to diagnosis and to explore opportunities for a more shared approach to the process. Historically, the act of diagnosing a disability has been attributed to professionals; however, we see evidence or a shift to a more collaborative and/or parent-driven process.

Moving beyond "let's wait and see."   For some parents, the process of advocating for a formal evaluation, whether medical or school-based, came after experiences with professionals adopting a "wait and see" approach. Andrew reflected on this phenomenon, describing a time during which he and his wife worked with their pediatrician to determine why their son was not meeting developmental milestones:

> Well, my son's always been a very quiet, he was a quiet baby. He didn't cry a lot. His affect was very plain. He seemed to be more content to be carried around in a papoose, close to his mom all the time, on her chest, and he slept most of the time. When he wasn't sleeping, he was disinterested or disassociated with his surroundings. He didn't focus on things in front of his face. His gaze was fixed. He seemed a little catatonic. We worried about that and called the pediatrician several times to think about what might be going on. Initially he gave us a diagnosis that my son may have cerebral palsy.

Andrew and his wife continued to express their concerns:

> Eventually though, with the pediatrician's help, we got the referral to Child Development Clinic, where the doctor did a work up on him and gave the diagnosis of autism based on her findings in the study. And we started immediately with the services from the Family and Infant Toddler Program that provides early intervention services in our state.

The experience of Andrew and his wife underscores the importance of listening to parents closely in order to hear and act upon their concerns. Andrew and his wife demonstrated persistence and advocacy that eventually resulted in an evaluation, diagnosis and intervention, but their story raises concerns about the length of time that it often takes for families to convince professionals that further action is warranted.

Like Andrew, Lulu also experienced the "wait and see" approach. She remembered a year long process of raising concerns to her pediatrician about her son's language development:

> I mean I started asking probably at maybe the 12 month checkup so I was saying he's really not talking and the pediatrician was doing the "it's fine, wait and see" kind of thing and by 2 when he still wasn't really talking, she said, "okay we'll refer" and I found out later that I could have and should have just called the local Family and Infant Toddler Project myself to get him assessed.

In retrospect, she reflected that going through the pediatrician as a gateway for a diagnosis, while common, was not the only way she could have initiated the process for her son to get early intervention. In her current work as an advocate for adoptive parents, Lulu recommends that families explore a variety of avenues to access services when they suspect that something is not right.

Other families encountered differences of opinion among professionals regarding how much time to wait before moving ahead to evaluate a potential disability. For example, Maggie found her family physician to be far more responsive to her concerns about her daughter's development than were school professionals. As she explained, she had years of early childhood teaching experience, so when her daughter did not seem to be reaching typical developmental milestones, she was able to use that knowledge and expertise to communicate her concerns to her daughter's pediatrician. Maggie shared:

> She didn't really put more than two, maybe three words together until she was three years old and then she started speaking more in sentences, so that was a red flag right here because I have the daycare. I see a lot of children and a lot of patterns, language development, and fine motor, gross motor skill development so with her not talking then, those red flags are going up. Something's not right.

She described her next steps:

> So I went to our physician and I told him all the things that I see and don't see and so he recommended she go to the child development clinic and so we did that and they said "yes, there's some issues here," so before she even hit kindergarten, we had a list of things that she needed help and support in and one was memory, short term memory.

Ironically this step occurred after she had approached her child's school about her concerns and had been told that it was too early to do any testing. Maggie reflected on the fact that the reason she was able to access early supports for her child related to her professional role and her ability to convey her concerns to a pediatrician who was willing to listen to her. She was grateful for the supports her daughter received prior to kindergarten, yet was concerned that these were provided primarily because of the time and energy she put into the process. Once the ball was rolling, she found that the elementary school professionals became advocates for putting appropriate programming into place.

The power of parents' drive to understand. In the process of seeking out information and advocating on behalf of their children, parents play a powerful role in the diagnostic process. The story of Will and his wife Abigail, whose daughter has an extremely rare genetic disorder, provides a compelling example of the ways in which parents' drive to pursue knowledge about their child's disability can outpace the depth and speed of professionals' ability to get to a diagnosis. Will credited Abigail for being the one who accurately diagnosed their daughter when she was a little over a year old. After months of extensive research and consultation with professionals, Abigail found a You Tube video that depicted the exact symptoms of what their young daughter was experiencing. This discovery led to connecting with an expert who confirmed the diagnosis that his wife had identified. Will described their journey to diagnosis:

> And so she started to have these episodes or these attacks where it seems like she is in pain and she would lose use of an arm or just kind of be almost like in paralysis and so working with our pediatrician, we looked at, thought it was things with her digestion and different things and it just kind of progressively started getting worse ...and so we thought she might be having seizures and so, of course Abigail went to You Tube and watching a lot of kids have seizures and things like that and it didn't really look like our daughter and so then we started seeing a neurologist and they thought it might be a mitochondria disorder and so we did the spinal tap and did all that stuff, and that came back negative but the University of Utah does a lot of mitochondrial disorder research and so one night my wife was on the internet looking at the University of Utah, looking at videos of kids with these mitochondrial disorders and there was a link to her actual condition.

Because their daughter's diagnosis was so rare, their role in finding answers about how best to meet her needs was significant. When asked whether he felt that he and his wife were in the driver's seat will responded affirmatively. He eloquently revisited the night his wife made the discovery:

> So I'm asleep, it's probably like 1:00 or 2:00 in the morning and Abigail comes running upstairs and says, you need to come look at this video and I say to her, "I'm not looking at another kid having a seizure online. I'm done looking at these videos of kids. I don't want to watch" and she said, "This is the last time I'll ask you. You need to see this." And I went downstairs and there was a girl online having an episode *[emotional]*—haven't told this story in a long time-just like her. I mean, it was the spitting image and we had no idea what it was until that point and it was like, that's her, that's what's happening and so the next day we called the neurologist and he said, "yeah, this could be it."

Will and Abigail's story reminds us of how powerful parents' desire to understand their child is, and how helpful that drive can be in the process of diagnosing disabilities, particularly those that may be complex. As professionals, it can be easy to discount parent involvement in the process as being too "pushy" or "demanding," but it is important to honor parents' "need to know" and the valuable information and knowledge that they contribute to the process. At the same time, it is important to recognize that not all families are equally positioned or have as much time and access to information as others.

Remaining focused on the child as a whole and unique person. A number of parents talked about the ways in which their knowledge and understanding of their child as a whole person and a human being made it possible for them to cope with the complexities of a diagnosis and to see the child from a more strengths-based perspective. Jamie, a young mother of a child with hearing and vision loss, talked about the power she derived from pointing out the difference between who her daughter appeared to be through an official diagnosis, versus who she was in person. As she described:

> I like it when people read us first on paper and then see us. I want you to read on paper her diagnosis. I want you to read on paper I'm a single black mother with a child with a disability. Then I want you to see us. Once you see the stats, and then see her and compare the two, your mind is blown. On paper, she seems more involved than she is. She's surpassed the doctors' predictions of what she wouldn't do. We are proof that you cannot judge a book by its cover. She is the top of her class and doesn't have an IEP any longer. She makes you forget the disability and just see her.

Georgia, too, described the difference between thinking about disabilities "on paper," and considering them in light of her children's strengths and personalities. She described the transition she went through as she moved from thinking that her children were "just quirky" to being overwhelmed by their diagnoses, to finding new ways of thinking that were more strengths-based and holistic. She described the approach that she and her husband took:

> Like it's huge for us to say that "okay, in spite of all of this stuff, you're a whole human being. You're a valued part of society and our family. You're talented in a lot of different ways. You're a great kid and a great family member." All that self-esteem stuff is really important to us 'cuz they hear enough negative weird stuff in the world. We talk about disabilities being your super power. We joke about all the kids have bionic hearing and bionic noses – we joke about that a lot.

Other parents too, talked about the importance of moving beyond the disability labels assigned to their children as part of the process of diagnosis to seeing their children—and having others see their children—as whole people. We return to this idea in subsequent chapters but want to reinforce here what research and parent narratives have emphasized: that a diagnosis of a disability should not cause any parent to feel that their child is somehow "broken" (Kingsley, 1987; Yuan, 2003).

Yuan, the mother of a son with Angleman Syndrome, wrote that "When I first learned that my son had a significant disability, no way did I think that I could be a good mother to him" (p. 207). Although she had concerns about her own competence as a parent, she recognized that "There was not anything "broken" about my son. He was just far more complex, more sensitive, more responsive, in more unusual ways, than any one I had ever known before. As I learned from necessity how to interact with him, read his subtle signs, love him, I became better at being a mother" (Yuan, 2003, p. 207). Kingsley's 1987 essay entitled *Welcome to Holland* conveys a similar sentiment, describing having a child with a disability as being similar to dreaming of a vacation in Italy, only to find out you will be spending time in Holland. She notes that the loss of the dream of going to Italy is "significant…yet if you spend your life mourning the fact that you didn't get to Italy, you may never be free to enjoy the very special, the very lovely things … about Holland" (n.p.).

Djenne's husband Michael conveyed similar ideas in his reflections on raising Malik:

A parent who has a child with a singular disability is like a parent given lemons and asked to make lemonade. But imagine someone walking in while that parent is trying to make lemonade and pours vinegar in the mix. Both ingredients separately are tantalizing, but together they create a major challenge to create a recipe that is palatable and perfect to that family. Things when combined together present a unique challenge. That's what it has been like for me having a child with multiple disabilities. I feel like I'm on one of those cooking shows. I've been told to make something that will be palatable and tasty in the end, but the only choices I am being provided with are ingredients that don't really go together in my mind. And there are always one or two cooks on those shows who have the creativity to take what they've been given and make it work for everyone. As a father, I feel the responsibility to make it all fit together, present beautifully and taste good. Sometimes I succeed, other times I don't.

Each of these stories serves as a reminder of the fact that while the journey to a diagnosis is important and useful in many ways, finding the "correct" disability label by no means captures the totality of the child with a disability or the family who loves and supports that child.

Professional Advocacy and Knowledge

Along with parents' efforts to ensure proper diagnoses of their children and/or to re-frame their own experiences with diagnosis and disability labels, some parents talked about how professionals who adopted an advocacy stance were invaluable in helping them to understand their child's disability and the need for services. They identified these occasions as being extraordinarily helpful in easing some of their stress as they came to terms with diagnosis and began to look for appropriate interventions for their children. For example, She' Ra Monroe at first doubted a professional diagnosis of Down syndrome for her newborn son. She recalled:

So when I delivered they told me that they thought he had Down syndrome and I promptly told all of them that they were crazy. "No, no, no, goodbye, I'm not talking to you guys anymore. I'm done," I said. Three months later I finally came to terms with it, and then we started, partly because he had medical conditions that needed to be addressed.

As She' Ra Monroe began to acknowledge her son's diagnosis, she was also able to fully appreciate the level of support and care professionals extended not only to her son, but to her as a parent. In particular she recalled a visiting nurse who was pivotal in helping her come to terms with her son's disability and to access support:

And the way I first came to know about services was his visiting nurse. She came in to do some wound care for the hernia surgery and she was just awesome. Really just awesome. Shaped our lives in so many ways. I cannot speak enough about her.

She' Ra Monroe articulated how important the relationships she built with early care providers were in providing her the support she needed to raise her son as a single mother. These supports contributed to her sense that a community was supporting her son throughout multiple transitions. Her story is illustrative of the fact that some parents may need extra time to process information about a disability diagnosis, and that professionals need to withhold judgment and continue to offer support when it appears this is the case.

Transitions

Because diagnosis is not a single event, the transitions from one level of service to another also present numerous challenges to families of children with disabilities. A medical diagnosis or diagnosis of "developmental delay" (used for children receiving services from birth to three under IDEA, Part C, and children ages three through nine under IDEA, Part B) that at one point qualifies a child for early intervention will need to be re-visited once the child is of school age to determine whether they meets the special education eligibility requirements for services provided to students ages 6–21. At times this can result in new "diagnoses" or labels. For example, a child who received services under the broad category of developmental delay in preschool might receive a new diagnosis of intellectual disability following a re-evaluation conducted once the child reaches school age. Parents expressed how important it was at these junctures to have professionals who advocated for services or supports using their knowledge of the system to make sure kids were not falling through the cracks.

Holly's story speaks to this sequence of events. As an infant, her son presented with emotional and behavioral challenges. She noted:

> When he was born we knew he wasn't all there. Just very unhappy in his own skin, just very moody, cried all the time and he wasn't happy until he started walking and crawling. Very overwhelmed with senses and he would get off the bus from preschool and just fall apart for like 30 minutes, crying.

She acknowledged that his preschool teacher's advocacy helped secure support as he transitioned to kindergarten:

> So we had a wonderful teacher and I can't think of her name anymore, but he went to kindergarten and she wrote up that she thought he needed an aide and a one on one, he was special needs.

Using that information Holly was then able to engage in her own advocacy for her son, when his kindergarten team felt that 1:1 support was not necessary. Although this early experience became the first of many in which Holly had to fight for adequate programming for her son, it highlighted to her the importance of working in partnership with professionals who advocate for their students.

Kelly was struck by the fact that when her daughter transitioned from birth to three services, to early intervention services for preschoolers, the team was aware of the changing criteria related to diagnosis. She appreciated their advocacy to ensure that there would be no gap in services. As she recalled:

> Yeah, so it was very interesting because even though she met her milestones with some small challenges, it sort of seemed to be understood and accepted by everyone who's worked with her pretty much all through her life, that she needs to keep getting these services – which was not what I expected. I expected to have to fight for them and I didn't have to, so when she was getting close to three, I remember the team talking about she's going to transition into the early intervention program. They knew that she was going to be due for her three-year reevaluation soon after she turned three. They were concerned that she wouldn't qualify so they did her reevaluation before she turned three so that she would, and it was all very above board, you know what I mean? It didn't feel sneaky but it was just everyone saying we want to keep her eligible.

In Kelly's mind, professionals used their knowledge of the system as well as their knowledge of her daughter's needs to ensure that she continued to receive support. Through these stories, a different kind of parent-professional relationship emerges, in which parents begin to see professionals as being "on their team" instead of against them. Professionals who demonstrate a sense of care in the process of identifying (and in some cases, re-identifying) a disability may be more likely to engage in positive and collaborative relationships with parents.

What's in a role? Collaborating with multiple professionals. The process of diagnosis can also introduce parents to a range of professionals they need to collaborate with in order to manage the needs of their children, and many find the realities of working with multiple providers to be a significant challenge. Depending on the complexity of the child's needs, the number of appointments and consultations may be very time consuming; at the same time, all involved benefit when efforts are made to ensure collaboration across disciplines and expertise.

Kelly emphasized the essential nature of having a point person to assist her in navigating the system and learning how to parent a child with significant needs. In particular, the visiting nurse who supported her following the adoption of her daughter became vital for managing the numerous interactions with professional service providers:

> When our daughter came to live with us, I remember the foster mom kind of giving us a list of all her upcoming appointments, like a follow-up appointment with the orthopedic surgeon. She had appointments at the Children's Specialty Clinic because that's where they followed her, for she was on methadone until nine months old and that was for the neonatal abstinence syndrome. So she had all these appointments including with Family Infant and Toddler Program because this other foster parent had started the process and had already enrolled her, and she had a VNA nurse who did home visits who was fantastic. Unbelievably helpful. Probably the most helpful of any support we had.

Kelly's experience raises an important systemic issue: namely, the importance of identifying one person that parents can turn to for help, especially when their child has complex needs. In chapter 4, we describe the multiple roles that parents often take on in situations like Kelly's, noting both the realities of this situation for parents and the need for more supports.

CHAPTER SUMMARY

The path to identification of a disability varies for each family. Whether diagnosis comes as a result of parent advocacy, professional advocacy or both, the process involves information gathering, sharing and filtering by both parties and ultimately sets the foundation for future collaborative experiences. Additionally, diagnosis is not a fixed moment in time or a singular event. The process of learning about the presence of a child's disability can be repeated over the years and in different contexts and often involves a complex and changing set of emotions for families. The stories we have heard from parents suggest multiple opportunities for improved collaboration, beginning with the very first interactions that parents and professionals have with one another. Based upon what parents have told us, we offer some suggestions for both parents and professionals.

1. *Promote open communication and transparency around the process of identifying a disability.* Professionals need to recognize that institutional (i.e., educational, medical, legal etc.) definitions and ways of thinking about disability are complex and are generally unknown to most parents prior to their personal experiences

with disability. Open and transparent communication between families and professionals is critical in introducing the processes that lead to identification of a disability and navigating subsequent phases as they evolve. It is critical that parents experience the early stages of diagnosis as a time in which they can ask questions and develop an understanding. There should be no "secret handshakes."

2. *Consider optimal ways to present information about a diagnosis to families.* Professionals need to carefully consider how information about a child's disability is presented, particularly in the initial phases of identification. Parents need professionals to be forthcoming with information and services, but the ways in which that information is delivered need to take into account each family's circumstances, cultural backgrounds, strengths, learning styles, and needs. Parents' early interactions often shape how they approach or navigate future interactions; thus it is important to be mindful of the tone and nature of early conversations. She Ra' Monroe's story reminds us that while some parents are ready to hear information about their child's diagnosis, others may need more time and space to think about what it means for their child to have a disability and the impact that will have on the family as a whole.

3. *Take into account the emotional nature of disability determination and diagnosis.* Parents' stories indicate that the process generally involves a range of emotions. Some of the earlier literature references ways in which Kublher-Ross' cycle of grief (1969) may come into play for families. While this cycle may be representative of some parents' experiences, it may be less linear than portrayed, and/or accompanied with other emotions, including relief at finding an answer, hope for the future, or a sense of urgency related to what needs to come next. Although some parents may relate to the cycles of grief framework, others do not relate to it and may in fact reject that the idea that grief is part of the process of understanding disability. Importantly, families' stories suggest that the emotions parents experience in relation to their child's diagnosis do not occur just once; rather, they may occur over and over again as a child transitions to a new set of services, new definitions of disability, or improvement or decline in the child's progress.

4. *Consider different cultural contexts and interpretations of disability.* Some of the stories we collected remind us that the terms commonly used to describe disability in education, medicine, and law may not be shared or accepted by all families. Our western views of disability typically locate it within the individual and portray disability as something to be "overcome" or accommodated for through the initiation of supports and services. Professional approaches to defining and considering disability give primacy to research and science and to an "objective" view of disability. Parents may see value in research and the expertise of professionals, but their perspective may also be shaped by their personal experiences with their child, religious and cultural beliefs, and so forth. Professionals are bound to professional standards and ethics that may come into

conflict with parents' perspectives, but they can affirm and discuss with parents the fact that there may be multiple ways to view and understand disability.

5. *Support access to reliable information.* Several families spoke about the challenge of "information overload," especially during the initial phases of coming to understand the processes through which disability determination occurs, their child's strengths and needs, the services and supports available, and the nature of particular disabilities. It is critical for professionals to provide information regarding available family supports (e.g., the federally-funded parent centers and deaf-blind projects within each state), as well as tips for locating and evaluating information available from professional sources as well as the web.

6. *Recognize the multiple ways that families contribute to the process of diagnosis.* The families we have spoken with provide multiple examples of their role in the process of diagnosis. Although this process was once considered to be primarily a professional activity, it is no longer the case, as many families gather information from a variety of sources, contact professionals, and engage in other efforts to advocate on behalf of their children throughout the process of diagnosis. Parents' roles as educators and advocates need to be recognized and considered throughout, both for their content (e.g., the information that parents provide regarding their child's strengths and needs) and for their intent (e.g., the level of effort and energy that families are willing to expend). Parents who have less access to information and resources, to professionals, and/or to the dominant language may still advocate for their children during the process of diagnosis, but their advocacy may be demonstrated through their expressions of love for their child or their anger about the system. These kinds of advocacy, too, are valuable.

7. *Recognize advocacy among professionals.* Some families shared stories about the process of diagnosis that were fraught with challenges and less than ideal relationships with professionals. Others were able to identify one or more professionals who brought knowledge, consistency, care, and a sense of advocacy to the process. These stories of positive relationships, open communication, and a willingness on the part of professionals to change their minds provide evidence that the process can (and does) work well in many cases. It's important to understand that parents' early experiences in collaborating with professionals are shaped by the journey to diagnosis. A positive start with a family's first team paves the way for future positive experiences, whereas a negative start may negatively influence families' views of parent and professional partnerships.

8. *Validate the family experience and journey.* Every family has their own journey of discovery and road to resilience. In fact, each individual in the family does. Having a child with a disability affects each member of the immediate and extended family and friends differently. Oftentimes parents have the responsibility of managing their own emotions and those of the siblings in addition to the reactions and responses of others in their immediate circle. It is crucial that families have a safe place to process these emotions. Educators and other professionals and service providers must seek to understand how a family is managing their emotions, what

is required for the family's day-to-day maintenance and what support systems are in place. This can help a professional to know a family's ability to be an active participant in the medical or educational team.

SUGGESTED QUESTIONS FOR REFLECTION AND DISCUSSION

For parents and professionals:

1. Why is important to view the process of diagnosis as multi-staged, rather than a singular event?
2. What transitions may lead to re-visiting a diagnosis or how a child is eligible for special education services and what implications does this have?
3. What strategies are effective for being transparent about eligibility processes and communicating proactively with families?
4. What information about early diagnosis should families share with schools?
5. What additional factors need to be considered when professionals are discussing the special education evaluation and identification process with families from diverse backgrounds?

SUGGESTED ACTIVITIES

For parents:

1. Consider Djenne's advice to professionals to ask parents how they would like to receive information. As a parent, what is your preference for how information is communicated to you by professionals? Do you prefer to meet face-to face? Phone calls? Via Email or text? How will you communicate this information to your child's case manager or other key professionals?

For professionals:

2. Consider Lindsay's story about being frustrated about the lack of transparency in the special education evaluation and eligibility process, and her perception that navigating that process equated with knowing a "secret handshake" or speaking a different language. Write a letter to a parent explaining the special education evaluation process using as little jargon as possible. In the letter clearly articulate the purpose of a special education evaluation as well as resources parents can use to seek more information.
3. Initiate a discussion and/or a short survey with a parent to find out how they would like to have information presented to them. Consider:
   • What are the preferences of the families with whom you work regarding how information is communicated and discussed? Do parents prefer texting? Email? Telephone? If your school has a policy on the use of technology, how will you communicate this to parents?

- What are the learning styles of the parents with whom you work (e.g., do parents identify themselves as visual, auditory, kinesthetic or tactile learners)? How might these preferences influence how you communicate information to families?

REFERENCES

Aceves, T. C., & Orosco, M. J. (2014). *Culturally responsive teaching* (Document No. IC-2). Retrieved from http://ceedar.education.ufl.edu/tools/innovation-configurations/

Blanchett, W. (2010). Telling it like it is: The Role of race, class and culture in the perpetuation of learning disabilities as a privileged category for the white middle class. *Disabilities Study Quarterly, 30*(2). doi:http://dx.doi.org/10.18061/dsq.v30i2.

Blue-Banning, M., Summers, J. A., Frankland, H. C., Nelson, L. L., & Beegle, G. (2004). Dimensions of family and professional partnerships: Constructive guidelines for collaboration. *Exceptional Children, 70*(2), 167–184.

Fadiman, A. (2012). *The spirit catches you and you fall down.* New York, NY: Farrar, Straus and Giroux.

Fernandez, N., & Inserra, A. (2013). Disproportionate classification of ESL students in U.S. special education. *The Electronic Journal for English as a Second Language, 17*(2), 1–22.

Harry, B. (2008). Collaboration with culturally and linguistically diverse families: Ideal versus reality. *Exceptional Children, 74*(3), 372–388.

Harry, B., & Klingner, J. K. (2006). *Why are there so many minority students in special education?: Understanding race and disability in schools.* New York, NY: Teachers College Press.

Herrara, S. G., Perez, D. R., & Escalmilla, K. (2015). *Teaching reading to English language learners: Differentiated literacies* (2nd ed.). Boston, MA: Pearson.

Heward, W. (2012). *Exceptional children: An introduction to special education* (10th ed.). Upper Saddle River, NJ: Pearson.

Jegatheesan, B., Miller, P., & Fowler, S. (2010). Autism from a religious perspective: A study of parental beliefs in South Asian Muslim immigrant families. *Focus on Autism and Other Developmental Disabilities, 25*(2), 98–109.

Kalyanpur, M., & Harry, B. (2012). *Cultural reciprocity in special education: Building family-professional relationships.* Baltimore, MD: Paul H. Brookes Publishing.

Kingsley, E. P. (1987). *Welcome to Holland.* Self-published. Retrieved from http://www.our-kids.org/archives/Holland.html

Kublher-Ross, E. (1969). *On death and dying.* New York, NY: Simon and Schuster/Touchstone.

McCabe, H. (2007). Parent advocacy in the face of adversity: Autism and families in the People's Republic of China, *Focus on Autism and Other Developmental Disabilities, 22*(1), 39–50.

Sleeter, C. E. (1987). Why is there learning disabilities? A critical analysis of the birth of the field with its social context. In T.S. Popkewitz (Ed.), *The formation of school subjects: the struggle for creating an American institution.* (pp. 210–237). London: Palmer Press.

UNDERSTANDING PARENTS AS
ACTORS AND EXPERTS[1]

We became actors in the play about the life of a medically fragile little boy. At the time Malik was borne my husband and I were in the ministry and had a 13-month-old daughter. What did we know about colobomas, trachea-esophageal fistulas and failure to thrive syndrome? Not only did we have to learn a new skill as parents, we had to learn a whole new language, both medical and educational. We had no written script and the characters kept changing and increasing in numbers with each new medical diagnosis. As soon as we learned our lines, the script seemed to change.

(Djenne)

A cliché in education is the catch phrase, "parents are the experts." But what does that phrase really mean? If we abide by that philosophy, why do so many parents feel that their knowledge and expertise are undervalued by school systems? Why do so many professionals classify parents in two ways: those who "don't care" and those who are "the squeaky wheel" (or worse)? In this chapter we explore different dimensions of parental roles, action, and expertise as expressed by the parents we interviewed. We offer this set of stories and lessons as an antidote to simplistic views of parent involvement, arguing instead that parents play a range of complex roles that serve to meet the needs of their families and themselves. Each of these roles suggests different ways in which parents become actors in their children's lives who deal with daily demands and realities, convey their knowledge, become advocates, and create change. Families embrace many roles, and no two families play these roles in exactly the same way.

Although the literature on family and school collaboration has explored the idea that parents and professionals may take on different roles within IEP, transition, and other planning contexts (e.g., deFur, 2012; Turnbull et al., 2011), our conversations with parents attempt to take a deeper look at what it means to be the parent of a child with a disability, and in many cases, to be that child's "case manager." Parents' need to advocate for their children may compel them to engage in information gathering, filtering, networking, advocating and leading. Alternatively, their advocacy may take place at an individual level, through demonstrations of love and care for their children, advocacy for certain kinds of services, or even anger at a system that does not seem fair. Understanding how parents define what being the expert means may help foster a deeper appreciation of parent knowledge and create opportunities to welcome their expertise and contributions on special education teams. This chapter begins by identifying key roles that parents of children with disabilities identify in the development of their expertise, followed by perspectives of parents regarding the degree to which their knowledge and expertise is valued within IEP meetings. We conclude by sharing strategies parents use to improve their sense of equity and parity on special education teams: practices they believe convey to professionals that their expertise is valued and important. Throughout, we acknowledge the need for professionals to understand parents as key actors, change agents, and experts in their children's lives, no matter what specific roles they take on.

BECOMING EXPERTS AND ACTORS: KEY ROLES OF PARENTS

Adopting a Role

When we ask parents to talk about their expertise and roles, most begin with a discussion of the explicit knowledge they have about their children's needs and the multitude of ways they share that knowledge with professionals. For some parents, this information is particularly important during times of transition or when advocating for specific services. For others it is an essential component of making sure that all team members are on the same page to ensure consistency in care and services. In discussing their knowledge and expertise, parents often articulate the numerous roles they adopt in order to manage the complexity of raising and advocating for a child with a disability. Many articulate the importance of having professionals who "truly know my child," with the idea that "knowing" needs to go beyond understanding of a child's academic needs to include knowledge of the whole child.

Parents as Case Managers

Although the term "case manager" is often used in the context of professional roles, many parents view themselves as the case managers of their children, noting that they are the ones with ultimate responsibility for coordinating all facets of their child's life, including multiple service providers and interventionists. Some parents view this role as a natural one, while others take it on out of necessity. Some raise questions about the degree to which it is in fact appropriate for family members to take on this role when their lives include other children, jobs, partners, etc. Several stories illustrate the range of approaches that parents take with respect to case management.

Early in her son's life, Bethany created a visual display to share with service providers to help them understand the vast network of individuals providing service to her son as well to help convey an understanding that she viewed herself as his ultimate "case manager." Bethany shared, "I kept hearing that everyone was my son's case manager, but everyone was a case manager in their own realm and so there were six or seven of them and I was ultimately the case manager who connected all of those hubs." When children have complex needs, oftentimes there can be a variety of agencies and professionals providing services. Parents see themselves as the cornerstone of service delivery who must ensure that the child's needs that the child's needs are getting met. This often includes managing opposing personalities in order to keep the focus on what parents view as their long-term goals.

For Holly, this process of "managing" the team became quite burdensome. As lines of communication broke down between the agencies serving her child, she found herself making multiple phone calls and having numerous separate meetings outside of team meetings to make sure each individual was clear about her perspective and what her son's needs were. Managing the relationships of all the team members was a central piece of how she ensured that her son's needs were getting addressed. Holly was very upset about this, recalling:

> It's ridiculous because everyone has their own agenda, everyone has their own defenses, so like I want to have a conversation with different people on what they're doing. But I can't have it at that meeting because school's jumping all over them for something and then DCF [Department of Children and Families] is putting their two cents in, which is fine because I do like our DCF worker a lot, and then I have the LEA [Local Education Agency] saying we should do this, so I can't, and nothing is settled. It's awful.

She remembered counting 40 emails that circulated among team members with regard to picking dates for one meeting. Her frustration mounted as her son's behavior escalated to the point where she had to call the sheriff's office on a frequent basis. At one point staff from the sheriff's office stepped in as respite providers on days her son was sent home from school or was struggling at home. Her son experienced five different school settings in multiple locations with rotating teams of professionals. Holly played the role of case manager by juggling multiple personalities and coordinating up to 20 service providers in meeting the needs of her son. She found the experience exhausting, yet she felt driven to do it because of the intensity of her son's situation.

Another parent, Maggie, described herself as a "juggler" who was tasked with coordinating the integration of all the different types of services her child accessed – some school related, some not. As she described:

> The parent is a juggler, although the balls interact and overlap, but I feel like the parent is the one who has all the balls, is the one touching all of them. There's mental health, emotional health, education. There's social life, the family interactions and just at home life and how things go there. That all this is part of the whole picture of your child's life and making their life run smoother and part of their overall education.

B.B. took the idea of serving as her daughter's case manager even a step further. Her daughter was identified as having developmental delay before the age of two, so B.B. recalled learning early on that many people would be a part of her family's life. Her approach was to take on the role of case manager both within and outside of school, including in the context of IEP meetings. As she put it:

I don't know if it's made it go better but starting really in the earliest levels, I've always understood the fact that teachers come and go and my partner and I are her parents forever and so when we go to an IEP meeting, I'm in charge. I'm in charge. And I bring real things real directly, I'm very direct. I lay it on the table with a big comma. And then I ask people what they think. And so what we've developed over time is a problem solving group. Problem solving but preceding the problem solving, I always start with strengths. ...There was one time in middle school when the special educator went immediately to, "you know, these are her deficits." I stopped the meeting and said, "Let's talk about Marjorie's strengths first. What does she do really well? What are the areas we can build on so she feels good about herself as she's learning these other things?"

B.B. went on to talk about her role in helping to establish a sense of trust and partnership with special educators and other professionals:

I think it also depends on trust. The teacher may be new to Marjorie, but I'm coming from 13 years of monthly meetings with teachers and special educators. Because we insist on it. And it depends on the individuals. ... I think you have to be invitational as a parent. You have to sort of say, this is my experience, what's yours? And when we put the two experiences together ... we have a bigger picture, and then from that bigger picture we can make better decisions. ...I think it's also good facilitation at meetings and since I facilitate most of the time, it's good (laughs). Sometimes I'll back up depending on who's doing stuff, but I think in my experience, we end up sitting there on the table as equals and kind of, with the best interests of this particular child in the forefront, we pool our resources and haggle it out together, sometimes debate different kinds of things.

This notion of parent as case manager is one that professionals may overlook or underestimate. B.B. acknowledged that her direct level of involvment in meeting facilitation was not always appreciated by professionals, but she persisted, seeing this as one of her key roles as a parent. On the other hand, some parents who took on the role of case manager experienced some resentment, feeling that the responsibility was outside of what should be reasonably expected of them. This question speaks to some larger systemic issues as well, including the need for systems of care that make it easier for professionals and service providers from different disciplines to communicate and cooridinate with one another, especially in cases where children have complex medical, emotional/behavioral, and/or educational needs.

Parents as interventionists. In addition to serving as a case manager or coordinator of professional service providers, many parents of children with disabilities articulate the active role they play in providing intervention to their child. Parents are often expected to implement early intervention services, and may continue to provide ongoing support and intervention to their school age child during the hours outside of the school day. Here too, parents experience mixed feelings about their roles as interventionists. On the one hand, family members may feel that intervening on behalf of their child's health or education is part of their natural role; on the other hand, the expectations around intervention may appear daunting.

An example of the challenges of being a parent and an interventionist was provided by Andrew, whose son received school and home based services to address his learning needs related to autism spectrum disorder. Andrew and his wife were actively engaged in networking with others and using their own resources to inform and enhance their son's education. Andrew recalled referencing books on child development and tracking his son's progress towards meeting developmental milestones. Additionally, he and his wife spent hours working with their son to develop eye contact. He described an exhausting routine early in his son's life where he and his wife were juggling work and providing intervention:

> She's coming in and I'm going out. And so she's doing the tuck to bed and then she gets some sleep and gets up in the morning and does the morning feeding, getting him washed and clothed and I come stringing in. I take him off to daycare, come home and go to sleep. Get up in the afternoon, run over to pick him up, we start daddy "face time" and the weekends it's the other way around. She's doing it and I'm working and sleeping and so we're giving 100% coverage by parents.

Similarly, Lina felt it was important to assist with interventions for her child, but was frustrated by the reception she had from professionals when her approach to intervention differed from theirs. She applied her training as a nurse to assist the medical professionals in resolving her daughter's feeding challenges. At first, she faced resistance when sharing her perspective that oral feeding should continue to be a goal despite concerns by medical staff that her daughter might aspirate. She recalled:

> Yeah I said "I would aspirate also if you squirt stuff in my mouth that I don't want and leave me flat on x-ray table." So they said, "It's your choice. You can go ahead and do it and if she aspirates that's what it is." She never aspirated. She never had aspiration pneumonia.

Lina's story captures a paradox in the view of parents as interventionists. On the one hand, professionals are generally positive about the idea of parents providing intervention, especially in a child's early years. On the other hand, a parent's knowledge of her child may influence how those interventions are provided and may come into conflict with professionals' views of how they should be implemented.

Other parents described more positive experiences in their roles as interventionists. She' Ra Monroe spoke of the importance of creating bridges between home and school, noting how much she appreciated it when professionals would work with her son on skills related to his life at home. Likewise, she envisioned that she also played a role in providing intervention. She commented:

> I'm there for him to solidify or to reinforce a lot of the learning. I'm by no means a teacher but I can give him the things they give me to teach him. I offer some different input on what might be motivators for him. I bring a lot of that into the school…so I bring all sorts of tools and stuff from home to create that bridge.

Maggie commented on her relatively positive experiences in collaborating with school professionals, noting that she felt empowered to share her knowledge of her daughter's learning style. She knew her daughter's challenge with memory was assisted by music, and used this knowledge to create songs that helped her daughter recall information during long evenings of homework support. Later she and her husband accessed music therapy through their own resources as an additional intervention for their daughter. Maggie noted that over time, she had been able to convince school professionals that she had information to offer to them regarding the best approaches to working with her child, reminding them that although she was not an expert in assessing the root causes of her daughter's disability, she understood the ways in which it affected her. As she put it:

> When you see your children grow up, you know what the symptoms are. You might not know what they mean, whatever the disability or the issue, but you've seen them grow up. …I may not be able to tell you what it is, but I'm the expert and can tell you this is what I see. … Professionals are not always seeing the whole picture. They're sort of seeing okay, we'll take this and we'll put a label on it and we'll run the ball with one play in mind. You have to look more than one play here because things kept showing up. You have to keep looking back to the parent as, "you are an expert here."

Other parents viewed themselves as consultants or experts in the process of identifying research-based interventions that held potential to be successful with their child. For example, Will and Abigail found that the information they shared with the team was often the most contemporary information available to assist professionals in developing interventions. In fact, Will noted that "we provide all the information; we provide links to information and things like that. There's not a ton of information out there because it's a rare disease so there's only like 700 cases in the whole world." This situation created some conflict in Will's mind. On the one hand, he and his wife wanted their child to have the most "cutting-edge" interventions, and they believed it was their responsibility to share what they knew with their team. On the other hand, Will was at times frustrated that his team was not better versed in the professional literature.

As Bethany summarized: "We've been doing this for 13 years. Most of them are coming in for one. I respect their professional expertise and their knowledge and I expect them to respect mine. Raising my kids is my life's work."

Parents as champions and advocates for their children. Many parents also spoke about their roles as advocates. Advocacy sometimes coincided with other roles (e.g., being a case manager or interventionist), but it was distinct in that it involved a conscious choice to play a strong role in decision-making, especially when alternative perspectives were offered regarding their child's services and supports. Several parents told stories about the ways in which their advocacy involved making sure that school personnel, health and mental health professionals and others truly understood their child. Greta, whose son Leon was diagnosed with developmental delay, and later anxiety and ASD, talked about how she communicated with teachers to help them understand his personality and learning needs:

> I keep an open dialogue with professionals to help them and my child succeed. I prepare teachers before they teach with a document about Leon and expect them to read it. I tell them "Read it to help you get him so you can prepare for him." I then follow up with the teacher to see what questions they have. I ask them what I may be missing and how can I help you do your job better as a teacher.

Djenne has found a similar approach to be helpful, noting that in the absence of documentation, it could be tiring to tell her son's story over and over again. She recalled:

> During Malik's first 3 years of life, he had a doctor and therapist for every part of his body: 10–12 in total at any given time. I was constantly in a position where I had to explain over and over again his condition and medical updates. To assist the professionals and to save myself from having to repeat the same story ad nauseum, I created a document entitled, "All About Me." I had a notebook with all of his information all ready for others to read. It's a two-page document that provided anyone working with Malik a snapshot of who he was from a medical, educational and cognitive perspective. It also includes his likes and dislikes and communication patterns. Whenever I am in a new situation, especially with a doctor, I ask them to read the document before they treat Malik so that they can make "informed" decisions.

B.B. used a story telling approach to ensure that others' knew about and could appreciate Marjorie's strengths and accomplishments:

> A strategy that I've learned is to know the people who are part of the team and to use their history with Marjorie as storytellers. … The thing that new people can't believe really is that Marjorie didn't talk until she was eight or nine years old. And they don't realize how far this kid has come. So to sort of give them that information.

Other parents advocated for their children by articulating high expectations and insisting that team members hold these same expectations. Jamie put it this way:

I always say to her teachers: "Don't treat her differently unless I ask you to do so for a specific reason. Have high expectations. I have higher expectations as a parent. There's no failing and no excuses. Practice makes perfect. You have to be dedicated to get what you need and want."

She went on to talk about how, as a single parent, she recognized early on that she would need the support of professionals to ensure positive outcomes for her daughter. Importantly, she wanted them to know that she expected a relationship that involved mutual respect for one another's expertise:

I set the tone early in pre-K. The staff and I know one another's expectations and we live up to both. If you don't see me a lot, you're doing a good job. I'm not going to come to your job and tell you how to do it. In the same way, I expect the same respect for me knowing my child the best. We need to respect each other's parts in the class and at home. That's my definition of a good team. This has worked great for me and the teachers.

Clearly, each of these parents found effective ways to advocate through ensuring that the professionals in their children's lives knew a lot about them, knew what made then unique, and knew what parents' expectations were, both at home and school.

A number of parents talked about their development as advocates as being an important part of their own growth and identity. Georgia, for example, noted that her early struggles to communicate with school personnel about her three children with disabilities had been replaced by a sense of self-confidence that empowered her to act on behalf of her own children as well as others. Melissa conveyed a similar story. She noted that her early experiences with advocacy centered around her daughter, who was never identified as eligible for special education but did receive some support for her anxiety, as compared to her later experiences in advocating for her son with learning disabilities. Melissa recalled that "When I advocated for her, I was a single mom, living in subsidized housing, and I was treated like a second class citizen...Now, I've been working for the school district for almost 10 years and things are really different. It plays out in the IEP context—I can see how I've become more confident." At the same time, she noted that in spite of growing in her own advocacy skills and advocating on behalf of other parents, she still needed support from others to continue to obtain appropriate services for her son's learning disabilities. She reflected on the idea of advocacy as a form of privilege that in her case, came through her development as a person and professional and her connections with others:

Privilege and power bring advantage and strength...My ability to advocate in my son's IEP meetings comes from my privilege of having people in my life— like my friend Zoe [a professor at a local university]—who suggest things. I worry about other parents who don't have this. There should be an advocate for all parents, right in the schools.

As was true for parents who saw themselves as case managers, some parents had mixed feelings about learning to become advocates for their child. Susan, for example, majored in Deaf Education as an undergraduate and received a master's degree in Deaf Education from Gallaudet University. A few years later she became the mother of a son who was deaf. In her case, she was an educator first and a parent second. Although she saw the need to advocate for her son, she talked about her initial resentment of the role, noting:

> I just wanted to be a mother or an educator—not both. Although I had practiced advocacy with the parents I had worked with, I had no clue how to do so with my own child. But it was the beginning of my own journey of self-education. I was mad at God for putting me in this position, one I didn't ask for and didn't want. But eventually, I was able to work through my grief and fear and to come to the realization that I could use my experiences to help other parents. I have made it my career.

The stories of parents as advocates send a powerful message. Parents talk often about how they feel they have been called upon to take on a role they did not expect, or were not trained or feel qualified for. They are learning as they are doing: as one parent noted, they are "learning to fly the plane as they are putting it together in the air." Many parents do not even realize they are developing incredible coping and advocacy skills that will equip them in the future. The challenge for professionals is to identify opportunities to support parents in developing skills as advocates and recognizing these as a source of great strength. We will return to the idea of advocacy as an expanded role and as a way to build families' capacity in chapters 7 and 8.

Parents as "just parents."   Along with the roles identified above, some parents talk about feeling that at certain times, they want to be "just parents." The idea behind this term is that of being with one's child "in the moment," interacting with the child as a mother, father, grandmother, grandfather, etc. In using this term, parents are not trying to discount the complexities of being "just parents"; rather they are acknowledging that interacting with one's child in some of the other aforementioned roles (i.e., case manager, expert, interventionist, and advocate) can feel exhausting and quite different from most people's views of parenting. Lindsay acknowledged that there were times when she and her husband just had to take a step back. She recalled how emotionally fraught the process of evaluating her son was and how when services finally fell into place and she felt confident the team was performing well, she chose to temporarily disengage from the process as a strategy to reclaim a sense of balance in her life. As she described:

> It's like "Let's have a meeting when we need one." Otherwise I'm just operating under "no news is good news."…We just kind of needed a break from how intense that was and we fully expect that intensity will come back

at some point with social interactions becoming more and more complex and so we're kind of like "Let's just enjoy this somewhat stable time for what it is." We're kind of stepping back, basically.

Parents talk frequently about wanting acknowledgement for the multiple roles that they play, including acknowledgement for their desire—at least some of the time—to leave those roles behind to parent in a more "typical" fashion.

In addition to this sense of wanting (and needing) to leave other roles behind, we have met parents whose lives are so overwhelming and complicated that the possibility of taking on any role other than "just parent" is remote. They may be balancing multiple jobs, dealing with siblings, confronting challenges in their own health or relationships, trying to make ends meet, and simply "getting by." For these parents, the daily act of parenting is a task that requires tremendous energy and a singular focus on what is in front of them at any given time. Some feel that they fall short when they cannot take on additional roles; others feel judged by professionals who wonder why it is so difficult for them to make meetings, follow up on plans, or respond to requests to fill out the multitude of paperwork that accompanies special education.

Many of the parents we have spoken to talk about how this desire to "just parent"— for whatever reason—is a strong one that may come up often or every now and then. It is important for school and other professionals to take time to know when parents have had enough of balancing multiple roles, when they are confronting too much to be asked to do more, and when they just need to leave all of it behind to be with their children and families in a different way. It is important that we recognize and value all that it means to "just parent," and to make space for this important and necessary request from families.

BACK TO THE CLICHE: UNDERSTANDING PARENTS AS EXPERTS

We began this chapter by talking about the cliché "parents as experts" and the degree to which that phrase actually plays itself out in family and school partnerships. It is a phrase that educators and other professionals use often, but also one that needs to be explored and understood deeply. In our experience, families often feel that although professionals often use phrases such as "you are the expert," the subsequent conversations and actions of professionals do not seem to affirm the statement. In this section, we explore some of the reasons why parents do not feel that their expertise is valued, as well as the strategies some use to be sure that their voice and knowledge becomes key to collaborative relationships and processes.

Feeling discounted. One of the dynamics that families often share is that school based teams discount their child, their families, or the information that they bring to meetings about their children. Some experience this as a feeling of outright dismissal, as in the case of Sarah, a special educator whose son Ben was on the autism spectrum. She recounted one meeting held in her son's school district (not the same one as where she worked):

> Nothing makes you appreciate the professionalism of your own colleagues as when you are at an IEP meeting for your son and the special ed director calls your son the wrong name and admits she has never met him before. And clearly is texting under the table. And the principal sits bent over looking at the floor. And both get up to leave with barely a goodbye.

Other parents talk about feeling frustrated when their knowledge of their child appears to be overlooked or when issues that seem particularly important or urgent are ignored or postponed for discussion by professionals. Djenne's husband Michael told this story:

> When Malik had his TEF surgery, I did some research and suggested to the doctor that he might need a g-tube at the same time. The doctor did not agree to do both surgeries simultaneously. After the surgery, Malik continued to exhibit signs of failure to thrive and the doctor came back to me and admitted that I was right and that we need to go ahead and give Malik a g-tube. He apologized that we had to have a second surgery and for not taking my recommendations in the first place. From that point on, this doctor validated our expertise as parents and a great team approach was formed when making decisions for my son.

This story had a positive ending; still, the consequences were significant and could easily have had a negative impact on Malik.

Parents also talk about feeling confused when they present information that is ignored or debated, only to learn later that when professionals present this same information, it seems to carry more weight. Jane, for example, recalled turning to her son's pediatrician to reinforce a point she was trying to communicate to school professionals:

> At the time my son had a pediatrician that had been with him since birth who was very supportive of us and I remember on at least two occasions and probably more, trying to make a point to the school but them not really hearing me. I didn't feel like they were understanding what I was trying to say or they were just flat out disagreeing with it and on at least two occasions I asked the pediatrician about this subject and he agreed with me and I asked him to write a letter. One time he wrote a letter and one time he actually came to a meeting and he said the same thing I did and they were like oh, okay, it was very immediate acceptance and agreement with him. I remember feeling simultaneously thank goodness he's here and why did he have to be here? He was saying the same thing I was.

Lulu experienced a similar dynamic in her role as an advocate for adoptive parents. In her professional role, she often suggested to other parents that she

71

accompany them to meetings so that school professionals would be more apt to listen. Most of the time, this strategy worked well and the parents she worked with felt that outcomes were better. In contrast, Lulu found that in her own meetings, she was not always heard or did not always have the energy to fight with professionals over a service or decision that she did not believe was appropriate for her child. She wondered out loud how it could be that her voice carried weight when she was viewed as a professional, yet could be ignored when she was viewed as a parent.

Like Lulu, Kelly experienced a great deal of dissonance regarding her role as a parent and education professional. Her team knew that she was an educator and at times treated her somewhat differently based on her professional role and knowledge. At other times, her position did not seem to make as much difference. As she explained:

> And then the other piece that's challenging is it seems like whenever the information about [my daughter] is being provided to any professional, it's more valid if it comes from a professional… It's really particularly interesting because I know that they know that I'm a professional and I know that they give me, I can tell, I know that they give me a different level, they assume a different level of knowledge and credibility on my part. But I still can tell at times that until I give them this information on a piece of paper, signed by a physician, it's not gonna be as real as it is just with me telling them and I don't really know why that is but I think it's a very real phenomenon.

Affect and emotion.   Another barrier faced by many families is the role that affect and emotion play in their knowledge of and communication about their child. For many parents, the feelings they have toward their child are inextricably bound with what they know to be true about their child. Professionals have the opportunity to view knowledge as an objective enterprise, but parents do not. Parents may have a range of experiences (including their own professional experiences) and knowledge of research-based practices, but even those with the most knowledge of educational, medical and other practices must balance that knowledge with what they know about their child as a person. Moreover, they cannot separate any kind of knowledge of their child from their accompanying feelings of love, protection, and desire for their child to have a good and happy life. At times, however, parents feel that their emotions are not recognized for what they are or that an emotional response will diminish a professional's view of who they are. Lindsay talked about this in her discussion of the process of diagnosis, noting that no matter how hard she tried, she cried in almost every meeting leading up to her son's diagnosis. She was perplexed by this, noting that as a successful businesswoman, she had never before let emotions interfere with her ability to get her points across to others.

Melissa's comments focused on the ways in which professionals did not equally value some parents' backgrounds, affect, appearance and speech. Her work as a school and community liaison had given her plenty of opportunities to witness the ways in which negative perceptions of certain parents made collaboration almost impossible. She spoke about the need for professionals to "assume good intentions and have an openness for people who are different from you."

> I think it's acceptance of people and where they're at and if [parents] have the heart and mind. It's not about their money. It's not about their assets, it's about who they are as people. You could swear like a truck driver but if what comes out of your mouth is from a good place of advocating for your child, for your kids, you should not be judged for that.

Other parents described more positive experiences in which professionals supported them and helped them to deal effectively with their emotions. Greta talked about the ways in which several of her son's teachers had helped her to move away from feelings of sadness and worry to a more positive view of him:

> One Kindergarten teacher always said how wonderful Leon was. She said it so much that I began to believe it. Before that, I was just so caught up in the thick of what was wrong with him, his being sick and not sleeping or eating. She pointed out what was good over the past year and what he accomplished. She was very encouraging…In third and fourth grade, it got even better. I have said to these teachers "You have no idea how you've changed my thinking because you believed in Leon." This is when he made the most academic strides because of these teachers' support. Grace and patience from them showed me that I really did have a great kid who has nothing wrong with him. He is who he is.

The role of anger. A key part of the emotional/affective element of parenting described above relates to the idea that parents at times experience strong feelings of discontent with special education processes and/or education in general, including feelings of frustration or anger. In fact, parents may feel that on occasion, they are given no choice but to become angry or to evoke strong statements in order to get what they need for themselves or their child. This creates a difficult dynamic in which parents find themselves acting in ways that may not be in keeping with their basic beliefs about working with professionals. Parents who have talked to us about this experience comment that for the most part, they are committed to collaborating with school and other professionals to plan IEPs, make medical decisions, plan interventions, evaluate outcomes, etc. Even so, they identify moments in time when they feel at "wits end" with the collaborative process and are driven to display anger to achieve the outcomes they desire. Jane captures this tension when reflecting on her own style as compared to parents who used anger more frequently to get what they need:

> And again, I come back to—gosh, I think this all the time—that I'm actually pretty good at this and a lot of times it's the parents who don't really collaborate and they are very aggressive and a lot of times they get the services but I still

don't think that's the right way to go about things. I've had several times over the years that I think "Well, look at so and so—their kids gets this and this and they're the kind of parent that goes to the meeting and just launches an attack."

These tensions aside, many parents spoke about the need and the positive outcomes that resulted from giving in to anger at key moments. Djenne told a story about a time early in Malik's life when she stood up to a doctor in ways she hadn't anticipated, with results that worked for her:

The day after Malik was born he was rushed to our local children's hospital to be prepared to surgically reconnect his esophagus. The surgeon that initially came to meet us was very patronizing. He quickly explained the surgery, wanting us to sign the permission forms. When we questioned him about the things that we did not understand, he became agitated. He said to us, "Trust me. It's just a simple plumbing job. Sign the papers so I can get on with it." Here I was, recently having delivered a baby, in shock and feeling forced to make a life or death decision for my child, faced with an arrogant and insensitive doctor. How could I leave the care of my child in his hands? It dawned on me. He's not the only doctor in this hospital and if he didn't respect or work with our family in the way we expected, then we did not have to allow him to perform the surgery. That was my first lesson in advocating for Malik. Doctors can be fired! Fortunately the doctor we ended up choosing was the expert in the gastro field and an incredible person.

It is no surprise that parents sometimes become angry, or that they need to express their opinions clearly and take a strong stand to make things happen. Parents have strong feelings for their children, and an approach invoking strong advocacy or even anger may sometimes be warranted. The challenge here is that most parents prefer not to have to engage in angry conversations, threatening language, or statements such as "I'll be bringing my lawyer to the next meeting." These kinds of interactions may result in desired outcomes, but they are also draining from an emotional standpoint. They take a toll on parents in the sense that they may cause them to behave in ways that are not generally a part of their repertoire; for some, the resulting feeling is that they are compromising who they believe themselves to be. An additional cost comes for parents who may not like behaving in this way, yet find that the success it brings in terms of outcomes is tempting.

Susan talked about this kind of an experience, noting that after many unsuccessful attempts to get her son's school to make accommodations for his learning disabilities, she adopted a very angry persona and would frequently yell or make threats during meetings. It was not a role or way of being that she had wanted to take on, but she slipped into it and stayed there for quite some time. As she noted, "Unfortunately, I became *that parent*—the one that gets labeled as the 'squeaky wheel,' the one no one wants to see at meetings…For awhile it got me what I wanted, but it took its toll on me and eventually stopped working as well." Susan experienced a great deal of internal turmoil over this situation, but for a period of time, she believed it was the only way to get the services and accommodations she felt her son deserved. Fortunately, she later found other ways to advocate that were more measured and intentional, less costly to her as a person, and much more effective.

Jamie shared a more positive experience, in which she was upset with her daughter's teachers, but found a way to present her dissatisfaction without resorting to pure anger:

> I had a run in with the teacher when she wasn't treating Taylor right and was being rough with her. When I went in, they expected me to act like the angry black mother. I showed them the opposite. I went in calm, pointed out what they did wrong, how I expected them to fix it and asked them what they needed in terms of support from me. That teacher passed down the message to the others about the type of mother I am and my expectations. So now I have a positive reputation in a situation that could have remained negative.

The lesson to be learned from these stories of anger is that strong feelings may be evoked in the lifetime of a team or parent-professional relationship; in fact, it is likely that they *should* be evoked, considering what is at stake for children and families. But when communication breaks down and the majority of meetings are characterized by difficult interactions, both parents and professionals can become engaged in patterns of behavior that are not optimal for their partnership or themselves as individuals. Jamie and Susan's stories serve as reminders that when parents have the tools to channel in more positive ways, teams can experience more effective collaboration. We discuss this in more detail in chapter six, but what seems important is for both sides to recognize that emotions can run high in family and professional relationships, and that by recognizing this as part of the process, rather than a flaw of the other person, there are more opportunities for all to be heard. Parents *are* the experts, but their expertise does not always seem to be valued. The collaborative process needs to allow for space for them to be heard, over time, and through a range of emotions and stages.

Bringing Parents' Voice and Expertise to the Process

When families feel that professionals don't value, welcome or trust their contributions, it further marginalizes their role in the collaborative process. Families want to feel heard and to believe that their ideas hold merit and are given fair consideration. Some families expect that this will happen, and most often, this expectation seems like a reasonable request on their part. Others recognize that being heard may require more intentional and strategic behaviors on their part. They feel that if they can contribute in ways that improves the context and climate of meetings and interactions, there may be a higher likelihood of having their voices heard and their actions reciprocated by professionals. In our research and interactions with families, we have heard numerous stories of the strategies that families engage in to increase their sense of voice and equity in the process, that in turn seem to engender more positive relationships with professionals. Examples include parents' efforts to reinforce their own expertise through expressing openness to professionals, establishing open and frequent communication, and ensuring that information is shared freely between home and school.

Expressing openness and gratitude for the family and professional relationship. A number of the parents we interviewed provided examples of the ways in which their willingness to be open to professionals contributed to the development of positive relationships. In turn, professionals seemed more likely to value their expertise. Parents' offerings and openness with professionals were expressed in multiple forms, including parents' willingness to tell a story about their child or family, to offer materials related to their child's disability, or to bring snacks to a meeting. For example, Lina's daughter's medical needs were very complex and required numerous interventions by a variety of service providers. Lina valued the willingness of service providers to come to her home to watch how she provided care as well as their desire to include her in decision-making and experimenting with new equipment. She expressed gratitude to those who came to see her and her daughter. In turn, she felt that her openness towards professionals made it more likely that they would reciprocate by searching for ways to meet her daughter's needs. She related this example:

> I think that because of the fact that I let people come into my home, the professionals I work with give more back. The [physical therapist] is very good at introducing me to different equipment, like a tricycle, fitting special kids into a tricycle....So they had her try on those tricycles and then they said this is a better one for her and I go wow, I saw other kids doing this also. That was impossible for me to think she can ride a tricycle...that was a very good experience.

She' Ra Monroe talked about how her willingness to step outside of her comfort zone when communicating with school professionals contributed to the team's understanding of her particular expertise and led to a greater sense of responsibility among team members. In spite of being concerned that her skills as a parent would be questioned, she once told her team about a harrowing experience when her child let himself out of her apartment in the middle of the night. She' Ra was concerned that this story would engender negative judgment from school professionals; instead, her willingness to share this experience was rewarded by their supportive responses. She was touched by the sense of caring and empathy that team members displayed, and was grateful to the special educator who went on to create a social story for her son that addressed this event and She' Ra's concerns for him.

Maria offered a simple strategy for demonstrating her appreciation for teachers—bringing food to meetings. As she described, "You could see it as a little bit of bribery, but I'm really doing it because meetings are so much more relaxed and easy going when the teachers have food. I have the ability to bring them something that makes them happy, and they show me by really listening to me when I ask for things for my son."

Creating time and space for communication. One of the great frustrations that family members—and teachers—frequently share is that the structure and constraints of IEP meetings negatively impact a team's ability to share and receive information important to the development of a child's program. They talk about the fact that the traditional IEP structure does not allow nearly enough time for parents and school personnel to fully discuss the child's needs at home and at school and/or for parents and teachers to build positive and collaborative relationships. Although this barrier is often a structural one that is beyond the control of school teams, some parents provided ideas for expanding and opening communication, even within these constraints. Lulu, for example, talked about the need for both families and professionals to be respectful of the use of meeting time:

> Really that piece is such a cliché but parents really are the expert on their children and I think, a lot of what I see it goes back to that piece about clear agenda for meetings because they often see professionals getting frustrated in meetings because we're sort of, the parent is sort of rambling about stuff that's not really on the agenda but pertinent to what's happening to the kid. I'm often watching the special educators look at the clock because we have an hour and we're not even talking about the IEP goals yet. It sort of goes back to like making sure that there's other times and venues for the parents to talk about that stuff and they understand that, so they aren't saving up all the little concerns about homework or social stuff and for me an IEP meeting for where we really need to adjust goals or whatever it is. I think that's why parents do that because they feel like okay we've got everyone here.

Lulu's point speaks to the need for all team members to be sure that IEP meetings are not the only opportunity that parents have to discuss issues confronting them and their children. At the same time, she notes the need for parents to be sure that their comments are on target with the purpose of the IEP meeting.

Greta talked at some length about the ways in which she tried to use a supportive approach when advocating for her son:

> His team and I have decided that email is the best communication, because we can communicate pretty quickly this way. I want to be an advocate, not a thorn in the teacher's side. I am an encourager for my child and his team. Positive encouragement is key. The fact that my child struggles, he can't help this. I don't want services to be disruptive to his learning, but the teachers know that his needs to be addressed. I try to find a balance between supporting the team and advocating for my child.

In She' Ra Monroe's experience, holding team meetings outside of school provided a way to ensure that all of the different professionals had time to communicate and share ideas. She' Ra Monroe appreciated the fact that her son's pediatrician convened these meetings. As she enthusiastically described, "This is not the IEP, this is amazingness." Bethany also favored meetings that occurred outside of school; in her case, within her home. She believed it provided professionals with additional insights into who her son was and a context for understanding him from a strengths-based perspective. Scheduling those meetings prior to a new school year also addressed the need for ensuring that the professionals providing his care were adequately trained. Both women felt that meetings held in alternative settings changed the power dynamic inherent in school-based meetings and gave parents the sense that their voices and expertise truly counted. Home based meetings may not always be possible, but when they do occur, they may have lasting and powerful consequences. Attention to the context and timing of meetings seems to be an important component of validating parents' voices, opening up communication, and creating more reciprocity within the IEP process.

Talking across professions. Ultimately, whether information is being shared through traditional meetings or other avenues, parents acknowledge the importance of having school-based teams recognize the family's role in ensuring that information flows to other service providers. Parents who see themselves as case managers want recognition for the role they play in information distribution. Djenne explained that although she did not want to take on all of her son's case management, she felt validated when school professionals acknowledged her efforts to share information from her son's doctors and incorporated it in decision-making. Lindsay talked about a similar idea, noting a shift she believes has occurred in the medical system. She urged others to consider the implications of different approaches to information sharing for special education teams. As she explained:

> It almost seems that a generation or two generations ago you went to a doctor, you didn't bring a lot of your own information, you didn't challenge what the doctor said, you took what they said and did it. It seems like the whole special ed area… still runs like an old school doctor's office where you show up and they tell you what you will or will not do. Instead it needs to be a case where parents can say things like, "here's my information" and "here's how we are going to make it work for all of us" and "this is what I don't agree with." It should be okay for me to say that. I shouldn't be shut down for not agreeing.

In Lindsay's vision, school-based professionals would hold a portion of the knowledge and expertise required to meet the needs of the child, but parents and outside professionals would make an equal contribution. The statement "parents are the experts" would take on a new and expanded meaning in which family and professional knowledge and expertise would be given equal footing and weight in decision-making.

What is important to note here is that in our current age of access to information, many more parents have opportunities to combine their personal knowledge of their child with readily available research-based information for the purpose of shaping their goals and desires for their child's future. Parents *are* the experts, but the very notion of expertise is changing rapidly in an open-access, digital world where many of us can learn things that were previously limited to the purview of professionals. Although not all parents have the opportunity or time to devote to gathering information outside of their personal experience, many can and do spend time conducting research and expanding their knowledge of their child's disability and potential interventions. Parents' expertise is as valuable as ever, and it may be greater than ever. At the same time, when parents do not feel their knowledge and expertise is valued, it diminishes the ability of IEP teams to function collaboratively. Recognizing the complexity and multi-faceted nature of parents' roles is only one part of the equation. Teams must reflect on structures that are in place to facilitate home and school collaboration and evaluate whether those structures promote or erode equity and the degree to which parents feel appreciated and valued in the process.

We close this chapter with the second half of the quote that opened it: the story of how Djenne and Michael came to understand and activate their roles in Malik's life:

> We had to become experts in managing our own emotions and then managing the opinions, personalities and recommendations of the numerous service providers and doctors in our lives. Malik had at least 10 therapists and doctors that we were in contact with constantly. Initially we leaned heavily on the expertise of these professionals, following their direction. As time went on, however, we realized that we lived with and cared for Malik on a daily basis. We knew him the best and what was best for him. Through research and seeking to understand what worked and didn't work for Malik, the script became more familiar to us. We realized that it was really our script to write because we were ultimately responsible for the decisions being made for Malik's well being.

CHAPTER SUMMARY

We began this chapter by asserting that although we often characterize parents as experts in their children's lives, parents do not necessarily feel that their expertise is recognized or valued. Moreover, professionals may not always recognize the many roles that parents play in their children's lives, including case managers, interventionists, champions and advocates. Some parents seem to appreciate and embrace these multiple roles, but they may also find them difficult to fulfill and/ or to question their purpose. In fact, some family members indicate that at times, they would prefer to be parents only—"just" parents—who function more like other parents whose children do not have identified disabilities. Additionally, parents may feel that even when they do their best to play active roles in their children's lives, their voices are not always heard. Drawing upon these stories of what seems to work and not work, we offer the following suggestions to parents and professionals:

1. *Spend time talking about the roles that parents play both within and outside of school and how these intersect with various aspects of the child's life.* Although it takes time, professionals need to know about the full constellation of activities and demands that make up a family's life and the roles that parents want or need to play. Most often, children's needs extend beyond the walls of the school and it is helpful for professionals to know what roles parents play outside of the context of education. This may be especially important when professionals want parents to assist in providing interventions at home, as some parents may be in a better position than others to fulfill this role. The "All About Me" document that Djenne describes is a good example of a communication tool that can be used to convey key information about the child as well as parents' roles to school and other professionals.

2. *Clarify the roles that parents want to play within the context of educational planning, including IFSP, IEP and transition planning meetings.* As indicated in the stories presented in this chapter, parents have different desires related to the roles they will play in educational planning and decision-making. *All* parents should be given opportunities to be heard and to share their expertise, but participation may look different across families. Some parents will want to take on more active roles than others, and most will want to adjust their level of interaction within teams over time and across situations. Parents and professionals can help to avoid role confusion by clarifying norms around participation and adjusting roles when families have a need to increase or decrease their participation. As we will discuss in subsequent chapters, the developmental nature of collaboration suggests that parent and professional interactions will shift over time; thus, it is important for all parties to remain flexible and open to changing relationships within school planning contexts.

3. *Build trust by listening, expressing gratitude, engaging in the process, and acknowledging parents' contributions.* A common theme in the stories presented in this chapter relates to the need for all members of collaborative teams to feel valued, heard, respected and trusted. These characteristics are built over time, so it is important for professionals to listen carefully to what parents have to say and to build the ground work for trusting, reciprocal partnerships that encourage positive discussion and problem-solving over time. Again, it is important to remember that parents' roles and their innate sense of love and advocacy for their children will result in different types of contributions and responses to challenges that may arise as their children enter into and progress through the special education system. It is key for all team members to remain focused on the child and to build on common purpose to appreciate what various members are contributing to the process. Melissa's reminder to "assume good intentions" is critical in this regard.

4. *Be intentional about the flow of information and how different types of information are valued and considered.* Both parents and professionals acknowledge that we live in a world of "information overload." It is critical for collaborative teams to remember that information comes from multiple sources and needs to be managed and communicated in ways that are accessible to all team members. If we are to truly recognize parents' expertise and the multiple contributions they make as actors in the process of raising and educating their children, we will need to think carefully about how different forms of expertise and knowledge are conveyed and considered in decision-making processes. Chapter 5 focuses on this issue in greater detail, highlighting the importance of joining parent and professional knowledge in the collaborative process.

SUGGESTED QUESTIONS FOR REFLECTION AND DISCUSSION

For Parents:

1. Think about the roles you play in relation to what was discussed in this chapter. Do you see yourself as a case manager? Interventionist? Champion/advocate for your child? Which roles are most comfortable and/or desirable for you? Which roles would you prefer not to take on?
2. How might you convey your role preferences to school and other professionals? What kind of supports might you need if you were to decide to increase or decrease your role in some aspects of your child's life?
3. How do you currently convey information about your child and family to school and other professionals? Is there a more efficient or effective process for letting others know about your child and family?

For professionals:

4. How often do you communicate with families outside the formal structure of IEP meetings? What is the nature of that communication, and in what ways is it meeting the needs and preferences of the families with whom you work?
5. How do you intentionally create mechanisms for parents to participate and share their knowledge? What changes could you make to the current structure or norms of IEP meetings to ensure that parent knowledge is shared and valued?
6. How might you learn more about the roles that parents play and want to play in their children's lives? Why is it important to think flexibly about the nature of these roles?

SUGGESTED ACTIVITIES

For parents:

1. Using Djenne's idea as a model, develop a one page "All About Me" that you could share with the various teams with which you work. Include information that

you find yourself sharing year after year with school and other teams, as well as other essential information about your child's personality, strengths, needs, etc.

For professionals:

2. Create a list of questions that you might ask of families who are new to your caseload that will support you in getting know more about their child, their previous experiences with schools, their knowledge of their child's disability, and their hopes and desires in terms of the roles they will play in their child's life.

For both:

3. Hold a "Family Night" in which parents and professionals participate in a round robin discussion about each person's knowledge, expertise, and ideas. Next, break into small groups facilitated by parent and professional leaders. Assign a "collaborative challenge" to each group (e.g., identify strategies for improving home-school communication, identify favorite family-friendly websites, design a "getting to know you" activity, etc.). Following discussion in small groups, report answers to the larger group. Assign one person to record groups' ideas and another to facilitate the conversation. If the activity is successful, consider planning another Family Night with a different focus.

NOTE

[1] Portions of this chapter appeared in Kervick, C. T. (in press). Parents are the experts: Understanding parent knowledge and the strategies they use to foster collaboration with special education teams. *Journal of the American Academy of Special Education Professionals.* Reprinted with permission.

REFERENCES

deFur, S. (2012). Parents as collaborators: Building partnerships with school and community-based providers. *TEACHING Exceptional Children, 44*(3), 58–67.
Turnbull, A., Turnbull, R., Erwin, E. J., Soodak, L. C., & Shogren, K. A. (2011). *Families, professionals, and exceptionality: Positive outcomes through partnerships and trust* (6th ed.). Boston, MA: Pearson.

JOINING PARENT AND PROFESSIONAL KNOWLEDGE

Being acknowledged as the expert on our child can be a double- edged sword. Yes, I know my child best and what's best for him. However, I recognize that I have certain limitations as a parent and that I rely on the service providers who have expertise in their respective fields to provide the knowledge I don't have. This reciprocal relationship of shared expertise is what develops trust. In some cases, it's doesn't matter if the provider has an expertise in his disability. I know many will not. The willingness of a provider to research and learn on their own, and the ability to contribute ideas based on this acquired knowledge is enough. A parent recently expressed her frustration with a service provider who was looking to her to tell him how to carry out his role. "He has the same access to information about my son's disability that I do. Why do I have to always have to be the one who is looked to for education and training? I am the parent."

(Djenne)

In Chapter 4, we explored the ways in which parents develop knowledge of their child's disability and cultivate and express that knowledge through enactment of a variety of roles. We emphasized the importance of creating conditions within the collaborative relationship that encourage professionals to listen to and value the critical knowledge and expertise that parents bring to the table. We also discussed some of the strategies that parents employ to underscore their expertise, noting that changes in technology and communication have created a new set of conditions for thinking about the nature of parent knowledge.

In this chapter, we introduce some key concepts associated with professional knowledge and explore the potential for families and professionals to negotiate their collective understanding in order to engage in shared decision-making. We describe some of the expectations that parents have for professionals, including professional knowledge of research and "cutting edge" practices and interventions. We discuss the importance of using data in making decisions, and explore the potential to view data in multiple ways. Additionally, we talk about the ways in which discussions among professionals and parents need to be driven by values.

THE NATURE OF PROFESSIONAL KNOWLEDGE

Although our research has not fully explored professionals' view of their own knowledge base around disability, it is important to consider the general nature of professional knowledge before diving into the topic of creating the conditions for a collaborative relationship that embraces the expertise of both families and professionals. Not surprisingly, the topic of professional knowledge is complex, involving the interaction of policy and research, professional standards, professional judgment and practice. Each of these is described briefly and in relation to the more general topic of family and professional collaboration.

Policy and Research

In recent years, federal education policy has placed increasing emphasis on the need for general and special educators to use research-based practices in the classroom as well as in interventions provided to students on IEPs, 504, and other support plans. The No Child Left Behind Act (NCLB) passed in 2001 makes explicit reference to the use of scientifically-based instruction as a primary means to improving academic achievement for all students (Turnbull et al., 2011), defining scientifically-based research as "research that ....involves the application of rigorous, systematic, and objective procedures to obtain reliable and valid knowledge relevant to education activities and programs" (20 U.S.C. S 7801(37). Similarly, the 2004 re-authorization of IDEA calls for professionals to use scientifically-based instruction and the use of related services and supports based "to the extent practicable" on peer reviewed research (IDEA, 2004).

These policies have had a dramatic impact on the field, resulting in a national conversation about the definition of "scientifically-based research" and "evidence-based practice." Although the distinction between the two is often debated, most special education scholars view "scientifically-based research" as an umbrella of practices that have been proven to be effective and include a basis in research. In contrast, "evidence-based practices" are considered by some to be the "gold standard" of scientifically based practices (Cook & Odom, 2013; Odom et al., 2005). They refer to instructional practices only (as compared to practices that may be implemented with family members or professionals) and must be determined effective through the use of large-scale research studies using purely objective and quantitative data collection and analysis methods. Results must be confirmed across studies and include evidence of strong effects for students with disabilities, with the majority being published in peer-reviewed journals (CEC, 2014; Cook & Odom, 2013; Odom et al., 2005). The federal government maintains a website known as the "What Works Clearinghouse" that documents practices shown to have met the criteria for classification as an evidence-based practice (www.whatworksclearinghouse.gov), and today's teachers are expected to be familiar with these practices. A point that is often raised is that not all education practices currently in use can be traced back to large scale, rigorous, peer-reviewed research. As such, both family members and practitioners are often left to identify and draw on knowledge that may be considered instead to be the "best available empirical evidence" (Whitehurst, 2003), leaving open the possibility for discussion and the application of family and professional wisdom in the selection and evaluation of practices (Cook, Shepherd, Cook, & Cook, 2012; Turnbull et al., 2010). The most recent re-authorization of NCLB in 2015—the Every Student Succeeds Act (ESSA)—maintains an emphasis on using "evidence-based practice," though the legislation reflects Congress' decision to refrain from trying to pinpoint a specific meaning of the term "evidence based" in the legislation and appears to give more leeway to practitioners in selecting interventions that may not meet the previous "gold standard" of evidence-based practice (Sparks, 2016; West, 2016).

Professional Standards

The language around the use of scientifically-based research and scientifically-based instruction contained in IDEA and NCLB is also reflected in the professional standards guiding the special education field and the preparation of special education teachers and leaders. The field's largest professional organization, the Council for Exceptional Children (CEC), includes professional standards referencing the use of evidence-based practices in PK- 12 instruction (https://www.cec.sped.org/Standards/Special-Educator-Professional-Preparation/CEC-Initial-and-Advanced-Preparation-Standards). In turn, these standards guide the curriculum of nationally accredited programs that prepare future special educators, as well as the licensing requirements in many states. Currently, programs that are nationally accredited in special education must demonstrate how their programs prepare special educators to meet seven professional standards. The first five standards address what special educators need to know and be able to do in order to assess, teach and support learners with disabilities; while the remaining two standards focuses on the need for special educators to understand and apply ethical practices and professional standards, including collaboration with families of children with disabilities. Although programs have the ability to include specialty areas within their curriculum, requirements for programs to align with the standards helps to ensure that special educators from around the country are prepared to demonstrate a common set of skills considered to be representative of effective and current practices in the field. Additionally, accredited preparation programs need to ensure that special education teachers demonstrate skills expected of all teachers (e.g., standards articulated by the Council for the Accreditation of Educator Preparation [CAEP] and the Interstate Teacher Assessment and Support Consortium [InTASC]). The focus on demonstration of standards through performance-based assessments thus serves to define much of the knowledge base of special educators.

Professional Wisdom and Practice

As is the case for most professions, special education teachers' formal knowledge – attained through demonstration of professional standards and knowledge and use of evidence-based practices (or EBPs)—is also supplemented by the professional wisdom and clinical judgment that come with experience in the field. As indicated above, both researchers and policy makers acknowledge that use of practices determined to demonstrate the "gold standard" of evidence-based practice is not fully attainable, at least at this point in time. For one thing, the evidence base for many practices may be difficult to establish (Cook et al., 2012). Some practices may be difficult to measure using large scale, randomized control-group designs; other times, researchers have been able to establish effectiveness of a given practice with one set of students with disabilities (e.g., students with learning disabilities) but not another (e.g., students with emotional disturbance). Some research studies have been successful in including children from diverse backgrounds, while other studies acknowledge that students from culturally and linguistically diverse backgrounds may not be fully represented in their samples. Other researchers (including our team) acknowledge that the complexity of school and family context, the "messy" nature of human interactions, the individuality of students, and the nature of knowledge itself, raise questions about the degree to which all human behavior can or should be studied "objectively." Researchers and practitioners asserting this point of view maintain that other research methods – including those defined under the qualitative research position – help to shed additional light on what it is we mean by "effectiveness" of a practice for a particular student (Glesne, 2015).

Moreover, many believe that the determination of what constitutes evidence-based practice needs to be validated and established in context. Terms such as "professional wisdom," "family wisdom," "practice-based evidence," and "clinical judgment" enter the conversation and help to define a more interactive and contextual approach to the ways in which research and knowledge inform practice for individual students and their families. For example, the American Speech-Language-Hearing Association (ASHA) makes explicit reference to the role of clients (e.g., families) in determining evidence-based practice (www.asha.org). In a 2005 official policy statement, ASHA described evidence-based practice as being defined by the use of current, high-quality research evidence that is integrated with practitioner expertise and takes into account client preferences and values in clinical- decision-making. Because EBP is centered on the needs of families and clients, the task of the service provider is to interpret best current evidence from systematic research and take into account the ways in which evidence-based practices may or may not be a good match for a client/ family's preferences, environment, culture, and values regarding health and well-being. Although CEC's definition of evidence-based practice appears on the surface to be less focused on family culture, preferences, and needs, a number of researchers (e.g., Cook et al., 2012; Turnbull et al., 2010) have emphasized the need to ensure that the selection and use of EBPs takes into account the family's goals, culture, and preferences, as well as effectiveness demonstrated on a case-by-case basis.

PARENT EXPECTATIONS OF PROFESSIONALS AND THE PROGRAM

It is probably safe to say that many families are not totally aware of the multiple professional standards that exist with respect to special educators' acquisition and application of research-based knowledge. At the same time, our research and experience suggest that family members have strong opinions and multiple perspectives on their expectations for professionals and the quality of interventions being provided to their children. Parents want professionals to be knowledgeable and to share a sense of urgency regarding their child's needs, to create individualized programs that use cutting- edge research, and to be experts on the services they are providing to their children. Some parents feel generally satisfied with professionals' knowledge of their child and the practices they use with children, while others feel that professionals are not adequately addressing their child's needs. The parent-professional balance in terms of knowledge acquisition and use is a delicate one: both family members and professionals have expertise, want their expertise to be recognized, and at times, need to negotiate differences between parent and professional knowledge. This balancing act requires that both recognize what the other has to offer and remain open to bringing both kinds of expertise to bear on the education of the child in question. In this section, we explore what parents have told us with respect to the need for professionals to "know my child," and to be aware of and skilled in the use of research-based interventions. We explore parents' definitions of "family-centered practices" and need for these practices to be rooted in a deep sense of empathy for families. We also examine the need for professionals and parents to feel comfortable with the potential ambiguities of research and decision-making.

Knowing and Appreciating My Child

Parents talk frequently about the need for professionals to "know my child." Their sense that their child should be recognized as an individual with specific strengths and needs seems to be a universal and foundational aspect of the establishment of effective family-professional partnerships. Parents feel strongly that whether selecting a program or placement for a child or advocating for a service, professionals should appreciate the unique qualities of their children and view their individual needs as a focal point for decision-making. It is surprising then, to find how many parents feel that this basic aspect of professional knowledge is lacking among professionals. In our research, we asked parents to elaborate on this so as to identify what it is they want professionals to know and how they think this knowledge can be effectively conveyed.

Holly talked about the ways in which some professionals seemed to place their adult needs above the strengths, needs, and goals of families and children. She talked about wanting to have professionals "leave their personal feelings inside" so as to recognize that educational goal-setting should be based on a child's personal qualities, individual needs, and individual success, as opposed to the personal biases and convenience of professionals. She' Ra Monroe reflected on the need for professionals to use their knowledge of individual children to promote creativity and individualization. She drew parallels to what she had learned as a nursing student:

There is more than one way to skin a cat and yeah, you know, there is this whole philosophy of, in nursing it's called patient centered goals or client-centered goals, depending on who is in your charge for that day. … And yeah, there's just so many ways to meet personal needs, meet individual needs. No child is by the book… You know like you look at every single child as "I am going to make that child the best he's going to be" and then turn around and say that to every single child you meet. Really, it's not a tiring goal, it's not something that's meant to make you feel weighted. It's something that's supposed to make you rise to the challenge.

Will had relatively positive experiences collaborating with his daughter's team, but he echoed the idea that professionals need to "rise to the challenge" of understanding the strengths and needs of children with disabilities. He advised professionals to "be open about what's available." He felt professionals "need to be the ones to come out and say, 'hey, I think we should provide this service.'" Lindsay was concerned about whether some educators working in education truly cared about the needs of children. She implored, "I just feel like if you're not in it to help kids you should work somewhere else. I really think it's that basic because if I think you're truly there to help kids, you will collaborate."

Other parents talk about their gratitude for the times when educators made it clear that they knew and valued their children. Greta noted "I am most proud when the team expresses how great Leon is as a child and the social progress he has made. Leon is a really cool kid and is fun and kind. Learning will come, but his character is developing wonderfully." B. B. spoke about the need for teachers to know and care for the children with whom they worked:

My daughter's such a positive kid. They all love her, and she works hard for them when they love her. But if you don't love the child, you're not going to get that from them. You have to like or love the child and you have to affirm them.

Melissa made a similar statement, noting "If Cody likes you, even if he has a level of respect and says 'oh, so and so made me work hard today,' but still likes you at the end of it, that's crucial to me." Clearly, families felt that professionals' willingness to really get to know their children and to convey their appreciation to parents was a key ingredient in their child's success. Parents who experienced the sense that "this professional really knows my child" often linked that attribute to the child's success in school as well as to the establishment of a strong and positive family and school partnership.

Research and "Cutting Edge" Interventions

Along with the need to "know my child," most parents want professionals to have knowledge of the research base that will inform the design and delivery of their child's services and interventions. In our experience, parents have different levels of understanding about that research base: some are themselves very knowledgeable and others prefer to have professionals locate and convey what the research says regarding children similar to theirs. Other parents have strong ideas about their preferred interventions, even in cases where interventions could be shown to be lacking in a solid base of evidence. No matter where parents fall on this continuum, most have an expectation that professionals will have some knowledge of their child's disability and what to do about it; if this is not the case, they expect professionals to develop it.

Will, for example, did not expect teachers to know everything about his daughter's genetic disorder, but he felt it was critical for them to research options and to propose what he referred to as "cutting edge interventions." He was convinced that his daughter's school-based team had good intentions; at the same time, he was often frustrated that team members lacked an understanding of recent interventions that might make a difference to his daughter's program. As a special educator by training, he acknowledged the challenge of knowing everything about every possible disability category; at the same time, he felt that school professionals were obliged to learn as much as they could. He described the ideal situation as one in which parent and professional knowledge would be "intertwined," noting the ways in which professional expertise should extend parents' expertise:

> I want the professional to be the expert. I want to show up to a meeting and find that they're the experts on verbal apraxia. They're the expert on how to improve my daughter's fine and gross motor skills. They should be telling me what it is my daughter needs and it should be right. It should be exactly what she needs, so that as a parent, I'm an expert, but I'm not an expert in verbal apraxia and I shouldn't be. …Sometimes I don't feel that I get a sense that the professionals in the room when I go into those meetings are exerting their authority professionally. That to me is the hardest thing: knowing that I know that there's something out there that could help our daughter but we're not getting it.

Andrew expressed a similar sense of urgency around the need to identify research-based interventions for his son. His frustration with his son's program stemmed from his perspective that school professionals lacked adequate data to support their selection of specific interventions. During the years before his son entered kindergarten, Andrew found that the professionals providing home-based services for his son "seemed to be very sympathetic and that's not really what we wanted. We wanted knowledge and action." Later, when his son transitioned into kindergarten, he described his experience as receiving "cafeteria style education, where [my son] gets services as long as that's what they are serving." Furthermore, there were no data to support whether the services his son was receiving were effective. He explained, "So your SLP services are wonderful but without results, without data, I don't know if they're working or not working." Andrew described his belief that professional competence was a necessary condition for family support:

It's like calling the fire department. You expect a truck to come and you expect them to have the right equipment and the right firefighters, the right skills and they're going to help you and when they don't show up and they don't put out the fire, you got your hands full. So I think that, you know, as human service providers, they need to be firefighters and rescue people... because that's what parents want. That's what parents need. It feeds their hope. I like to go home, go to bed and close my eyes and go to sleep and know that somebody has actually got my back.

Stories from parents like Djenne, Will and Andrew highlight the fact that although parents want to their voices and expertise to be honored, they do not feel that it is their responsibility to take full ownership of identifying interventions and collecting data to determine their effectiveness. As Djenne put it, being acknowledged for one's expertise can be a "double-edged sword" if professionals do not also take on the responsibility for developing expertise in particular areas of disability and an individual child's needs.

STRATEGIES FOR JOINING PARENT AND PROFESSIONAL KNOWLEDGE

Along with identifying tensions existing in the space between parent and professional knowledge, families have talked with us about practices and strategies that they have used with success. Some of these strategies are identified in the professional literature (e.g., family-centered practices, acknowledging diversity, and data-based decision-making), but family members often had their own interpretations of these practices and how and why they worked for them and their school partners.

Employing Empathy and Family-Centered Practices

For many, the use of family-centered practices offers a way to join parent and professional knowledge and value the contributions of each. A number of the parents we interviewed spoke at length on this topic, defining "family-centered practices" as approaches used by professionals that honored parents' expertise, fostered the development of personal connections with families, and conveyed respect and empathy.

She' Ra Monroe spoke eloquently about the need for professionals to form close connections with families for the purpose of drawing out their knowledge and expertise. In her words:

Form a personal relationship, a professional personal relationship. Ask the parent "how's home?" Because you'll get a lot of information, you'll get a lot of like stuff a person does or a parent wouldn't think of or know is pertinent knowledge. Ask about that background. Ask about things that don't even really relate to the child.

Other parents talked about the need for professionals to communicate about smaller issues as they arise rather than putting them off for later. Lulu, for example, noted that "There's easy ways to communicate about little blips as they come up rather than saving them for the meetings and having them become big problems by then." Similarly, Georgia talked about the value of brief opportunities for communication with professionals:

Just being available to chat. Even if it's before school for like two minutes, like you catch the teacher. Oh this thing happened right before school, I just wanted to let you know. Or like you send an email. Like my younger daughter is famous for getting anxious about something the night before. We have no idea what's going on with her. We just see the anxiousness but she can't spit it out until the night before and so we can email her teachers and give them a heads up and they'll email us back and we know that it's okay.

Bethany noted responsiveness and flexibility as additional characteristics of a "family-friendly" approach:

And then being family friendly in the logistics of your teaming. In other words, right now, because I'm home schooling, I bring my kids to the meetings. I mean, what am I going to do with them? [My son] has so many appointments. I can't hire a babysitter every time I have something for [my son] and the team is marvelous. Sometimes they'll even set out coloring. I always bring something for them to do, but they welcome them. They say hello to them and they trust that they can manage themselves and we have our meeting, so, and they always make a time that will work for me and they ask me directly, "will this work for you?" And they always start with, "is there anything you need to add to the agenda and any updates from home?" So it really feels like we're working together.

For many families, the concept of family-centered or family friendly practice is built upon a strong foundation of empathy on the part of school and other professionals. Lina came to understand the importance of empathy after her daughter was born with severe disabilities. A professional nurse by training, Lina found herself re-examining her own practices after becoming a parent of a child with a disability. She advised:

Think from their standpoint, or step into somebody else's shoes. Yeah. Because I found before I had a child with a disability as a nurse, I did not understand much of special needs kids. I work pediatric units in hospital and I didn't know, I wasn't able to be sympathetic with them. Now I do because I have a kid like this of my own. I provide extra love to those special needs kids.

Georgia talked about the importance of demonstrating empathy through acknowledging the effort that parents of children with significant disabilities make in coping with everyday life activities:

I always feel like I am constantly struggling to keep my dignity, to not like, completely lose it. People don't get it. There's this whole other world that parents have to inhabit and then they send their kid off to school and say okay, we made it to school, like every day is a victory when we get to school. Most days its like 10 or 15 minutes late because somebody had a tantrum, they couldn't find a sock, they didn't want to eat. Something was off the train and then we get them to school. I feel like saying "Okay, you take care of this child for six hours, I'll be back."

Other participants provided examples of how professionals cannot only show empathy but honor parents' expertise in the process of forming collaborative relationships. Lina advised professionals to be open to parents' ideas about how to implement interventions. She learned quickly about strategies that were most effective for feeding and caring for her daughter, but was frustrated by professionals who felt that she should employ different techniques to do so. Over time, her team came to trust that Lina knew how to approach her daughter's unique challenges. She noted that professionals needed to demonstrate flexibility and to:

Let them (parents) do it their way. That's okay. They've been doing it their way for years and they know how to take care of their own kids. Or if they voice a concern, you listen to them. You have to think from their standpoint. That's what I've learned over the years.

Katie felt that if professionals reached out to parents and tried to understand their own goals and expectations for the child, it would result in more individualized and effective programs. She advised, "I would encourage professionals to say, 'what are your goals, what do you want, what do you see, how do you visualize this and what can I do to make this collaboration work?'" Jane felt professionals needed to "view the family as an equal participant to the process," and "keep in mind that everybody's there for the same reason, the same person."

Throughout these comments, it is clear that parents value family-centered practices that demonstrate empathy, build upon the relational aspects of family and professional partnership, take into account the full nature of family's lives, and place family goals at the center of decision-making and planning. Embracing and using family-centered practices goes a long way to building the sense that parents' expertise is important in shaping a child's education. And as Djenne's opening quote asserts, the "reciprocal relationship of shared expertise is what develops trust."

Collecting, Analyzing and Using Data to Make Decisions

Increasingly, education has become a "data-driven" world. Within special education, teachers and parents recognize the value of collecting, analyzing and using data to inform instruction and decision-making for students with disabilities. Many of the parents we have encountered have spoken about the need to be sure that professionals are collecting and using data to ensure that students are receiving a high quality education that leads to positive outcomes. Andrew, for example, noted the importance of having professionals "make a convincing argument for the services they provide. Until they can develop a trajectory and produce data…they shouldn't be speaking eloquently about the value of certain interventions." He went on to note that the task of engaging in data-based decision-making was a "daunting task," but that "it's what keeps it appropriate."

Although some parents used the term "data" to describe quantitative data collected in relation to various strategies and interventions, others used the term more broadly and/or emphasized the need to contextualize data gathered in the decision-making process. They wanted professionals to recognize how the nature of their family life could shed light on the interventions that seemed more (or less) likely to work with their child. In speaking about how parent knowledge could be joined with professional knowledge, Georgia noted the need for professionals to think about the idea of "theory to practice" in the context of the full picture of a child and family:

> I would say it's different when educators, good intentions are awesome, theory is awesome, experience with kids who aren't yours is awesome but unless you've been in the trenches, you have no idea. It's like my husband said, that it's kind of like if you were a drug counselor but you never had an addiction problem before. How could you ever understand the full scope of what's happening? You have a little window into it, the empathy, but you haven't really had your heart attached to it before.

Other parents referred to story telling as an effective way to share data with professionals. B. B., for example, was frustrated that Marjorie's teachers did not always acknowledge the progress she had made over the years. Rather than presenting the "facts" of Marjorie's growth, B. B. found that it was more compelling to tell stories and to engage previous educators in story telling when new professionals were present:

> One of the things I learned across time was to involve her previous teachers in describing her progress. There are two or three people that have been with Marjorie since she started receiving early intervention. You know, teachers don't believe parents. So what I've learned to do is to have her early intervention teachers tell the story of how every single benchmark you put in front of this child, she's exceeded. And the teachers believe them.

These collective stories about data point to the possibility of joining parent and professional knowledge by emphasizing the need to use data in decision-making *and* to ensure that data are contextualized and substantiated by what children do across home and school environments. They also suggest that it is helpful to consider both quantitative and qualitative data, including stories that reflect children's interests, needs, and accomplishments. Most parents have many stories to tell, and while not all may be relevant to educational planning and decision-making, many are.

93

Professionals who are able to listen to stories with an ear for what matters may learn a great deal about a child's learning and family life. B. B.'s point that teachers do not always believe parents is important, as it reminds us to pay close attention for what counts as data and whose reports of information are most valued.

Understanding and Respecting Diverse Experiences and Values

As indicated in Chapter 2, the changing demographics of today's schools make it all the more important for special educators and other school professionals to be prepared to work with families from diverse backgrounds, including families whose backgrounds may be very different from their own. The families we have spoken to mention a number of ways in which they feel that their backgrounds have served to support or impede their interactions and ability to collaborate with professionals. Specifically, they talked about how professionals' perceptions of their knowledge base, their socioeconomic status and racial, ethnic and cultural backgrounds affected the degree to which they felt that they achieved equity in collaboration.

A prevailing theme that emerged was parents' sense that although their professional status or cultural or socioeconomic background should not have an effect on how they were treated by professionals, it often did—sometimes in positive ways, and sometimes not. Parents whose backgrounds included professional experience in education, for example, noted that they were sometimes given more respect because of their own experience. Will talked about this, noting that the fact that he was a special education administrator created a different tone for his daughter's IEP meetings. He appreciated the efforts that special educators made to create a positive and collaborative environment, but was also disturbed that this same treatment was not always given to parents who were not professionals or were diverse in terms of their background, race or socioeconomic status. Lulu and Kelly, both education professionals, had mixed experiences in terms of the degree to which educators appreciated their experiences and backgrounds. Both felt that their teams gave them additional credence for their knowledge some, but not all, of the time. She'Ra Monroe and Lina worked in the medical field, and found that some of their professional perspectives could be generalized to the education field and were acknowledged as being useful by school personnel. Even so, Lina's earlier story about professionals' skepticism regarding her feeding techniques left her with a sense that her knowledge was not always valued equally by team members.

Both Melissa and Georgia shared important insights about the ways in which they sense that professionals' views of them changed over time as they gained knowledge through professional experience and increased their socioeconomic status. Georgia, who homeschooled her older children for a number of years, recalled that her first experiences with school professionals were not particularly positive. When Georgia raised concerns about her daughter's social and emotional levels as compared to peers, she received a message from school personnel that their daughter's challenges were primarily related to their parenting style. She recalled feeling "pretty crappy" about that. Later, after she completed a master's program in special education and entered a doctoral program in educational leadership, she felt that she received much better treatment. Although she appreciated the fact that her knowledge base and confidence had grown and that she seemed to garner more respect from other members of her children's school teams, she had reservations about the reasons for some of these changes. She wondered if some of the changes also related to the fact that she was an African-American woman about whom teachers made multiple assumptions:

I think the change I'm not crazy about is that socioeconomic stuff where I was a mom who came to meetings in my jeans and tennis shoes and a hoodie talked a certain way. That attitude that I felt was very different compared to now. Information or help was offered in the early days felt different. The tone felt different. At the beginning I thought, wow, I don't really want an argument but they feel like they want an argument, like why is that? What is this resistance about? I'm just asking questions and wanting information. Why are they taking this kind of defensive mode? And overall it left a bad taste in my mouth.

Melissa talked about similar experiences, remembering that "So when I was advocating for my daughter, I was a single mother living in subsidized apartments. My daughter received free and reduced lunch. I can remember being treated like a second class citizen." Melissa went on to take a job in her district as a family liaison, and later, as an administrative assistant in the superintendent's office. She described how much more valued she felt when advocating for her son as compared to her daughter:

It's definitely different the way that I'm viewed and respected than when I was a single mom. And of course, that's given me some more confidence. And so when you, when you feel better about yourself and your circumstance, the strength comes out in the demands. You definitely, privilege and power brings that strength where it's an advantage. I can see where I definitely didn't have that for my daughter and the things that she went through. My son definitely has that advantage.

Having worked for several years with parents who were from low-income and culturally diverse backgrounds and were generally disenfranchised from schools, Melissa had become very sensitive to the ways in which issues of power, race, and class influenced family-school partnerships. She reflected on her own approach with parents whom others found to be "difficult" or hard to reach, noting that her success in working with them came from her understanding her own struggles as well as being open to recognizing the strength that lies in all families:

I feel that I gave people a sense of belonging and acceptance and leadership opportunities. And the respect was given and they just gave it back freely. I was not judgmental of how they lived, what their house looked like. I complimented them for the things that I saw in their children and in themselves. And so I'm very proud to have had the opportunity to engage and to have those relationships that I shared. I think some of it was easier for me than for some of the other folks that were parent-involvement coordinators who didn't have the struggles I did in my past. I've been in a lot of struggling spots so it was very easy for me to talk about my past and to build those relationships.

Melissa went on to talk about how this culture could be changed over time. She felt strongly that all educators needed to participate in anti-bias training and to be interviewed to see if they were able to be open and respectful of all parents. She acknowledged that it might take additional work for professionals from middle class and majority backgrounds to fully understand all families, yet believed that the idea of collaborating without judgment was something that could be learned:

It's like somebody who's middle class who's never experienced maybe what an inner-city African American person would have experienced could potentially have a judgment. Some of that judgment comes from non-exposure or just a lack of interest. So I think a lot of it has to do with where you hold yourself. If you think that that person that you're dealing with is your equal, then you're on the same place, no matter if you talk the same, act the same, and so how you get to that place is believing that the individual that you're collaborating with is a good person and has the same intentions that you do.

Most importantly, she felt it was important for educators and other professionals to have a deep understanding that "Parents even, parents when they're struggling themselves, they really want the best for their students. They just want their kids to be successful. I've never met a parent that doesn't want better for their child than what they've endured." Jamie, a single black mother, wanted something similar—for professionals to look beyond her racial and socioeconomic status and to feel that professionals "care about *who* we are, not *what* we are."

Each of these conversations touches on the importance of ensuring that professionals develop the skills to have a deep understanding of their own cultural values, to be aware of their potential biases, and to treat parents from all backgrounds in open and nonjudgmental ways. Over and over, we heard parents who had managed to use their cultural capital to navigate the system make statements such as "If this was so hard for me, what must it be like for parents who have a lot less than I do in terms of resources and access to information and support?" Clearly, the expertise and knowledge of both parents and professionals can only be shared in an environment of mutual respect and understanding for one another. Professionals need to be vigilant about these issues for all families, and perhaps moreso for families who have fewer resources and/or combat bias and negative stereotypes based on factors such as culture, race, and socioeconomic status.

Acknowledging Not Knowing

Finally, we wish to acknowledge that although parents have high expectations when it comes to the knowledge and expertise of professionals, many also understand the complexities of the special educator's job and the impossibility of knowing everything about every child with a disability. Instead, parents looked for honesty within the process, including transparency about the times when they professional did not have all of the answers about effective interventions and supports. Djenne's opening quote is worth repeating here:

> In some cases, it's doesn't matter if the provider has an expertise in his disability. I know many will not. The willingness of a provider to research and learn on their own, and the ability to contribute ideas based on this acquired knowledge is enough.

The joining of parent and professional knowledge thus requires acknowledgement that no one member of a team can know everything, no matter who that team member is. When new knowledge needs to be sought out, families seek transparency in the process and evidence of professionals' willingness to learn more and to advocate on behalf of their child. In the best of situations, knowledge is viewed as a fluid and co-created construct that is enhanced when professionals and families share information and expertise, engage in problem-solving, respect one another's viewpoints, and recognize when more information and expertise are needed.

CHAPTER SUMMARY

In the early days of special education, it was often assumed that professionals held most of the knowledge of disability and special education processes, and that part of their role was to "impart" this knowledge to parents. As a result of increased recognition of the expertise and knowledge that parents hold, as well as the information-rich age in which we live, it is clear that the artificial boundary between parent and professional knowledge can no longer be drawn. It is also clear that collaboration is enhanced when parents and professionals bring their different kinds of knowledge to bear in ways that benefit the child. Although the similarities and differences between professional knowledge and parent knowledge are complex, it seems that some of the tensions arising in collaborative and data-based decision-making arise because parents and professionals have multiple experiences with and different understandings of terms such as "knowledge," "expertise" and "data." Professionals are bound by the law and by ethical codes to draw on scientific research in their teaching and provision of interventions, and this fact may contribute to the condition in which professional knowledge may be privileged over parent knowledge. At the same time, parents' knowledge is drawn from experience, family wisdom, and a deep understanding of their child. It is often accompanied by knowledge of the research that may be similar to or even greater than the professionals' knowledge of research.

Parents who have talked about their knowledge and expertise have much to offer in terms of enhancing the possibilities for parent and professional knowledge to be joined together. As such, we offer the following recommendations:

1. *Take steps to ensure that children and families are known and appreciated.* A fundamental building block for collaboration and for the joining of parent and professional knowledge and expertise is a family's sense that their child is known and appreciated by professionals. In chapter 4, we offered a few ideas of ways that professionals and families can take time to know one another and to build a shared understanding of the child, their family, and the educational context. In order to know one another, families and professionals need to listen well and to be intentional about learning as much as possible about one another. Not surprisingly, families who feel confident that their child is known, cared for and even loved are generally more trusting and engaged in the collaborative process.

2. *Implement and evaluate research-based practices that make sense in the context of the child and family.* Families and professionals may have different levels of knowledge of effective practices for children with different disabilities. The collaborative process needs to encourage open dialogue about the research that is known to both parties, with time and space to discuss whether or not any particular strategy is well-aligned with the family's culture, goals, context, and knowledge of the child's preferences and needs. Families acknowledge that it may not be possible for professionals to know everything about the disabilities and learning profiles of all of the children on their caseloads, but they do expect that professionals will seek out research that promises to bring about the best results possible for their child. Data collection and analysis are also important steps in the collaborative process. Families want to know what works and doesn't work for their child and they expect professionals to regularly collect and report data on their child's progress. Similarly, they expect professionals to listen to the data they have to share, whether it is provided in more traditional formats or though stories about their children's successes and challenges.

3. *Employ empathy and family-centered practices.* Parents who feel that their expertise is valued often talk about the value of family-centered and family friendly practices in the collaborative process. Moreover, they place empathy at the heart of family-centered practices. Professionals who pause to understand family context and who recognize that family's lives are multi-faceted convey a sense of empathy that contributes to a sense of reciprocity in educational planning and decision-making. As Djenne suggests, the feelings of reciprocity that come through the development of shared expertise helps to build the a sense of trust that is fundamental to positive and collaborative family-school partnerships.

4. *Remain open to and respectful of parents' diverse backgrounds, values and experiences.* We offer the idea that it is time to move away from a dichotomous

view that contrasts parent knowledge and professional knowledge, to a view in which parents and professionals strive for deeper understanding of what knowledge each possesses and how it might be enjoined to create better outcomes for children. This challenge requires professionals to take a deep look at their own views of knowledge and to examine any potential biases they have with respect to parents' backgrounds, experiences, and expertise. This includes understanding the impact of racism and the intersectionality of race and disability. The ability for professionals and families to be open with one another, especially when their backgrounds are dissimilar, requires introspection and sometimes, support from the outside. Opportunities to engage formal activities – such as anti-bias training and parent-educator support groups—as well as informal activities—such as journal writing and discussions—may serve to deepen our views of ourselves and the ways in which our interactions reinforce or detract from the idea of collaborating to develop shared expertise.

SUGGESTED QUESTIONS FOR REFLECTION AND DISCUSSION

For parents and professionals:

1. What are your own definitions of "parent knowledge" and "professional knowledge"? Do you feel that the knowledge you have about children with disabilities is heard and respected by others? Why or why not?
2. What strategies might special educators and other school professionals use to gain more information about the home context of children on their caseloads?
3. What are some ways IEP teams can be more explicit about the types of interventions they are using and share data in an accessible way? What kinds of data are most meaningful to professionals and parents?
4. How might schools gather feedback from parents on their experiences with collaboration and particularly their sense of equity on the IEP team?

SUGGESTED ACTIVITIES

For parents:

1. As a parent of a child with a disability, consider your preferred mode of communication with professionals. What forms of communication (e.g., email, texting, phone calls) do you find most helpful when communicating with professionals? What questions do you wish professionals would ask you, in order for them to gain a deeper understanding of your child's needs and your expertise as a parent? Write down your answers to the questions above and consider sharing them with your child's case manager.
2. To what degree do you feel comfortable sharing information and participating in decision-making about your child's education? Explore reasons why your

expertise may not be fully valued and share this with someone you trust. How might you act on this information?

For parents and professionals:

3. Explore your personal cultural history and beliefs by answering the questions below. Share answers to the questions with someone you trust or in a small group setting:
   • What cultural background do you identify with? What rituals, customs and/or religious beliefs were important to you when you were growing up? How do these influence your ideas about raising and educating children?
   • What was your family like when you were growing up? As a child, what beliefs did you develop about parenting? In what ways do your early experiences with your family influence who you are today?
   • What was your educational experience like when you were in school? How does your personal experience influence how you interact today with education professionals and families?
   • Looking back at your answers, what do you see as strengths when you are talking about your child/other people's children? Can you identify any places where you may have a harder time relating to people whose backgrounds were different from your own? How might this information help you as you think about family-professional collaboration?
4. Make a Venn Diagram that places a child with a disability in the center. Fill in the circles of the diagram to identify what families know about the child and what professionals know about the child. What information and knowledge do both share? What information might be missing and who would be the best person to gather that information?

REFERENCES

Cook, B. G., & Odom, S. L. (2013). Evidence-based practices and implementation science in special education. *Exceptional Children, 79*(2), 135–144.
Cook, B. G., Tankersly, M., & Landrum, T. J. (2009). Determining evidence-based practices in special education. *Exceptional Children, 75*(3), 365–383, doi:10.1177/001440290907500306
Cook, B. G., Shepherd, K. G., Cook, S. C., & Cook, L. (2012). Facilitating the effective implementation of evidence-based practices through teacher–parent collaboration. *Teaching Exceptional Children, 44*(3), 22–30.
Council for Exceptional Children (2014). *Council for Exceptional Children standards for evidence-based practices in special education.* Arlington, VA: Council for Exceptional Children.
Every Student Succeeds Act (2015). *Every Student Succeeds Act, S. 1177.* Retrieved from https://www.gpo.gov/fdsys/pkg/BILLS-114s1177enr/pdf
Glesne, C. (2015). *Becoming qualitative researchers: An introduction* (4th ed.). Boston, MA: Pearson.
Odom, S. L., Brandinger, E., Gersten, R., Horner, R. H., Thompson, B., & Harris, K. R. (2005). Research in special education: Scientific methods and evidence-based practices. *Exceptional Children, 71,* 137–148.

Sparks, S. (2016). NCLB rewrite sets new path on school research. *Education Week.* Retrieved from http://www.edweek.org/ew/articles/2016/01/06/nclb-rewrite-sets-new-path-on-school.html?qs=Sarah+Sparks+evidence+based+practice

Turnbull, R., Turnbull, A., & Wehmeyer, M. (2010). *Exceptional lives: Special education in today's schools* (6th ed). Upper Saddle River, NJ: Pearson.

Turnbull, A., Turnbull, R., Erwin, E. J., Soodak, L. C., & Shogren, K. A. (2011). *Families, professionals, and exceptionality: Positive outcomes through partnerships and trust* (6th ed.). Boston, MA: Pearson.

West, M. R. (2016). *From evidence-based programs to an evidence-based system: Opportunities under the every student succeeds act.* Retrieved from http://www.brookings.edu/research/papers/2016/02/05-evidence-based-system-opportunities-under-essa-west

Whitehurst, G. J. (2003). *The Institute of Education Sciences: New wine, new bottles.* Paper delivered at the Annual Conference of the American Educational Research Association, Los Angeles. Retrieved October 29, 2003 from http//www.ed.gov/rschstat/research/pubs/ies.html

ENHANCING COLLABORATION[1]

Collaboration is when there is communication back and forth between teachers and special educators and parents, and parents play a role in the education of their children...So collaboration is everybody – everybody has a stake in the game.

(Maggie)

In this chapter, we explore the structural and interpersonal conditions that appear to foster collaboration and a positive and action-oriented approach to meeting the needs of students with disabilities and their families. We begin by re-visiting and expanding upon key frameworks for collaboration that were touched on in Chapter 2 and contribute to our thinking about what constitutes effective collaboration. We then build upon these frameworks by describing parents' views of effective collaboration. Many of the comments offered by family members extend the previous research and thinking about collaboration, offering insights into new possibilities for collaboration in our digital and information-rich world.

WHAT MAKES IT WORK? DEFINITIONS AND CHARACTERISTICS OF COLLABORATION AS IDENTIFIED IN THE LITERATURE

As a backdrop to understanding collaboration within the context of special education, it is important to remember that the IDEA does not explicitly define collaboration or collaborative processes; however, the law's emphasis on ensuring parent participation in decision-making and its due process provisions imply a need for parents and professionals to collaborate with one another. Collaboration may be considered a necessary condition for ensuring that parents give input into key processes associated with special education, including IFSP, IEP and transition plan development, eligibility determination, and the identification of interventions and strategies that are likely to promote success for students with disabilities. Collaboration is key to the formal meetings and processes associated with these aspects of special education, but the need for collaboration also transcends those processes. Parents talk frequently about the importance of a deeper form of collaboration that is ongoing, rooted in relationships, and evident across multiple contexts and situations. Much of the research conducted on collaboration has attempted to identify its presence or absence within formal meeting processes; however, we find that it is equally important to consider it as an ongoing and iterative process related to a broader set of principles, conditions, skills, and behaviors.

Underlying Principles of Collaboration

Although the literature contains multiple definitions of collaboration, most authors suggest that collaboration is a somewhat abstract construct that includes a particular set of underlying principles, involves at least two parties who are engaged in a mutual problem-solving process, and includes a set of observable behaviors and outcomes (Friend & Cook, 2013; Thousand & Villa, 1992). The defining principles of collaboration include the presence of intentional and explicit agreements among parties that they are going to engage with one another using collaborative approaches. Agreement to adopt a collaborative framework signals that those involved will *not* be making decisions based on hierarchical arrangements or "chains of command." Some have referred to the "voluntary" nature of collaboration, noting that even within contexts where IEP and other meetings are required by law, participants choose to interact with one another using a collaborative style as opposed to other decision-making styles (Friend & Cook, 2013; Thousand & Villa, 1992). Collaboration requires hard work and attention to the process; as such, individuals and teams engaging in collaboration need to be committed to its success. The literature also talks about the need for participants to experience a sense of parity. That is, members of a collaborative group need to place equal value on each member of the group and their expertise and unique perspectives (Friend & Cook, 2013). The group needs to have at least one commonly agreed upon goal; for teams, this goal relates to the success of the student around whom the team has been formed. In order to achieve mutual goals, team members also need to believe in and be skilled in the use of collaborative approaches to problem-solving (Wheelan, 2016). The commitment to problem-solving is at the heart of any effective team, because most of a collaborative team's work involves setting goals that reflect the collective wishes of the team, and identifying and evaluating strategies designed to meet those goals.

Underneath it all, team members need to develop collaborative relationships that support goal identification and achievement. As such, collaboration requires a sense of trust and shared responsibility for the team's accomplishments and especially for the attainment of agreed upon outcomes for the student with a disability (Friend & Cook, 2013; Thousand & Villa, 1992). Teams embracing these principles—agreement to engage in collaborative processes, a sense of value and respect for each team member and their perspective and contributions, shared goals, a positive approach to problem-solving, and trust and shared responsibility—appear to be much more likely to work through challenges that inevitably arise as teams take on the complex tasks that confront them in their quest to support students with disabilities and their families over time.

Characteristics of Effective Collaboration

The basic principles of collaboration are also associated with a set of behavioral characteristics that may be viewed as conditions for, as well as outcomes of, effective collaboration. Different authors speak about these in different ways; here, we present the five-point framework offered by Thousand and Villa (1992) that to many, captures the essential characteristics of collaborative teams. It is generally agreed that successful collaborative teams need to have regular meeting times that include opportunities for team members to have *face-to-face interactions* with one another (Thousand & Villa, 1992). Although technology offers promise for more virtual forms of communication and collaboration, it seems that some level of direct interpersonal interaction is a necessary condition for collaboration. The literature suggests that face-to-face interaction is best achieved in groups of five to seven. Larger teams may find it necessary to meet in smaller groups some of the time, with full team meetings used as a way to communicate important information to all members. Successful teams are also characterized by a sense of *positive interdependence*, meaning that team members share norms and goals, distribute roles and tasks, and celebrate the team's accomplishments as they arise. Roles commonly used in collaborative teams include facilitator, recorder, timekeeper, recorder, and encourager. Ideally, these roles are assigned to various team members and rotated on a regular basis. Teams of professionals and parents often confront legal requirements that identify specific persons as facilitators and/or recorders (e.g., special education case managers are often expected to facilitate meetings and ensure that notes are taken); however, roles such as timekeeper and encourager may be assigned to parents.

Importantly, collaboration also requires each team member to make *effective use of social and interpersonal skills*, including listening, giving and receiving feedback, problem-solving and conflict resolution. It is widely acknowledged that these skills are complex and may need to be supported and developed over time (Friend & Cook, 2014). Still, the extent to which any group can consider itself a collaborative team is dependent upon each member's willingness to bring their best social and interpersonal skills "to the table" (Mostert, 2010; Wheelan, 2016). Closely related to this is the concept of *individual accountability*, which asserts that the desired outcomes of group goal-setting and problem-solving can only occur if each member of the team carries out the responsibilities assigned to them. Many teams find that the use of team processes—such as using agendas and distributing meeting minutes that note action items and responsibilities assigned to individuals – tend to increase accountability among team members. Some teams begin meetings by referring back to agreed upon assignments to determine whether or not these have been carried out according to plan.

Finally, successful collaborative teams are characterized by their willingness to engage in regular *group processing and monitoring*. Teams accomplish this by setting aside specific times to reflect on how the team is doing with respect to its accomplishment of tasks and development of positive relationships. Some teams prefer to do this at the end of each team meeting; others find it more feasible to reflect a few times a year on their progress. Although this aspect of collaboration may feel somewhat difficult or contrived, acknowledgement of its importance can provide the time and space for group members to have honest discussions of how the team is functioning. Like all good relationships, members of collaborative teams need opportunities to pause, reflect, and revise their approaches. They do this when team members feel safe with one another and have trust in the process. This is not the easiest aspect of collaboration, but it is a critical one.

Stages of Group Development

Discussions of the underlying principles and defining characteristics of collaboration suggest that true collaboration is not easy to achieve. As such, it is important to recognize that there are developmental aspects to collaboration. A branch of the literature with connections to the disciplines of psychology and group dynamics (e.g., Tuckman & Jensen, 1977; Wheelan, 2016) asserts that most teams develop over time through a set of distinguishable stages. Although authors assign different names to these stages, they are best known as "forming, storming, norming, performing" (Tuckman & Jensen, 1977). The *forming* stage is identified as the beginning of collaboration, generally occurring when a new team forms or when team membership changes to a degree that it feels like the team is beginning anew. This period of development is often characterized by high group conformity and agreement, reliance on one or two individuals to direct the process, and a "politeness" that some characterize as the group's "honeymoon phase." Teams that pay close attention to this stage can use it to clarify the team's scope of authority and use of decision-making processes, as well as to create a clear set of norms, structures and routines, including the use of agendas, minutes, and roles.

Whether teams spend a short or long period of time in the forming stage, most eventually move into the *storming* phase in which conflict, disagreement, and lack of clarity about roles and authority emerge. It is important for teams to recognize that conflict is not only inevitable, but is a healthy part of the collaborative process, for it is only when team members come to recognize and feel comfortable expressing different points of view that a truly collaborative approach to problem-solving can occur. Successful navigation of this stage requires the team to learn how to manage and even embrace conflict. Teams that are successful in doing this move on to the stage of *norming,* whereas those that are not may feel stuck in storming for long (and uncomfortable) periods of time. In the norming stage, teams tend to re-group and readjust their expectations and goals. Their experience with conflict serves as a reminder of what is and is not important to team members, thereby clarifying where it is that the team wants to go. It is in this stage that teams tend to re-visit their structure and operating procedures, improve upon their skills in problem solving and conflict resolution, and become more sophisticated in their approaches to decision-making, compromise, and negotiation. There may be acknowledgment of differences in power and authority, but stage three teams can learn to work with these differences rather than to see them as threats to collaboration. Theories of group development recognize a fourth stage known as *performing.* Although not all teams progress to this point, most people feel that the feeling of being in a stage four team is palpable. Teams that are performing engage in regular problem-solving and conflict resolution, with members having a sense that they can "agree to disagree." The team seems to have an ebb and flow to it in which tasks are accomplished, relationships continue to develop, and the challenges that present themselves seem less daunting than they would have seemed in earlier stages.

Some have criticized theories related to stages of group development for portraying group development in terms that seem too linear or simplistic. In fact, most authors who support the concept of developmental stages acknowledge that team development may be more circular and recursive than linear (Wheelan, 2016). Wheelan stresses the importance of effective leadership within team development, noting that teams in the early stages often require a leader or facilitator whose stated role is to support the group in forming and working through conflict. As the team progresses to higher levels of functioning, the leader's role becomes less apparent and the team adopts a more distributed approach to leadership (Thousand & Villa, 1992). While theories of group development thus do not hold up in a textbook fashion for all teams, acknowledgment of the fact that teams need time, support, and leadership in order to grow often brings a sense of comfort to those who find collaboration a difficult and messy undertaking.

Recognition of the multi-faceted and developmental nature of collaboration may also help to explain why collaboration in school teams can feel so challenging. Many teams involving professionals and parents meet infrequently and/or are subject to frequent changes in membership as the child transitions to new grades, schools, and case managers. Furthermore, not all decisions made by special education teams are truly collaborative. The law authorizes the Local Education Agency representative to make financial decisions that may override the wishes of a parent and/or team members. In those circumstances parents may enact procedures to dispute those decisions through due process. This legal reality may impact the ability of teams to collaborate effectively. The challenges created by these conditions suggest that the establishment of true collaboration as defined by the literature may be extremely difficult to achieve. Acknowledging that, we find it all the more important to hear from parents about what particular challenges they face, how they would like to see collaboration defined, and what strategies might improve conditions for collaboration.

WHAT MAKES IT DIFFICULT? BARRIERS TO COLLABORATION AS IDENTIFIED IN THE LITERATURE

As discussed in Chapter 2, the literature on the nature of parent-professional relationships and collaboration has made much of the barriers to collaboration. As indicated earlier, many of the early studies of parent participation in IEP planning indicated that parents were not active participants and as such, could not be defined as being true partners in the collaborative process (e.g., Cone, Delawyer, & Wolf,

1985; Goldstein, Strickland, Turnbull, & Curry, 1980; Lusthaus, Lusthaus, & Gibbs, 1981; Vacc et al., 1985; Vaughn, Bos, Harrell, & Lasky, 1988). Later studies raised questions about the degree to which parents were actually satisfied with their roles in IEP planning (Harry, 1992), and/or to which teachers were open to more active forms of engagement. Subsequent research concluded that parents of non-dominant cultures and low socioeconomic backgrounds received direct or implicit messages about what they were or were not allowed to say, resulting in a perception among parents that decision-making was supposed to remain in the hands of professionals and not parents (Blue-Banning et al., 2004; Harry). Additionally, they explored the role that culture played in families' perceptions of disability, family structure, and authority, noting that different cultural values at times resulted in opposing views among family members and school professionals regarding the nature of disability and culturally appropriate responses to it (Blue-Banning; Harry; Kalyanpur & Harrry, 2012).

Other studies have focused on barriers to collaboration that are less relationship-based and more logistical in nature, such as the amount of time that school professionals have to engage in collaborative processes, and the realities of budgets that impose real or perceived constraints on how resources are allocated to students and families (Overton, 2005). Additional barriers include those that more directly affected families, including time for parents and others to leave work, child-rearing and other responsibilities to participate in meetings; difficulties finding transportation to and from meetings; and the realities of attending to other children and family members.

In the section that follows, we re-visit barriers to collaboration as they have been identified by the family members we have interviewed. Some of these reflect barriers identified in the literature; others do not. Following this discussion, we move to family members' more positive views of what collaboration can and should be, including some of the strategies that parents use to promote collaboration with professionals.

WHY IS IT SO DIFFICULT? FAMILY PERSPECTIVES ON BARRIERS TO COLLABORATION

Time: "There's Never Enough"

The IDEA requires school-based teams to meet at least annually to develop children's IFSPs and IEPs, with some states requiring an additional two to three meetings per year to discuss the child's progress. Although teams for children with more severe disabilities often meet more regularly, it is the case that many parents of children with disabilities meet face-to-face only once per year with service providers. Scheduling meetings is primarily the responsibility of the special education case manager. While parents can request meetings, the organizational process of setting up the meeting time and inviting team members typically lies with the special education case manager.

Over and over again, the parents we have talked to express concerns about the timing of when meetings get scheduled as well as the lack of sufficient time during the meetings to address all areas of concern. As Jane summarized, "There's never enough time." Kelly elaborated further:

> Sometimes I'll ask for a meeting or there will be a meeting, and I'll come in with a bunch of things in mind to address but the school team has their bunch of things in mind and probably doesn't realize that I have mine. It will end up that we can't do it all, there's always such a limited time... I know that it's often only 30 minutes and I know we can't adequately address much in 30 minutes and so there's always that thought about how do we use the time and what things do we kind of put off to the side for another time. Which probably won't exist.

Kelly also talked about the difficulties of scheduling meeting times that worked for all involved. She reflected on the challenges of balancing the needs of her family with the constraints of the school schedule:

> If I have to bring my toddler to the meetings, it's a very different kind of experience and I understand the reality of a school schedule, but the meeting that we had the second week of school, I would really have liked my partner to come too. But the only time they could meet was 7:30 in the morning so we had no option for the two year old so my partner stayed home with him and I went to the meeting. It wasn't the ideal time to have the meeting but I also knew, it's the only time they have.

Lulu reflected on similar challenges, noting that the schedules of the professionals on her son's team dictated their meeting time: "No one on the team was full time at school except the principal so to get everyone we needed, it had to be Wednesdays at noon." The mid-day meeting meant that Lulu—who worked a distance from the school—had to take the day off from work each time her team met. During one school year, the team met five times prior to Christmas, which proved to be not only an inconvenience, but a financial barrier as well. For Lulu, missing work meant missing out on part of her paycheck. At the same time, she felt she needed to be present for all of the meetings. When given advice from an advocacy organization to miss some of the meetings, Lulu responded "Are you kidding? I'm not going to have them meet without me about my kid without me there. That's not gonna happen." Lulu understood that the meetings were important, so she chose to live with the hardships caused by this schedule.

Money: What Is Available? Who Decides?

Identifying and paying for appropriate services. A second roadblock that participants identified was funding. By law, the decision to allocate funds for services ultimately resides with the school district or Local Education Agency (LEA) representative. The

LEA representative is typically the special education coordinator or school principal. Thus, although the law implies that parents are equal decision-makers in collaborating with schools, approval for funding is at the discretion of the LEA. Collaboration is based on the idea of equity and consensus-based decision-making; as such, many parents find that the realities of funding create an unequal balance of power that thwarts collaboration. Lindsay articulated this in her comment that "I still feel like collaboration with the school is not truly possible just in the sense that the school still holds all the cards." Issues related to funding can be a source of great frustration for families, especially when they perceive that the team is unwilling to provide services that may benefit their child. Holly's son attended six different schools until they found one with a program that appropriately addressed his academic and social-emotional needs. Her son's early years in school were characterized by turbulent times and frequent calls to the police. Finding a school where he finally began to thrive was a relief, yet she wondered why her team had not considered this placement sooner. She recalled:

> But [name of school] was the first school that he actually has done well at and I feel, I hold, actually, our LEA responsible for not even telling us about [name of school] because she doesn't like it. To me, she wasn't looking at the benefit of the child. She was looking at the price tag of the school because they're very expensive and that's her personal feeling ... .But it's the first school he's done well at.

The power of the decision-maker.   Closely related to the challenge of finite funds was the issue of control in the decision-making process. Katie felt frustrated by the role of administrators in controlling purse strings related to educational decisions for her son. She raised the following concern: "Because I see the problem being administrators more than I see special educators. I see it as administrators because it has to do with money. We only have this much money; we only have this many resources and this many needs." B. B. offered a similar point of view, arguing that power differences existed even among school professionals. In her experience, special educators who seemed to agree with some of the requests she made for her daughter Marjorie were reluctant to advocate for services and accommodations with administrators and other team members. She viewed special education teachers as a minority even within their own settings:

> They're not really teachers in their own schools. They're like guests in a larger unit and they need some identity development...so that they have then the courage to speak out and say, and to expect that things go the way they should go. When we have a lot of young white women teachers in our state who have been socialized to be nice. We have to break that social victim of politeness because a lot of things don't get said because people don't want to be impolite and the kids suffer.

Katie's frustration with administrators putting up roadblocks to funding services for her son led her to strong advocacy. She interpreted the law differently that did the school, feeling that its obligation was to provide her son what he needed regardless of cost. As she described:

I understand, this is the law and you have to do these things. He needs a one-on-one, he needs somebody to translate for him and if you don't have the money…I don't really care. You have to do it. You have to figure this out. That's your responsibility. I mean I think that we do have to, to a certain extent let them know. I'm not ashamed that I'm making you do, not you individually, that I'm making the system work for my child.

Clearly, the concept of collaboration as a process that utilizes parity in decision-making is one that does not always exist in reality.

Weighing the options. Will provided some unique perspectives on the issue of resources. He spoke about understanding the limitations of school budgets, yet found it difficult to ignore the fact that he knew that services existed that would benefit his daughter. At the time of the interviews he and his wife were trying to determine what services the school should be responsible for and which pieces might be supported through different funding avenues. According to Will:

We don't think she's getting enough language at the school. And that's not the school. I know how that works. I know what level the kids get of direct service in the schools and I know they have a lot of clients, and I understand that, so the next piece is going to be how much it's going to cost for us to go to see her [the specialist], how much is our insurance going to pay for, and then how much do I think the school is responsible for that extra speech and language services. I feel they are responsible for a lot of it because that's the biggest barrier right now for her, is the speech and language. That's coming up and we'll see what happens.

Will's perspective pointed to the challenges that families face as they navigate complex funding mechanisms within the special education, health care, mental health and social services systems. How do parents know what is appropriate and what is too much? How do families know if they are receiving all of the information necessary to make informed decisions about their children? How do the dynamics of the collaboration on the team impact access to resources? Andrew expressed concerns about what he experienced as a lack of transparency regarding what options actually existed and what he was told was available:

Not only do I have to get smart, I have to start looking out for the things I think are appropriate because nobody's telling me what they are, so nobody's fessing up to what they know professionally. And a lot of it seems to be cloaked in this economics. It's all about cost.

Jane captured this concern describing the issue of money and funding as being the "elephant in the room." She envisioned her role as one in which she was always seated on the opposite side of the table from the school team. In describing this metaphor, she noted:

> So, it's not in reference to any one specific team or any one specific point in the years but it's a generalization of how I've felt many times through the years …There's me on one side of the table and everyone at the school on the other side of the table. I often feel like I'm trying to convince everybody there of something and they're all united in how they stand on something and often it's in disagreement of what I'm trying to say so it doesn't really feel like we're a team sitting around the table very frequently. …And then even though it's never discussed directly in the meetings, just over and over again, I just know that what's driving a lot of their points is money and even if that's the case, it frustrates me to think that. It frustrates me to think that if there's a legitimate need that [my son] has, that we can't figure out a way to make that work just because there isn't money. I don't like that door being shut in my face.

When confronted with financial roadblocks, some parents felt they had no choice other than to agree with the school's plan. Others, like Katie, fought for services they felt were necessary. Lindsay and Maggie both had experiences where they used their own resources to pay for services and testing they felt the school was reluctant to provide. Although she was able to afford this for her family, Lindsay spoke about the inherent lack of fairness in this situation, noting that most families would not be able to afford an independent evaluation. As she stated:

> I just feel like it's a broken system still. I mean we only made it work because we poured money into it. That's the only reason I feel like it worked for us. I still feel like, in a parallel universe if we had not done that and we asked for an evaluation, it would have taken a year to get one and then he still would be home schooled in the second year. I mean, we threw money at it and that's how it got solved at the end of the day.

Challenges related to funding and decision-making are difficult and prevalent in the special education process. When parents experience a lack of transparency around information sharing, they can end up losing trust in their school team and the system as a whole. This can negatively impact relationships among team members, leading parents to feel frustrated and marginalized in the process. As Will pointed out, school districts do face financial constraints and must work within these to provide a free and appropriate public education for each child with a disability. The difficulty lies in creating a situation in which team members can make transparent and informed decisions that take into account families' needs and desires within the context of what is possible, and deliver on the promises of equity and fairness in the system. Although there is no easy solution to this barrier to collaboration, it behooves all team members to focus on trust-building and clarity in decision-making so that those around the table recognize the options and feel that the most educationally sound decisions are being made on behalf of children with disabilities and their families.

Challenging Personal Dynamics

A third barrier commonly identified by families was the complex nature of interpersonal dynamics among team members. The literature describes the presence of positive interpersonal skills as a key to effective collaboration, but the majority of the parents we have talked to over the years described at least one experience in which they found professionals to lack interpersonal skills. In some cases, they described individuals with whom they "clashed;" other times, family members felt that school professionals had their own interpersonal challenges. When parents felt that they needed to manage conflicts between professionals, they felt tired and discouraged about the possibility for effective collaboration. Holly described an instance of infighting among different service providers:

> And the LEAs are arguing so, the last meeting, there had to have been four conversations going on at one time, like different points of views with other people and I'm just sitting here like, are we done? Are we done because this was an IEP meeting and like there's a conversation here going on about why they want something, the school's having a conversation about what they already do, and it's just ridiculous.

At other times, parents felt singled out and marginalized as a result of being on the receiving end of conflict and negativity. Jane described a special education administrator whom she found particularly challenging:

> There was a different director of special education in my district at the time and she was, actually from what I understand, very much loved by the board. She was all about money and saving money and I think that made her a hero to some people but she actually came to some of my IEP meetings back then because there was some tension ... and she at two meetings actually yelled at me and it just was, there was no collaboration whatsoever. It was more me versus them than it ever had been before and that was in the beginning, that was my intro to this whole system and it was just, it was awful.

Experiences like Jane's and Holly's eroded their trust that the system was working on behalf of their children. Navigating tension among team members and providers is exhausting for parents, particularly when they feel a sense of urgency in addressing the child's needs. Andrew's comments were particularly illustrative:

> The feeling that there's actually differences between staff in the same school, there's a turf war about the battle lines. Who owns what? Where's stuff gonna fall? Who's going to be responsible for what, and all you're looking for is what's fair and appropriate. And it's a mystery because, in our case, we're told

that our town's school is going to be the service provider for our son and we have to wait for that to happen on their terms and they can't even decide what the terms are and that's disconcerting. And that goes right back to this as a parent, this is necessity and this is the mother of invention, right? Because as a parent, you're going to invent stuff that your kid can't get because that's what you gotta do. This is a desperate act.

Along with disagreements arising from differences of opinion about services, systems, and funding, parents also talked about feeling extremely frustrated about team members' general lack of understanding of their child and family context. This point hearkens back to our discussion in Chapters 3 and 4 about parents needing to feel that team members "know my child." Maggie remembered, "There were times when I felt like even though they would physically listen, they weren't hearing and they weren't reacting and that became frustrating." Jane, who tried to ask clarifying questions when she did not understand what school professionals were suggesting, felt that team members frequently misinterpreted her questions and became defensive:

I think over the years several times I've encountered someone who's very defensive and I think that is something that I struggle with a lot, even to this day because that kind of, I've encountered an SLP, a PT, and a case manager who were all, when I would try and discuss something got very defensive and that's a really really hard thing to work through because once someone's defensive, I mean, it's just really hard to make them not be defensive. To get them to understand you're just trying to have a discussion about something. You're not trying to say you're doing it wrong. …People have a lot of trouble getting out of the defensive mode. That's happened several times.

Additionally, many parents described the challenges that came from balancing not only IEP teams, but the multiple professionals outside of education who were sometimes part of their children's lives. Will described the challenges he and his wife experienced in integrating a range of services for their daughter with complex educational and medical needs. They had chosen to take a holistic approach to meeting their daughter's developmental needs that included traditional and alternative therapies. In their case, the school-based team was fairly high-functioning, but the various providers outside of the school had difficulties communicating with one another and the school professionals.

Language and Structure as a Barrier

Special education services for children with disabilities are provided in accordance with the regulations and procedural requirements outlined in IDEA. As parents quickly learn when they enter into the special education system, the profession is laden with jargon, discipline-specific terms, and a complex set of procedures, some defined by law and some embedded in local practice. Parents' frustrations centered on navigating the process, understanding their rights and interpreting IEPs. Challenges in interpreting the "language" of special education frequently had a negative impact on the level of engagement they experienced on teams and their sense of parity with other team members.

For Lindsay, this lack of clarity began when she was first introduced to the evaluation and eligibility determination processes. She found it challenging to understand what the process entailed and who would serve as the point person to manage the process and flow of information. She articulated her concerns:

> It's the whole transparency thing. It's what I harped on endlessly. I feel like in the business world, I mean if I work on a project, or I'm meeting with a client, you pretty much establish the point person right out of the gate, like within 90 seconds of the first time you have a meeting. ...I never had that sense for the first year to two years, who was actually, who is in charge, who do I follow up with, that I know if I follow up with you, you on your side are making things happen, on my side I'm making my things happen. There was never the most basic structure of a flow of work ever, and to me that is so crazy making still.

Not having a clear person in charge exacerbated Lindsay's frustration in trying to understand the evaluation process and understand her rights. In her view, what was needed was:

> ...someone who can translate the process and make it easy to understand and make you be able to think through like "okay, I get it. I can go onto step two and this is what we need to do." It's just made so much harder than it needs to be and you lose time. To me that is a real problem. You just waste and lose time that you really need.

Although states are required to inform parents of their rights through written documentation provided in a language that they understand, many parents found that these materials were confusing and if anything, served to complicate the process and make it seem more distant. Lulu felt that the parental rights handout she received was not sufficient to translate the terms involved and the decisions that needed to be made. Moreover, the language that was used did not convey to parents that they were a part of decision-making. If anything, she felt that the document was given to her as an afterthought and as a replacement for a verbal description of the process. She noted:

> I don't know, parents just have to stay on top of so much... the whole thing with the rights and the way they're offered and yes, they're offered over and over again but they're also always offered now in the "like, so I have to offer you these. Do you want them again?" It's always, which is true, you don't need 15 copies of them but I've never seen a special educator explain those to a parent in a meeting, never. I very rarely see anyone take them.

Lulu's experience served as an example of the need for special education and other professionals to pay attention to the quality of their efforts to share information with parents. When parents perceived that special educators were just "going through the motions" or worse yet, were withholding information, they could easily develop a sense of complacency or disengagement from the process. During a focus group meeting in which a group of family members were discussing some of the barriers to effective collaboration within IEP meetings, Jane came to a realization:

> I've been sitting here thinking, I've come to this new realization of sitting here and that's that I don't really care about the IEP anymore. The document itself just means nothing to me anymore. I don't even know what his goals are. I know how that came about, partly because the process of writing goals is just so overwhelming to me …he'd have like eight goals and objectives and everything else. But even more than that, what I'd ask is how's he doing on this and I would know he didn't make, he wasn't achieving them and nobody had anything to say to me and I didn't understand how they were really evaluating it so the whole thing just became …meaningless to me. They're not following through on anything. … I'm just realizing tonight that I don't even care about that, the IEP anymore. It's really sad.

Andrew echoed Jane's sentiment:

> I stopped caring about the IEP a long time ago. When we got told, right when I got told in first grade that "don't worry about how that looks on there because the system makes us write it a certain way" and they've been complaining about this system, they have a software system and that has to be presented a certain way. So when they just say "it has to be done that way" it doesn't make sense. That was almost a justification as to why it didn't need to make sense to me.

The structural and language barriers presented in this section present a distinct challenge inherent within special education. On the one hand, the legal provisions of special education are in place to protect families and children and to create a path for parent participation in educational decision-making. On the other hand, these same procedures and entitlements are laden with terms and technicalities that may be difficult to understand and may serve to disenfranchise the very people they are supposed to protect. In some ways, this challenge goes well beyond what teams can address in the collaborative process; in other ways, it challenges professionals to think about how the process can be explained and made more transparent to families.

How Can It be Better? Parents' Perspectives on Possibilities and Strategies for Collaboration

As discouraged as some families felt, many offered perspectives on the possibilities for improved collaboration. Some talked about specific situations in which they had experienced more effective collaboration, while others spoke about strategies they engaged in to help improve or streamline the process. During a number of our interviews, we asked parents to describe what "true collaboration" would look like and how it might be best achieved. Many of their sentiments reflected the core underlying principles and defining characteristics of collaboration that we included in the beginning of this chapter.

Mutual goals.   As noted earlier, a key component of collaboration is the sense of positive interdependence that is created when team members hold mutual goals and see their role as involving collective problem-solving for the benefit of the child and family. She' Ra Monroe talked at length about the importance of ensuring that each team member, including the parent, would participate in meaningful ways to advance the team's common goals. As she described, "There's a lot of mutual respect and mutual knowledge and true understanding of what the ultimate goal is." Katie articulated a similar point of view, noting that collaboration is "everybody working together for the same purpose." She experienced a true sense of collaboration in contexts when the team was really conscious of and advocating for her son's individual needs. Will, too, felt that collaboration was evident when "The school based team and the parents and child [are] working together to improve the life of, in this case [my daughter]."

Engagement and conflict resolution.   Another key characteristic of collaboration is the use of positive interpersonal skills, including the ability to listen, express one's feelings, and engage in discussion for the purpose of gaining understanding and resolving differences that arise. Many parents described these characteristics in their definitions of true collaboration. Jane, for example, noted, noting that "the first thing that comes to mind is equal participation. People truly engaged in a process. And people being open and interested in hearing what everyone has to say and discussing things." She recalled moments when a team member would listen to something that she shared about her son's interests and would then incorporate those ideas into his educational plans. At those moments she felt a sense of collaboration among team members. Kelly talked about the need for "true discussion" that would move people out of the polite phases of collaboration and into a place where multiple viewpoints and creative solutions could emerge. As she described:

> I appreciate it when there's discussion, true discussion that might feel a little bit like disagreeing but really is contributing something new, in addition to what somebody else has already presented. So for me true collaboration happens where there is such a level of trust with each other and comfort that you can have those discussions and not have to worry about offending or stepping on toes that get in the way of it.

117

Similarly, Lina spoke about collaboration being achieved when team members really listened to one another for the purpose of understanding others' points of view and building on those to achieve a positive outcome:

> Collaboration is everybody working together. We have differences naturally but we have to work over those differences and just make the client's life better. Just like work in the hospital. Everybody's different. You don't have to agree with somebody all the time but we have to work together as a team to provide the best services.

The notion that conflict should not be avoided, but rather, needed to be acknowledged as part of the problem-solving process emerged often in parents' discussions of how to improve collaboration. As the literature on stages of group development notes (e.g., Wheelan, 2016), conflict is a natural part of group development that occurs in almost all teams and needs to be mastered for collaboration be present. Similarly, a number of parents described how their own journeys began with a fear of conflict, and later, recognition of its value. Georgia talked about her early experiences with a second grade teacher who was not serving her child well. She recalled that her "gut" told her to pull her child out of the class, but that she was concerned about doing so:

> I think that in the early years, I just didn't know how to deal with conflict. I didn't know what to do. It was very overwhelming and I thought, "hmmm, okay." At the end of the day I'd say "Is this person going to treat my child well if I make a raucous? Is that relationship going to change?" Because that's not okay. We never saw eye to eye with that teacher, no matter what she did. She just kind of undermined everything that we wanted to do.

As the years went on, Georgia's confidence in her ability to engage in difficult conversations grew. She became much less fearful of conflict and found herself more willing to take it on in order to promote problem solving in her children's teams. Still, she noted that it took time for her to get to this place and that she had had to reconcile her earlier feelings about power, authority, and parent and professional roles. Her comments underscore the developmental nature of collaboration, parents' growth in collaboration skills, and the role of conflict over time:

> I think parents have to not be too hard on themselves when they can't quite get there during times of conflict. It's a complicated thing. It's hard because most parents feel like they're challenging something that it is in somewhat of an authoritative role or at least a power differential, Maybe not authoritative but a difference of power.

B. B. talked about her experiences with conflict and problem-solving, many of which had resulted in positive action steps for her daughter. In her experience, successful conflict resolution resulted from the development of trusting relationships over time, good facilitation skills, and frequency of communication. She described it this way:

And it depends, if you trust them, I mean I do trust them, but I'll ask them lots of questions and I'll say "I don't agree with that" or "That's really interesting" but I think you have to be invitational as a parent. You have to sort of say, "This is my experience, what's yours?" And when we put the two experiences together, and we've had many, many experiences of problem solving where everybody put information from their vantage point so we had a bigger picture, and then from that bigger picture we could make better decisions. But I think it's trust, it's frequency. … I think in my experience, we end up sitting there on the table as equals and kind of, with the best interests of this particular child in the forefront, we pool our resources and haggle it out together, sometimes debate different kinds of things.

Jamie offered a similar set of steps that she found could lead to effective problem-solving. She talked about setting the stage by clearly articulating her expectations and conveying to the team the positive role she wanted to play in her daughter's education. Then, when conflicts arose, she found it easier to remain true to her expectations while demonstrating her desire to find a mutually acceptable solution with professionals:

When there's a conflict, I consider everyone in the situation, ask advice, provide resources for the teachers. I lead them in developing an effective plan to solve the issue. It easier for professionals to collaborate when they see the parent's willingness to collaborate.

Greta, too, talked about how she used her role as an advocate to facilitate conflict resolution. She described how each year, she gave teachers a description of her son Leon that she expected them to read so that they could better understand him. When she found out Leon's most recent teacher had not read the report, she was disappointed. Rather than engaging in ways that would have escalated the conflict, however, she increased her engagement in a strong but professional way:

This year the teacher didn't read the report on file by the time school began. Every year I usually hand deliver it to the teacher and this year I assumed she could access it from the files. When I emailed her to ask whether or not she read it, she admitted she had not. The next day, I gave my son a paper copy to hand deliver to her to read and did a major follow-up with the teacher. The teacher got on board quickly and has become a strong advocate for my son.

As Greta noted "trust is a big issue. If someone doesn't respond well, I look and see how I can help in a different way. I assume the best of teachers and give them the tools to succeed." Clearly, Greta's attempts to be proactive helped to increase problem-solving, rather than to escalate unresolved conflict.

Although not all parents were as comfortable with team process and conflict resolution as B. B., Jamie, and Greta, these stories serve as examples of the ways in which conflict may be viewed as an opportunity for effective problem-solving and resolution. Comments about the need for trust, frequent communication, effective facilitation, and information-sharing serve as reminders of the importance of viewing collaboration as a developmental process that, when done well, can embrace conflict as an opportunity to hear diverse viewpoints, consider a range of solutions, develop common ground, and select solutions that are acceptable to all team members.

Parity and individual accountability. Parents' definitions of collaboration also included the importance of creating a sense of parity through a sense of shared responsibility and accountability. Maggie described this element of collaboration as having "skin in the game." She spoke at length about the contributions she made at home to enhance the skill development of her daughter. She did not feel that it was solely the professionals' responsibilities to provide interventions that might benefit her daughter. For example, after discovering that music therapy was an effective intervention, she found avenues to increase her daughter's access to music by hiring a recent high school graduate to integrate songwriting into her daughter's units of study. She stated, "Why not have, why shouldn't we be, I don't know, have some skin in the game so to speak? …Everybody plays a part in it and it's not someone pointing a finger at someone else saying, 'This kid is totally your responsibility.'"

Jamie offered similar statements, noting that she took her responsibility in the process very seriously. She spoke about her early efforts as a single parent to learn all she could about early intervention services and her continued efforts to foster collaboration by making her expectations clear to teachers. She saw her efforts to advocate and take responsibility for her daughter as key to her successful partnership with school professionals, noting "I always say, I feel good as a parent because I've afforded my child every opportunity to get what she needs."

Proactive strategies. Across our interviews and focus groups with family members, we have heard a number of stories of the strategies parents use to engage proactively and contribute to more effective collaboration within their school teams. These stories stand out for us because they contrast with the literature's earlier portrayals of parents as passive participants. They also stand in contrast to stories that special educators often tell about "difficult parents" who seem to them to be overbearing in the collaborative process. The strategies that have been shared with us are important because they underscore parents' commitment to their child's education, as well as their desire to contribute in intentional ways to the collaborative process. Family members who engage in these strategies maintain an advocacy role in the process, but do so in a way that is generally well received by educators.

One common theme among parents was an attempt to help school professionals get to know their child and family. We have spoken elsewhere about how important it is to most families to be sure that school personnel know their children in a holistic way. The parents who were proactive in this regard did not wait for school professionals to tell them that they had made an effort to get to know their children; instead, these parents took initiative to ensure that this would happen. Bethany gave a detailed description of the ways in which she made sure that her son's IEP team would come to understand him:

> We write a letter that describes who [my son] is as a person, what we want for him as parents, and answer some very basic questions. We let them know that he has cerebral palsy, and that it is not a progressive thing or something you can catch. It's a brain injury that affects his motor skills, including swallowing, including moving, including talking. We go through interests of his. He loves horses, he loves playing with his siblings, he loves going out on the boat. Give people an anchor to see him as a person. ... We've donated books to the library so that they have books on hand. We've come in and spoken to the class different years when that's made sense. Thank you notes are huge. Just recognizing how much all these people are doing. I mean, I was a teacher, I know how hard it is to spend this much time on one kid. Just trying to share.

Djenne and Greta's stories about developing materials to give to professionals so that they could more quickly and easily understand their children provide additional examples of proactive steps that some parents take to enhance collaboration.

Other parents talked about the importance of being present in their child's life at school. She' Ra noted that

> I'm present. Honestly that's my best strategy. When he was in day care, I volunteered for about an hour every morning and every afternoon, and everyone knew I was there. At his school now I'm just there. We do have to have formal meetings but I touch base with his teacher, his para, the principal, his special educator at least once a week. I just saw the OT at [convenience store] the other day and we had a little impromptu meeting there kind of just eating a Snicker's bar. Yeah, so that's my best way. I don't do email well and I don't do that like real formal thing really well. I'm just there, telling people "Hi, I'm here."

Djenne talks often about the importance of presenting research and data in ways that supported their family's preferences for Malik and over time, led to successful collaboration. She talked about the long process that led to a mutually agreeable educational placement for Malik:

> I remember walking into numerous IEP meetings with 10–15 professionals and service providers at the table. These meetings were initially contentious because Malik was caught between two school systems, one that tried to force our hand in accepting their programming for Malik and another that was actually meeting and implementing his educational goals. Over time, I had become a seasoned parent, having expanded my knowledge of my rights and his educational needs. I was confident that I was indeed the expert on my child. My role had transitioned from mother to advocate. Already being in the parent role, I sought to understand the perspective of the first school system. Although

I did not agree with their recommendations, I was now able to provide concrete evidence and data to support what I knew was the best placement for Malik at the time. I would go to each meeting with a list of 3 things: first, Malik's goals; second, the "non-negotiables" for our family; and third, the places where I was willing to meet the school in the middle and negotiate. This helped me articulate Malik's needs in a calm manner and to be able to make sure the IEP goals were in line with Malik's needs. It also evened the playing field, because I knew the "secret handshake" was in effect from some of the professionals and I had my own! Eventually this process won the respect of the service providers and Malik was able to remain in our preferred educational placement. Believe it or not, I had to do this twice. Once we won one battle, we moved to another state and the dance began again. By this time I had more experience, now playing the game with the right tools.

Djenne's story reminds us that from a parents' point of view, advocacy and collaboration are intertwined. Djenne and Michael had a preferred outcome for their son, and they achieved it through presenting data, trying to understand different points of view, communicating in a respectful way, and presenting the points on which they were and were not willing to compromise. The ensuing negotiation resulted in an outcome that may have been more preferable to Malik's family than to the school, yet it reflected a problem-solving approach that promoted equity in decision-making and left all parties with their dignity intact.

Understanding collaboration as a reciprocal process. Finally, a number of parents talked about the ways in which they had come to understand collaboration as a reciprocal process in which family members and school professionals could, over time, understand how their power together was greater than what each had to offer individually. This is a sophisticated understanding of collaboration, and one that comes primarily when people have a chance to experience teams in more advanced levels of development. It is also a point of view that embraces the ideas we talked about in Chapter 4 regarding the need for parents and school professionals to come to a deeper understanding about different ways of knowing. Andrew, who was at times frustrated by the lack of collaboration that he experienced on his son's teams, was still able to articulate the possibility for team members to recognize what each knew and did not know, and therefore, to learn from one another:

> Collaboration is in my mind, and however misguided this might be, collaboration is rooted in your professionals' understanding of the things you know and don't know. It's also related to your ability to articulate the things you know and don't know. Your ability to articulate the things you know and defer to a more articulate person the things you don't. Collaboration is the art.

This sense of collaboration as an art and a "third space" in which both parties work together for an outcome that neither could have achieved alone links directly to the concept that collaboration is characterized by a sense of "positive interdependence." It was not a view of collaboration that many families experienced all of the time, though many described specific instances when this was the case. Greta, for example, talked about reciprocity within collaboration as something that occurred as both she and her son Leon's teachers figured out how to deal with his learning challenges. She noted "The dialogue I've used with teachers is, 'What can we do and who can we put him with to help him have another successful year in school.'" She talked about the relationships she formed with teachers and counselors to support Leon's organizational skills and the "grace and patience" they showed her as he progressed through school, convincing her that "I really did have a great kid who has nothing wrong with him. He is who he is."

Stories like Greta's remind us that while "true collaboration" may be difficult to achieve throughout the entirety of family and school partnerships, it surfaces in times when families and professionals are focused on the child's needs and are determined to find creative and workable answers to the challenges that present themselves. It may be more difficult to achieve the "art of collaboration" when parents have a very specific goal that they care deeply about and need to take a strong advocacy stance. In the next chapter, we dive more deeply into the concept of advocacy, noting the ways in which it complements and extends parents' roles in the collaborative process.

CHAPTER SUMMARY

In this chapter, we returned to the literature to identify key principles and characteristics associated with effective collaboration, including the need for collaborative teams to engage in face-to-face interaction, positive interdependence, effective use of interpersonal skills, individual accountability and group processing and monitoring (Thousand & Villa, 1992). In addition, we explored the idea that collaboration should be viewed as a developmental process. The stages of group development identified in the literature (i.e., forming, storming, norming and performing) (Tuckman & Jensen, 1977; Wheelan, 2016) were offered as a framework for understanding that collaboration must be intentional and nurtured over time. Along with these frameworks for understanding and promoting collaboration, we identified barriers identified in the literature as well as by parents involved in our research and experiences. We noted that a significant amount of meeting time is spent determining special education eligibility, developing educational plans (i.e., IFSPs, IEPs, transition plans) and addressing procedural elements of the special education process. If parents feel disengaged from those processes and meetings, it can have a considerable impact on their sense of collaboration with team members. Whether the roadblock is time, funding, relationship management, or just navigating the complex language of the process, parents voiced clear ideas about how to improve collaborative practice. As such, we offer the following suggestions:

1. *Become acquainted with collaborative theories and frameworks that help to make sense of the process.* The old saying "knowledge is power" holds true when it comes to collaboration. Parents and professionals who have opportunities to become acquainted with how collaboration should work are probably in a better position to make it happen. Teams can use their knowledge of the principles and characteristics associated with collaboration to analyze what is and what is not working on a particular team and to address elements that can be improved. By understanding collaboration as a developmental process, all team members can learn to think of collaboration as a practice that can be improved over time. At the same time, it is important for professionals to recognize that most parents who enter into the special education process have not had opportunities to think about the meaning of collaboration or how to participate as effective team members.

2. *Consider structural and organizational barriers to collaboration that exist in schools and think about ways that these can be addressed.* The parents we have spoken to reiterate the ways in which barriers such as time, resources, power in decision-making perpetuate barriers to parent participation. On the one hand, we acknowledge that some of these challenges (e.g., time constraints, power to allocate resources) may constitute institutional barriers that cannot be addressed by parent and professional teams. On the other hand, we encourage teams to think about how these kinds of barriers might be addressed through systems level advocacy. How might schools increase opportunities for parents and professionals to interact with one another? In particular, how might schools invite families who have not been well-represented to experience more comfort with and a greater sense of belonging in special education processes and procedures?

3. *Acknowledge differences and the need to embrace conflict and to engage in conflict resolution.* Across our multiple experiences with both parents and professionals we have noticed that—at least at the outset – the notion of conflict is off-putting to many. We hear far too many stories about the fear that many people have of confronting others. Unfortunately, a lack of ability to present ideas that may appear to be in conflict or have the potential to result in difficult discussions usually results in one of two scenarios. Those who always shy away from conflict tend to feel diminished, powerless and/or frustrated over time, because it becomes impossible for them to express their true beliefs. Those who refrain from engaging in conflict most of the time may find that every now and again, their feelings of dissatisfaction erupt and are expressed in such a way that prevents healthy resolution of conflict. As acknowledged by the stages of group development, a more healthy approach is to accept the idea that some level of storming is not only typical, but helpful. When parents and professionals can establish trust and learn to express diverse points of view clearly and with respect for different forms of knowledge and expertise, team members are often able to engage in productive problem-solving. When team members can "challenge ideas, not people," ask clarifying questions, understand the "why" behind another's

point of view, and – occasionally – "agree to disagree," they are demonstrating a high level of collaboration and evidence of a highly performing team. There are many excellent materials available on conflict styles and strategies for conflict resolution, and we highly recommend that parents and professionals engage in learning about the benefits of respectfully challenging one another's ideas for the purpose of finding common ground.

4. *Promote strategies that increase parents' participation and empowerment in collaborative processes.* Throughout this chapter, we have made the case that collaboration is a learned skill, a difficult undertaking, and an art. It is our hope and expectation that school and other professionals will receive training in collaboration as part of their initial preparation for their profession; if not, we would hope that they will have opportunities to participate in ongoing professional development. The same expectation does not hold for all parents, because not all of them have experiences in fields where collaboration is specifically taught or practiced. Some parents may find that collaborative practices are consistent with they way they approach the world, but others will need to be supported in developing skills in collaboration, team decision-making, and positive conflict resolution. As such, we believe it is essential for schools and other organizations to help parents become connected with opportunities for development of their skills in advocacy and collaboration. Chapter 7 addresses this issue in more detail, but we find it important to emphasize the degree to which we believe that parents deserve to receive whatever support they need in developing and refining their collaborative skills over time.

SUGGESTED QUESTIONS FOR REFLECTION AND DISCUSSION

For parents:

1. As a parent, what strategies do you employ to foster collaborative practice? If you had one wish for your child's team related to collaboration what would it be?
2. What barriers to collaboration are the most significant within your school context? What steps might be taken to alleviate those barriers?

For professionals:

3. What strategies might you use to share information and foster collaboration with families outside the constraints of the IEP and other meetings?
4. What norms and expectations do you communicate to parents that help them to understand your approach to collaboration during team meetings? In what ways might you communicate to parents about how decisions will be made within the context of team meetings (including IFSP and IEP teams, eligibility determination teams, etc.)?
5. Many of the examples provided in this chapter refer to collaboration in the context of meetings; however, parents also talked about ongoing relationship-building

as a form of collaboration. What strategies do you currently employ to support collaborative approaches in your relationships with families? What additional strategies might you adopt?

SUGGESTED ACTIVITIES

For parents:

1. Reflect on your own skills within the collaborative process. What are your strengths as a team member? In what areas might you like to develop additional skills? Who/what might be able to support you in that skill development?
2. Make a list of the things you do to promote collaboration within your school teams. What is working? What is not working? Identify three action steps you can take to help improve collaboration on this team.
3. Develop a list of goals, non-negotiables and areas for compromise between you, your child and professionals that you are willing to negotiate before or during your next IEP meeting. Get the advice of another parent or professional to make sure your requests seem reasonable.

For professionals:

4. Initiate a discussion with parents on how best to collaborate with them in meeting the needs of their child. Using your knowledge of collaboration and the stages of team development referred to in the chapter (Tucker & Jensen), work with your colleagues to construct a set of norms that are likely to promote collaboration. Post these in the areas where you tend to meet with families, and review them on a regular basis.
5. Consider the challenges of infrequent meetings with families. Make a list of ways in which you model collaborative practice on teams for which you may only meet once or twice in a face-to-face context. Record your answers to other questions: What other strategies can you use outside of meeting times? How might you engage parents in playing a formal role within the structure of your collaborative team?
6. Think about all of the collaborative teams of which you are a member. To what degree do these teams reflect the five characteristics of effective teams as described by Thousand and Villa? Choose one area in need of improvement and make an action plan for improving it.
7. Explore resources in your school or community that are available to support parents in developing their collaborative skills. Share opportunities for workshops and conferences with families and/or attend an event with a group of families.

NOTE

[1] Portions of this chapter appeared in Kervick, C. T. (in press). Parents are the experts: Understanding parent knowledge and the strategies they use to foster collaboration with special education teams. *Journal of the American Academy of Special Education Professionals.* Reprinted with permission.

REFERENCES

Blue-Banning, M., Summers, J. A., Frankland, H. C., Nelson, L. L., & Beegle, G. (2004). Dimensions of family and professional partnerships: Constructive guidelines for collaboration. *Exceptional Children, 70*(2), 167–184.

Cone, J. D., Delawyer, D. D., & Wolfe, V. V. (1985). Assessing parent participation: The parent/family involvement index. *Exceptional Children, 51*(5), 417–424.

Friend, M., & Cook, L. (2013). *Interactions: Collaboration skills for school professionals* (7th ed.). Boston, MA: Pearson.

Goldstein, S., Strickland, B., Turnbull, A. P., & Curry, L. (1980). An observational analysis of the IEP conference. *Exceptional Children, 46*(4), 278–286.

Harry, B. (1992). Making sense of disability: Low-income, Puerto Rican parents' theories of the problem. *Exceptional Children, 59*(1), 27–40.

Harry, B. (2008). Collaboration with culturally and linguistically diverse families: Ideal versus reality. *Exceptional Children, 74*(3), 372–388.

Kalyanpur, M., & Harry, B. (2012). *Cultural reciprocity in special education: Building family-professional relationships.* Baltimore, MD: Paul H. Brookes.

Lusthaus, C. S., Lusthaus, E. W., & Gibbs, H. (1981). Parents' role in the decision process. *Exceptional Children, 48*, 256–257.

Mostert, M. P. (1997). *Interprofessional collaboration in schools: Practical application in classrooms.* Boston, MA: Allyn and Bacon.

Overton, S. (2005). *Collaborating with families: A case study approach.* Upper Saddle River, NJ: Pearson.

Thousand, J., & Villa, R. (1992). Collaborative teams: A powerful tool in school restructuring. In R. Villa, J. Thousand, W. Stainback & S. Stainback (Eds.), *Restructuring for caring and effective education: An administrative guide to creating heterogeneous schools.* Baltimore, MD: Paul H. Brookes.

Tuckman, B. W., & Jenson, M. A. C. (1977). Stages in group development revisited. *Group and Organizational Studies, 2*, 419–427.

Vacc, N. A., Vallercorsa, A. L., Parker, A., Bonner, S., Lester, C., Richardson, S., & Yates, C. (1985). Parents' and educators' participation in IEP conferences. *Education and Treatment of Children, 8*(2), 153–162.

Vaughn, S., Bos, C. S., Harrell, J. E., & Lasky, B. (1988). Parent participation in the initial placement/ IEP conference ten years after mandated involvement. *Journal of Learning Disabilities, 21*(2), 82–89.

Wheelan, S. (2016). *Creating effective teams: A guide for members and leaders* (5th ed.). Thousand Oaks, CA: Sage.

FINDING VOICE

Promoting Advocacy, Choice, and Leadership[1]

A child with special gifts is the fuel that will put in motion a parent's desire to learn, fight for the child's rights and look for the best opportunities to offer the child a healthy, productive and happy life. But a parent cannot ask for services available or fight for rights if she is not aware that those services and rights exist or cannot differentiate between eligibility and entitlement! Participating in a parent leadership training will give parents the tools they need to become empowered.

(Clara, former parent center director)

Before this leadership training, I felt powerless. Now I feel like I can do anything!

(Celia, PCL participant)

Previous chapters have addressed perspectives on how parents and professionals gain knowledge about disability, special education, and the processes that promote or detract from their ability to collaborate successfully with one another. We have presented the collaborative process as one that is complex, developmental, and rooted in relationships between families and school professionals. In this chapter, we explore the ways in which family members develop a sense of agency and voice in decision-making and collaboration. Although it is not the case for all families, a majority of the parents we spoke to for this project identified one or more experiences that helped them learn to advocate for themselves and their children, develop a sense of confidence in themselves, and in some cases, take on a leadership role at the school, community, state, or even national level. We begin by presenting tools that all parents can access to help develop their knowledge and advocacy, and then describe outcomes associated with specific efforts that we as authors have been involved with related to developing parent leadership. Throughout, we maintain that parents who are supported in finding their voice and engaging in advocacy and leadership efforts may be in a position to gain a sense of agency and empowerment that results in more positive relationships with school professionals as well as participation in larger and more systemic efforts to improve the lives of children with disabilities and their families.

RESOURCES AND TOOLS FOR PROMOTING
KNOWLEDGE AND ADVOCACY

Parent Centers

Many of the parents we have spoken with over the years have accessed their local federally funded parent center to gain information, support, and training related to their child's disability and the special education process. As described by the Center for Parent Information and Resources (www.parentcenterhub.org) on its home page, every state has at least one Parent Training and Information Center (PTI) funded by the U.S. Department of Education, Office of Special Education Programs (OSEP) to provide resources to families of children with disabilities, including information on early intervention, school services, therapy, local policies, transportation, and more. Additionally, states with high populations often have an OSEP-funded Community Parent Resource Center (CPRC) that offers similar support and training to families of children with disabilities who are from diverse cultural and linguistic backgrounds. Finally, OSEP funds state and multi-state technical assistance projects designed to improve services and results for children with dual sensory loss (i.e., deaf-blindness), as well as a national technical assistance and dissemination center for children who are deaf-blind.

Over the years, these national centers and PTIs, CPRCs and Deaf-blind projects and consortia in all 50 states and the U.S. territories have amassed a great deal of information that is publicly available in family-friendly language, and in some cases, in multiple languages. Most host workshops and conferences that provide parents with frequent opportunities to learn and share their experiences with other parents. PTIs and CPRCs are often directed by and staffed with people who are themselves parents of children with disabilities, bringing even greater authenticity to their work. Projects serving children with dual sensory loss and their families address a critical need to provide specialized services to children and families dealing with the challenges of multiple and low incidence disabilities. Clearly, these parent centers and projects provide an excellent resource for both parents and professionals; we believe that all parents who are new to the field of disability should be encouraged to become connected with their local and/or regional centers and to avail themselves of all that the centers have to offer.

Although resources offered through parent centers are important to many families, some of the parents we have spoken with did not learn about these kinds of support until later in their children's lives. Georgia noted the importance of ensuring that parents have access to support groups, but recalled that when her children were younger "I didn't even know about our local center." Melissa, who over time became an advocate for other parents, was concerned about inequities in the system regarding the provision of information to families. She described her own journey to becoming an advocate as one that evolved over time with the support of a friend who was a university faculty member in special education. Still, she noted that many parents lacked a "go to" person and/or were not given access to information about how to find support. As she put it, "I just can't stress enough that I feel like there should be an advocate for parents and I don't know if it could be a state thing where the state could provide a certain number of advocates per region."

Technology

As described in previous chapters, technology has played an increasingly important role over the years in helping parents to access knowledge and develop a sense of advocacy, particularly as it pertains to the sharing of information about disability-specific issues. Many of the family members we have spoken to over the years note that upon learning that their child had a disability, they turned first to the internet to learn as much as they possibly could. The power of technology and the internet cannot be underestimated. While the early studies of parent participation in the IEP process assumed that most families gained their information from school-based or medical professionals, rapid changes in the availability of information suggest that this is rarely the case today. Will, the father of a daughter with an extremely rare genetic disorder, talked about the fact that the hours of internet research he and his wife conducted in the early years meant that they almost always knew much more than other professionals about their daughter's condition. Although this at times created tensions and frustration for the family (e.g., when they felt that professionals had not done their "homework" or were not as knowledgeable of current research as they should have been), it also ensured that their voices and knowledge were a key part of every conversation regarding their daughter's education and health. The preponderance of readily available information also creates challenges on both sides of the table, in that both parents and professionals are called upon to be critical consumers who can distinguish between reliable and unreliable information. This is not always an easy task, especially for those who are not familiar how research is developed, conducted, published and disseminated. Here too, professionals and parents need to work together to develop a common understanding of what constitutes reliable, research-based information.

The following website addresses are some that parents have found most helpful and reliable over the years:

www.parentcenterhub.org
www.wrightslaw.com
www.pacer.org/pandr/
www.cec.sped.org/Tools-and-Resources/For-Families
https://nationaldb.org

TOOLS FOR PROMOTING CHOICE AND FAMILY ENGAGEMENT

Although it is beyond the scope of this chapter to present an exhaustive review of the literature on tools that promote choice and family engagement, our research and experience suggest that strategies falling under the umbrella term of "person-centered planning" are particularly useful for developing and sustaining positive and collaborative parent and professional partnerships. In this section, we describe the underlying assumptions of person-centered planning and describe three specific approaches representative of this approach. In addition, we describe a related process known as Choosing Outcomes and Accommodations for Children or COACH (Giangreco, Cloninger, & Iverson, 2011) that focuses on engaging families of children with intensive needs in educational planning. Finally, we include descriptions from families about their experiences with one approach known as Making Action Plans or MAPS (Forest & Lusthaus, 1987; Vandercook, York, & Forest, 1989).

Emergence of Person-Centered Planning

Person-centered planning (also known as personal futures planning) is an umbrella term used to describe a set of processes and strategies that allow persons with a disability, family members, and friends to share information about the individual with disabilities for the purpose of creating a profile of strengths, dreams, challenges, goals and needs that result in a long-term vision for the focus person (Shepherd, Giangreco, & Cook, 2013; Shepherd, Kervick, & Salembier, 2015; Wells & Sheehey, 2012). Person-centered planning approaches were introduced into research and practice in the late 1980s, in part to counter what was perceived to be an over-professionalization of traditional planning meetings, including IEP and transition planning meetings. In moving away from discussions and decision-making that were dominated by professionals, person-centered planning processes help shift the context of meetings to create a student and family focus and an environment more conducive to building trust, respect, communication, and positive and collaborative relationships among students, parents, teachers, service providers, and others (Furney & Salembier, 2000; Geenan, Powers, & Lopez-Vasquez, 2001).

As described by O'Brien and O'Brien (2000), the roots of person-centered planning can be traced to communities of practice devoted to the principles of normalization in the 1970s and 1980s. The normalization movement asserted that negative perceptions of individuals with disabilities—and in particular, those with intellectual and developmental disabilities – had led to segregation, widespread reliance on institutionalization of people with disabilities, and inadequate provision of services and supports, which in turn perpetuated low expectations (Wolfensberger, 1972). Proponents of normalization advocated for changes that would reflect a more positive and growth-oriented perception of persons with disabilities and recognize their right to live in their communities and participate in inclusive opportunities for employment, postsecondary education, and community living. The movement called for opportunities for individuals with disabilities to lead self-determined lives. The concept of self-determination has been defined as the state in which a person with a disability acts "as the primary causal agent in one's life and making choices and decisions regarding one's quality of life free from undue external influence or interference" (Wehmeyer, 1996, p. 22). Because person-centered planning promotes self-determination by basing planning and supports on the hopes and desires of individuals with disabilities and their families, it may be seen as an important alternative to more traditional forms of decision-making that rely solely on the basis of professionals' recommendations.

Although multiple definitions and approaches to person-centered planning exist, it is generally described as a reflective, strengths-based planning process attended by and focused on an individual with disabilities and a variety of people close to the individual (typically including parents), which results in a vision of the future for the individual with disabilities and plans for achieving that vision (Rasheed, Fore, & Miller, 2006). Flannery and colleagues (2000) delineated critical attributes of person-centered planning, including a focus on the individual's presence and participation in the process; determination by the individual and family members regarding who will be present at the meeting; a sense of familiarity among meeting participants; a focus on planning that is based on the individual's interests, preferences, and strengths, and leads to a vision of the future; development of an action plan that includes a clear process for monitoring implementation of the plan; and a flexible and informal approach to planning.

Person-centered planning gained its original momentum with adults with disabilities, however the idea of using strategies that put choice making and planning in the hands of individuals with disabilities and their families soon garnered attention in the literature on IEP and transition planning and related student and family outcomes (e.g., Salembier & Furney, 1994; Neece, Kramer, & Blacher, 2009). Claes and colleagues (2010) conducted an extensive review of person-centered planning, concluding that use of related processes may have positive outcomes on the development of the social networks, community involvement, choice-making, knowledge, and reduction of problem behaviors among young adults and adults with developmental disabilities. Other studies have asserted similar results, lending credence to the idea that person-centered planning can make significant changes to the nature of IEP and transition planning (Callicott, 2003; Childre & Chambers, 2005; Flannery et al., 2000; Meadan et al., 2010; Miner & Bates, 1997; Salembier & Furney, 1994; Shepherd et al., 2015; Wells & Sheehey, 2012), including higher levels of satisfaction among parents and students with disabilities regarding opportunities to talk about their hopes and dreams and to contribute to discussions of goals and action steps. Families have described person-centered planning as a productive and worthwhile process that encourages communication, brainstorming, and problem solving between families and professionals, resulting in a shift away from simple exchange of information between team members toward true collaboration (Childre & Chambers). Person-centered planning has been associated with increased

133

participation and empowerment among families (Salembier & Furney, 1994; Trainor, 2007), as well as increased cultural sensitivity on the part of teachers (Callicott, 2003; Sheehey, Ornelles, & Noonan, 2009).

In summary, a growing number of studies support the notion that person-centered planning processes are beneficial for students with a range of disabilities as well as their families. The fact that many of the empirical studies referenced above have been conducted primarily with older students with intellectual and developmental disabilities suggests that it is not appropriate to conclude that the approach results in positive outcomes for *all* students and families; still, the emerging evidence and direct reports from some of the families we have worked with suggests that person-centered planning may result in higher rates of satisfaction among students and parents, more effective IEP and transition planning processes, and more positive outcomes for students with disabilities and their families.

Examples of Person-Centered Planning Processes

Three commonly used person-centered planning tools are Essential Lifestyle Planning (ELP; Smull & Sanderson, 2005), Planning Alternative Tomorrows with Hope (PATH) (Pearpoint, O'Brien, & Forest, 1993), and the McGill Action Planning System (MAPS; Forest & Lusthaus, 1987; Vandercook et al., 1989).

Essential Lifestyle Planning. Essential Lifestyle Planning (ELP) is a person-centered planning tool that was developed by Smull and Sanderson in the late 1980s to assist the transition from institutional life to community-based services (Smull et al., 2005). The goal of the process is to develop a vision for daily living and supports for the individual with a disability that is rooted in the person's values and preferences and forms strong partnerships with service providers (O'Brien & Lovett, 1993). In order to develop a plan based on the ELP process, a facilitator is brought in to provide expertise in guiding the process. Throughout the process, the participants, including the individual with a disability, are viewed as experts in the content of planning, in that they are able to identify the important information that will contribute to building an effective plan (Smull et al., 2005). Key components of the process include identifying what is important to and for the person, clearly outlining the roles and responsibilities of paid service providers, building compatibility between the individual and the service providers, identifying systems of communication, and determining what is working and not working from the perspective of the individual and support providers. Research on outcomes associated with ELP describes an emphasis on positive outcomes and utility in identifying the critical and most valued elements of daily living and supports for individuals with disabilities (Rudkin & Rowe, 1999).

Planning Alternative Tomorrows with Hope (PATH). PATH is a planning tool that focuses on the dreams and long-term goals of an individual with a disability. Marsha Forest, Jack Pearpoint, and John O'Brien, who were also authors of the original MAPS process, developed PATH in the early 1990s. PATH has been used with children, youth, and adults with a variety of disabilities, including intellectual and developmental disabilities. It is a planning tool that helps individuals identify aspirations and develop the road map to achieve those goals (Forest & O'Brien, 1993; Pearpoint et al., 1993; Pipi, 2010). The process engages the individual with a disability and other team participants in identifying preferences for all facets of life, including community, employment, recreation, friendship, and housing. The purpose is to establish the future dreams of the individual and then articulate steps to achieving those dreams while assigning responsibility to team members to help the individual progress toward realizing the identified outcomes (Garner & Dietz, 1996). The process is composed of eight steps: (a) articulating a dream for the individual; (b) identifying a goal for the next year; (c) examining where the individual is now; (d) selecting people to support the journey; (e) identifying strengths; (f) developing action steps for the next few months; (g) identifying action steps for the upcoming month, and (h) choosing and committing to the first step.

A key characteristic of the PATH process is its use of graphics, pictures, and color to bring the vision of the individual's dreams to life (Pipi, 2010). It is sometimes used as a follow-up to the MAPS process, where the MAPS process is used to develop the long-term vision for the individual with a disability, and PATH is used to identify more specific action steps for the person's immediate, midrange, and long-term future. Pipi (2010) described the potential for PATH to be applied in different cultures. Her work involved using the tool within the context of Maori communities in New Zealand, where she found that PATH's underlying principles resonated with ideas about inclusion within the Maori culture. Additionally, she found that the medium, including the use of symbols, was powerful in evoking images to convey hopes and dreams.

Making Action Plans.   Originally known as the McGill Action Planning System, Making Action Plans, or MAPS (Forest & Lusthaus, 1987; Vandercook et al., 1989), is one of the most widely used person-centered planning strategies and an approach that can increase the involvement of parents and children and youth with disabilities in a variety of educational decision-making contexts, including the development of Individualized Family Service Plans (IFSPs), Individualized Education Plans (IEPs), plans for grade-to-grade or school-to-school transitions, and transition planning for students moving from secondary to postsecondary environments (Miner & Bates, 1997; Shepherd et al., 2015; Salembier & Furney, 1994, 1997).

Briefly stated, the MAPS process involves bringing a family together with key teachers and support persons (e.g., general and special education teachers, guidance counselors, physical and occupational therapists, speech and language pathologists, social workers, friends and relatives, potential employers, representatives from religious and community organizations, etc.) to engage in a one to two hour planning process in which participants respond to five broad questions about the student's history, dreams, fears, strengths and preferences, and needs. Individual responses are recorded and displayed publicly. Originally, most MAPS were recorded on flip chart paper, though a more recent trend has been to document the process using technology tools such as Google Docs.

Generally speaking, one person facilitates the five steps of the process and another records the responses of all participants using key words and graphics; however, it is sometimes the case that the facilitator also serves as the recorder. At the outset of each step of the MAP, the facilitator describes the purpose of that step and invites students and family members to give the first response to prompts posed for that step. Following family input, other team members add their observations and ideas. The MAPS process concludes with a review of the information gathered through the process for the purpose of identifying key goals and issues of importance to the family and student, which in turn become the driving forces for the development of more formal educational plans (e.g., IFSPs, IEP and transition plans, personalized learning plans, etc.). Table 1 shows the five steps of the MAPS process, including the purpose of each step and key prompts that may be used to elicit responses from team members.

Table 1. Five steps of the MAPS process

MAPS step	Purpose	Prompting questions
History	Identify key events in the focus person's life	"Tell us a bit about your background, including school and family experiences." "What key events or experiences have been most important?"
Dreams	Identify desired future outcomes for the focus person.	"What are some of your dreams for the future?" (Dreams may relate to education, community life, work, independent living, etc.) "What do you hope will happen for you/this person in the coming year? Five years from now? 10?"
Fears	Identify concerns for the present and future.	"What worries or concerns do you have for now or in the future?" "What might stand in the way of the dreams we've just discussed?"
Who Is...?	Describe the focus person, including strengths, skills, interests, activities, friends, etc.	"What words best describe you/this person?" "What should we know about you/this person?" "What are your interests, strengths, skills, etc.?"
Needs	Identify steps that need to be taken to achieve dreams and minimize concerns, including information to be used in the IEP, IFSP, transition plan, etc.	"Looking at the ideas we've talked about in the previous four steps, what needs to happen to make dreams come true and/or to avoid concerns?" "What steps need to be taken in the near future?" "What information needs to go into this person's IEP (or other plan)?"

Following completion of the MAPS, the team agrees to a process for sharing critical information. Generally speaking, this involves transcribing information from the flip chart paper onto a handout that can be distributed and used to express the family's hopes and dreams during subsequent formal meetings (e.g., IFSP, IEP, transition planning, etc.). If a Google Doc or similar document has been created, the team agrees on a process for sharing it at future meetings. Other schools conduct the MAPS process at the beginning of a scheduled IEP or transition planning meeting. This approach works well to integrate MAPS with legal documentation of the planning process, but it does require schools and teams to set aside a longer time for meetings.

Additional Family-Centered Planning Processes

Choosing Outcomes and Accommodations for Children (COACH). In addition to person-centered planning processes, additional family-centered planning practices have been developed and used to promote family engagement in the development of IEPs, IFSPs and other formal plans. One of best known of these is Choosing Outcomes and Accommodations for Children, or COACH. COACH, now in its ninth version since 1985, is an assessment and planning process designed to assist school personnel in working collaboratively with families to develop IEPs for students with intensive special education needs (Giangreco, Cloninger, & Iverson, 2011). A secondary aim of COACH is to assist families in becoming better consumers of educational services and partners in the educational process. Because COACH is designed for specific use with children and youth ages 3 through 21 with low-incidence disabilities, it is particularly helpful to families and school teams as they think about how to structure curriculum for students whose needs extend beyond what is typically reflected in the general education curriculum corresponding to their chronological age (e.g., students who require foundational communication and social skills to participate in chronologically-age appropriate inclusive placements) (Shepherd, Giangreco, & Cook, 2013).

COACH is divided into two parts, including six major steps as well as strategies for implementing COACH-generated plans in inclusive classrooms (e.g., scheduling matrix, tools for planning instruction). Of the six steps, the first three are directly related to family participation. The *Family Interview* (Step 1), is the heart of COACH – it provides a unique combination of features to assist families in selecting a small set of the highest priority learning outcomes for their child. Step 2, *Additional Learning Outcomes* (Step 2), assists in identifying a set of learning outcomes from both those listed in COACH and the general education curriculum. Finally, *General Supports* (Step 3) assists in identifying supports to be provided to or for students with disabilities across six categories so they can pursue the learning outcomes identified in Steps 1 and 2 (Giangreco et al., 2011; Shepherd et al., 2013).

A key feature of COACH is its link to assumptions and principles that serve to create a direct connection between the perspectives offered by parents and the curricular and instructional planning process (Giangreco, 2002; Shepherd et al., 2013). The process focuses on a *posture of listening* in which specific steps are structured so that professionals spend time asking questions that will help them better understand family's perspectives and understanding of their child. It also uses strategies intended to identify family member's perspectives on five *valued life outcomes,* for the purpose of ensuring that a family's values—rather than professionals' values—drive the planning process. Finally, COACH embraces the tenets and selected elements articulated in the selected elements of the *Osborn-Parnes Creative Problem-Solving Process* (CPS) (Parnes, 1992), in an effort to ensure that creative ideas are generated, selected and developed in ways that honor a family's intent (Giangreco et al., 2011).

Family and Professional Experiences with the MAPS Process

As authors, we have participated in numerous MAPS for students and families representing a variety of backgrounds and needs. Some of these MAPS were conducted and documented as research efforts (i.e., Salembier & Furney, 1994; Shepherd et al., 2015) while others have been written about in training materials (i.e., Furney, Carlson, Salembier, Cravedi-Cheng, & Blow, 2004; Morris & Shepherd, 2011; Shepherd, Hasazi, Kucij, Brick, & Goldberg, 2007), and/or conducted as part of our work with families and schools. Our experiences have included families of children of all ages (i.e., age four to over 21) with a range of strengths, abilities, and challenges. Participants have included children, youth and adults with intellectual disabilities, learning disabilities, emotional disturbance, attention issues, autism spectrum disorder, deaf-blindness, hearing impairment, speech and language impairment, multiple disabilities, and children considered gifted and talented but at risk of a disability. Through these collective efforts, we have learned a great deal about families' experiences in the MAPS process and the ways in which the process can serve as a tool for promoting school and family partnerships.

Enhancing knowledge and awareness. Many of the families and professionals we have worked with have remarked on the way in which the MAPS process enhanced the knowledge of all participants regarding the child's background, hopes, interests, concerns and needs. One MAPS process involved Peter, a student with intellectual and language disabilities, his parents, a transition coordinator, and his special educator. During the initial MAPS meeting, Peter was in 10th grade and was beginning work on a transition plan. A second MAP was conducted a year later to review his accomplishments and follow-up on plans articulated in the initial MAP. Although Peter was initially reluctant to talk in a team setting, he gradually opened up and participated more actively than his parents had expected. His mother commented on all that she learned through the process, noting that "Through this process we learned a lot about ourselves as a family and a lot about Peter," while his father remarked that "We have discovered through this MAPS process that Peter is probably capable of more than we might have expected, especially in the areas of employment and social needs, and the independent living we were worried about. We feel that these are all goals that he will definitely accomplish."

Another MAP included Michelle and the preschool teacher of her son Michael, an active and inquisitive five year old with characteristics of a child with ADHD. Michelle, who had immigrated to the U.S. from the Congo, noted that the MAPS process allowed her to share details about her life as a single mother with Michael's pre-school teacher, Natalie. Natalie found this information to be extremely useful, noting that it gave her ideas about what motivated Michael, his need for structure and male role models, and the richness of the community of friends who surrounded Michael and Michelle. A MAP conducted for Luke, a kindergarten student with autism and limited oral communication who was transitioning to first grade, also provided important information for his teachers. The first grade teacher who was assigned to have Luke in her classroom the following fall remarked that prior to the MAPS process, she had not really understood Luke and was worried about having him in her class. She appreciated the information his parents shared with her about his creativity, his interest in making things for others, and his emerging language and communication skills. The Needs page of the MAP provided an opportunity for the teacher and Luke's parents to identify a number of activities that would prepare Luke for the transition to first grade.

A post-MAPS interview with Jim Jackson, a teacher of Mohamed – an 18-year-old student with intellectual disabilities who came to the U.S. with his family from a refugee camp in Burma – revealed that the process helped Jim to learn a great deal about the family and personal life. For instance, Jim was not aware of the host family that had provided initial housing and support for Mohamed's family, or the complexity of Mohamed's family composition. Jim remarked after the MAPS meeting that "I never realized until the MAPS process just how many relatives Mohammed has in this school. His extended family is large and fluid, and they all support and look after him during the school day." In addition, Jim and other MAPS participants were visibly moved as Mohamed's sister and father recounted the horrible living conditions the family endured during the two years they spent in a refugee camp. This information helped Jim to better understand Mohamed's previous lack of education as well as his father's determination to ensure a better life for his children now that they were living in the United States.

Enhanced engagement for students and families. Family members and school professionals have also talked at length about the ways in which the MAPS process promotes engagement and participation among family members. Following a MAP conducted with Travis, an 11th grade student with emotional disabilities, and his mother Shelia, Travis' special educator talked at length about the fact that the MAPS meeting had promoted the most extensive and positive interactions she had ever observed between the two of them. She commented that:

> I was worried that Travis and Sheila would not get along, because they haven't in previous meetings. The way it usually goes is that Sheila starts talking and

Travis gets angry and leaves the meeting, but this time it was different. The MAPS questions made it possible for them to hear one another, even when they didn't totally agree on things. It was so amazing at the end to see Travis step up to identify the three things from the MAP that he thought he should work on.

Peter's special educator Jamie commented on the changes he observed in Peter and his parents over the course of the two MAPS. Jamie noted that during previous IEP meetings, he had talked a lot and generated most of the ideas, whereas during the MAPS meetings, Peter's parents "were really clear about the hopes and dreams they had for him. During the second meeting, they were much more vocal about their ideas."

Students have also commented on their increased participation in MAPS meetings. At his post-MAPS interview, Mohamed commented that the process "made me go to another level." He talked about the ways in which the process helped him to feel free to express his hopes and dreams for the future (e.g., getting married and having a family). He felt that the MAPS meeting marked one of the first times in schools that his family had really listened to him, which in turn gave him confidence that he could realize some of his dreams. His father and sister both remarked that "we haven't really heard him talk about these things before," while his teacher noted that "he is talking all the time now, and I attribute that to the experience he had in the MAPS process…We're putting him in the center ring, and he's performing, growing as we watch."

Promoting cultural responsiveness.   Finally, the MAPS meetings we have been involved with that included families from diverse backgrounds suggest that the process may help to promote cultural awareness and responsiveness. Although we have been careful not to push families to talk more than they want to during the History step of the MAP, family members have indicated that they appreciated having professionals listen to more in-depth descriptions of their lives, cultural beliefs, and family situations. Jim Jackson noted that although the need to translate the process into English was at times challenging within Mohamed's MAP (although Mohamed and his sisters were fluent in English, their father was not and preferred to have the process translated), he felt that the process "encouraged a high level of cultural responsiveness because it puts someone at the center of a room and gets at their hidden needs." Jim noted, "Students and their stories are very important… families like Mohamed's seem to appreciate having others listening to what they have endured before coming to this country." Further, he talked about the fact that the MAPS process helps achieve "a level of honesty that goes beyond what we are used to in our predominately white, Anglo Saxon experiences."

Members of a MAPS team including Jinnow, a mother from Somalia, her son Abdul (the focus person for the MAP), her daughter Maia (who also served as the translator), and Abdul's special educator, classroom teacher, and English Language teacher expressed similar thoughts. Jinnow articulated that the MAPS process had made it possible for her to talk about things that Abdul's teachers did not know about the family, including her strong sense of caring and desire for him to be successful in school. This was confirmed by the special educator who noted that "hearing about what life was like in the refugee camp and knowing that Abdul was allowed to roam freely at all hours of the day and night in that camp helped me to better understand some of his behaviors at school. It makes more sense to me now that the some of the rules and norms we have in school and in the community feel really confining to him." By having students and parents speak first during each step of the MAPS process, family members feel more validated and certain that their responses are the most important. Their values, which reflect their culture, beliefs, and history, are at the forefront of the process, rather than taking the back seat to what a school might think is best for a student. Jean, a single parent with custody of her nephew David, an 11th grader with significant cognitive challenges, talked about it this way:

I was so amazed at how it felt during the first MAPS meeting to have blank paper on the wall and to be asked about my dreams for David. I don't feel like the school people have always valued my ideas. They haven't really been listening to me. Before this, I'd come in and they would say things like "We think it will be best if David goes into such and such a class." But during the MAP, I got to say what I thought was important for him: things like, having a dream to go to Nashville to see two singers that he liked, or having him get a job in the local fire station so that he could wear a uniform. This was the thing that really made a difference for me, that I was going to have people listening to our family's dreams for him.

Although processes such as Essential Lifestyle Planning, PATH, MAPS and COACH require additional time and planning, it is clear that these family-centered approaches have the power to engage parents and students with disabilities in decision-making, with the result that IEPs and other plans are more likely to reflect the wishes and needs of families. To many, the additional investment of time is worthwhile because it results in more student and family-centered plans that reflect the family's values and goals and promote self-determination. In turn, the investment of time creates a stronger sense of buy-in and accountability among parents and students for attainment of goals and activities generated through the process.

Djenne provides this supporting evidence:

We recently participated in a MAPS session as part of Malik's transition process. One of our goals was to begin to identify areas of skill that Malik can use to be career ready after graduation. This prompted us to enroll Malik in a day program for the summer months so that he could begin to hone in on these skills and develop new ones. We used the information gathered in his MAPS to write goals for the summer (as well as in his IEP). This gave the directors of the program and Malik's aide concrete goals to implement and has already led to summer job opportunities.

TOOLS FOR PROMOTING LEADERSHIP AND ADVOCACY

Over the years, we have also learned a great deal about the importance of supporting parents in developing skills in advocacy and leadership. The IDEA's primary focus is on the need for parents to be active participants in educational decision-making for their children; although the term "advocacy" is not specified, it is implied in the sense that in order to express their ideas and wishes, parents generally need to take on an advocacy role. Additionally, certain provisions within the law emphasize parents' roles in leadership efforts that go beyond the team level and into the realm of policymaking. For example, IDEA mandates that every state include parents of children with disabilities as members of a state advisory council designed to identify and address the unmet needs of families of children with disabilities. Parent participation is also required on regional committees dedicated to implementation of the IDEA and the Education and Secondary Education Act. A number of research studies highlight the importance of involving parents in policy decisions; at the same time, the literature makes it clear that the reality of developing collaborative relationships and increased parent participation and leadership is complex and requires both school professionals and parents to be supported in developing related skills (Brame, 1995; Jeppson & Thomas, 1995; Koroloff et al., 1995; Mueller, 2009). The legal requirements to include parents as decision-makers at all levels are clear, but little direction is provided to special education teams and policy-makers about exactly how to include parents as equal participants (Mueller, 2009). Similarly, the mandate for parents of children with disabilities to be involved in educational decision-making implies that parents have skills in communication, collaboration and problem-solving that will allow their full participation, while some in fact have not had the opportunity to acquire such skills (Overton, 2005; Thousand & Villa, 1992).

The Parents as Collaborative Leaders Project

In 2004, faculty and staff at the University of Vermont and PACER Center of Minnesota applied for and received funding from the U.S. Department of Education to develop and implement a project designed to support parents of children with disabilities in developing their skills in advocacy, leadership, and policy development (Shepherd et al., 2007). At the time of the project, the PACER Center was designated as the national center charged with providing technical assistance to the 100 federally funded parent centers and community parent resource centers established across the 50 states and U.S. territories. The project, known as *Parents as Collaborative Leaders* (PCL) was implemented in six states across the United States and included direct support for 32 parents from around the country, as well as follow-up activities involving over 100 additional families (http://www.uvm.edu/~pcl/) (Shepherd & Kervick, 2016). The goal of PCL was to develop a research-based intervention that could be disseminated nationally to support parents wishing to take on more active leadership roles within their schools and communities, as well as at the policy level.

A central feature of PCL was its theory of action regarding leadership development among parents of children with disabilities. First, the conceptual framework of the project asserted that the development of leadership among parents of children with disabilities would need to go beyond providing information regarding special education laws and practices to include a distinct set of leadership and communication skills emphasizing the collaborative practices typically used in educational settings (Friend & Cook, 2013; Thousand & Villa, 1992). The term "collaborative leadership" was used to capture the idea that parents would be most successful if they developed an awareness of themselves as leaders, as well as a deep understanding of key principles and practices associated with collaboration. Second, the project had an applied focus, as it was designed to ensure that the acquisition of specific skills in leadership and collaboration would be supported through a mentorship model involving implementation of a "leadership internship" based on parents' individual interests and goals.

Drawing on this conceptual framework, the project began with the development of ten curriculum modules designed to support parents in enhancing their skills in leadership and collaboration, as well as an internship guide designed to support parents in increasing their participation and leadership in policy related activities at the local, regional and/or national levels. Figure 1 lists the titles of the ten modules.

1. Defining Parent Leadership
2. MAPS for Leadership
3. Critical Elements of Collaboration
4. Stages of Group Development
5. Tips for Leading Effective Meetings
6. Listening and Asking Clarifying Questions
7. Understanding Conflict
8. Re-framing Agendas
9. Solving Problems in Groups
10. Understanding Diversity

Figure 1. Ten curriculum modules of the parents as collaborative leaders project

The original PCL curriculum was delivered through a three-day leadership orientation conducted at the PACER Center. Each parent leader was paired with a mentor from their state who was on the staff of the parent center serving the community in which the family lived. During the final day of the orientation, parent leaders and mentors created an internship plan outlining a 30 hour internship experience to be carried out by the parent leader during a 6 to 12 month period following the workshop. Following completion of the orientation and internship, a majority of the parent leaders continued to support other parents in developing their own skills in advocacy, leadership, and collaboration, and/or to participate in additional leadership and policy development experiences. A number of evaluation and research activities were conducted to assess the effectiveness of the PCL approach, including satisfaction surveys and in-depth follow-up interviews conducted with participants from the original PCL project as well as participants in training activities conducted after the funded project had concluded. Themes emerging from these follow-up activities were important in helping us to evaluate specific aspects of the project that were most important, as well as to think more broadly about ways to support all parents in developing leadership skills. A summary of these themes follows, with reflections from participating parents.

Learning to lead. One of the primary lessons we learned from speaking with parents participating in PCL was that learning about leadership is complex and requires attention to a wide range of dispositions and skills. Parents told us that they appreciated spending time with other parents to learn skills in collaboration, communication, and conflict resolution in the context of parent leadership. One PCL participant, Helen, commented "I've been to other trainings where we learned a lot of information, but this curriculum introduced me to some new things I hadn't encountered before, such as collaboration with others, listening, and conflict resolution." Laurie reflected on the ways in which the orientation provided her with some deeper insights into her patterns of communication and conflict resolution. She commented that prior to the orientation, she had felt confident in advocating for her daughter with Down Syndrome, but realized during the orientation that she needed to add some other conflict resolution "tools" to her repertoire. "The training in conflict was really helpful," Laurie noted. "I had to learn that it's important both to stand my ground and to keep quiet sometimes. This was a real 'aha' moment for me." Suzanne told a similar story, noting that the orientation's focus on collaboration and conflict resolution helped her to think differently about her communication style. "As the parent of a child with a disability," she noted, "you experience a lot of raw emotion. I let that get in the way sometimes and I burned a lot of bridges because of it…As a result of the project, I learned that school districts don't fear angry parents, but they will pay attention to informed parents."

Applying new skills. Parents also spoke about the ways in which the skills they acquired through the curriculum orientation were critical to the success of their internships. Gabriella, who helped to develop a statewide network for families of children with autism in her state, noted "the internship process really helped me to strengthen my problem-solving and leadership skills. It greatly increased my enthusiasm for legislative involvement and advocacy." Laurie, whose internship included leadership of a newly forming board representing families of children with Down Syndrome, described how the skills she learned in the orientation were critical as she helped to guide the Board through a period of internal conflict.

As she described, "I really had to draw on my knowledge of collaboration and the importance of setting norms." Lian's internship involved organizing and recruiting parents for a legislative event, and supporting them in developing and presenting power points and personal testimonies. During her interview, Lian reflected "the orientation process was so important to my internship, because it helped me to think about my organization, strategies for outreach, and leadership."

Parents also appreciated the opportunity to develop a leadership internship in an area of interest where they thought they might be able to make a difference to others. Most parents started with a personal concern and brainstormed ways to address this concern for themselves as well as other parents facing similar challenges. This lesson reminded us of the power that comes from providing parents with opportunities to move outside of their own family circumstances to contribute to the lives of others.

For example, Annie's concerns about her ability to advocate effectively in IEP meetings for her daughter with learning disabilities became the inspiration for an internship in which she created a regional parent group that organized information and training sessions for parents interested in increasing their advocacy skills. Carmella, who described in an early orientation session how her challenges with the English language made it difficult to tell the story of her son with autism, went on to participate in an internship in which she recruited parents to tell their personal and family stories to legislators attending a legislative breakfast focused on the needs of children with autism from the Hispanic community. Helen, the mother of a son with a dual diagnosis of autism and emotional disturbance, originally described feeling alone as she tried to understand and meet her son's needs. Building on this concern, her internship included serving on several statewide committees focused on issues related to dual diagnosis. Suzanne built on prior connections with her local parent center by conducting her internship in that setting. Following the internship, she was hired as a staff member in the organization. Similarly, Anita's internship focused on a parent support group in a large urban area that brought together parents of children with vision problems and dual sensory loss. She was so successful in this endeavor that she was later hired to coordinate parent training and support groups for a local chapter of a national association geared to parents of children with visual impairments.

Personal growth through leadership. Parents also described the ways in which the PCL project helped them to experience a sense of growth, personal development, and increased confidence. Here, their comments reminded us of the importance of thinking about the ways in which affect, emotion and self-perception are related to the development of skills in collaboration, advocacy and leadership. Carmella spoke about the fact that although she began the orientation with little confidence in her language and public speaking skills, the feeling of support she received from mentors and other parent leaders who were bilingual helped her to quickly feel more comfortable speaking up in groups. Her sentiments were echoed by Lian, who remarked "the training helped me to feel so much more confident," and Bridgette, who cited the leadership orientation as giving her "greater confidence in speaking to people and groups in general." Bridgette noted that some of the activities she engaged in during her internship – such as accepting the nomination to be president-elect of the association, planning and conducting board meetings, and conference planning and publicity – required a level of public speaking that she had not possessed prior to participating in PCL.

Other parent leaders described experiencing an increase in their sense of self-esteem and self-determination, with one parent commenting that the orientation "really helped me to recognize my own strengths, skills, and talents." Celia framed her growth in confidence as a process through which she found her voice. "I felt powerless before the orientation," she remarked, "but the project helped launch me into action. I feel stronger now." Maria wrote about how the conversations she had with other parent leaders during the orientation "helped us build our understanding of our leadership and communication styles. I had an appreciation of others. I learned that each person has something I could learn from." She talked about how over time, she came to see herself as a leader and a person whose leadership was defined by her generosity to others:

> The leadership project helped me think of myself as a leader. I didn't see myself as a leader before, even though I wanted to make a difference. It was very empowering and important for me. I realized I could do this. I used to be a volunteer, but I have now taken on more leadership roles. I see myself as a leader and an instrument for others. I try to be proactive and fair. I am a quiet leader, a gentle leader. I listen and try to be centered.

In contrast to Maria's self-described "gentle leadership," Lian expressed a more extroverted style that she felt had been fostered through the PCL experience. As she put it, "I now feel really good as a leader. I think I can run for office! It would not be possible without the training we had. It made such a difference. ...My confidence level has grown. I'm going to change the law! I know now that we (parents) can move a law into action." The comments from these two parent leaders captured the project's attempts to validate different leadership styles and interests. A number of the parents noted that although they did not initially think of themselves as leaders, their definitions of leadership and appreciation of varied styles expanded as a result of participation in the orientation and internship experiences.

Valuing relationships and connections. The interviewees also spoke about the ways in which their participation in the leadership orientation and internships helped them look beyond their personal situations to understand the value and power of forging relationships with others. Several spoke about the connections they made with other PCL parent leaders during the leadership orientation, noting that they retained these connections well beyond the conclusion of the PCL project. Activities embedded in the curriculum included multiple opportunities for parent leaders to share stories and to learn from one another; for many, this was a highlight of the experience that helped them to see their personal challenges and successes in light of larger systemic and policy issues. As parent leaders moved into their internships, they continued to discover the ways in which relationships with others helped to fuel their personal growth as well as to enable them to meet their broader internship goals. A number of them talked about the ways in which their internships helped them to "feel good about helping other families." For Annie, the most meaningful part of the internship process was watching parents learn and feel empowered by the parent education meetings that she helped to establish in her school district. As she described it, "I was able to go to IEP meetings with some of them and see them apply what they had learned to advocate for their children. It was also great to see that there were parents in the group interested in taking on leadership experiences of their own." Similarly, Carmella identified the most powerful aspect of her internship as the opportunity to listen to and re-tell the personal stories of other parents of children with autism. She found it powerful to see how lawmakers attending her legislative breakfast were moved by these stories and eventually, took action on them at the state level. Suzanne, once worried about "burning bridges," came to realize the power of networking and reaching out to other parents for the purpose of making their collective voices known and bringing about change. She commented that her experience with the PCL gave her a more positive outlook on the future of children and other children and a stronger sense of connection to her school and community.

Several parent leaders talked about the ways in which their internship experiences helped them to make new connections with other parent leaders in their states who were engaged in similar change efforts. Lian commented that "I really appreciated the opportunity to work with people from all over the state in a collaborative effort to get information that would help families of children with autism," while Celia noted that her confidence grew as she began to meet and network with other advocates. Her previous sense of isolation began to shift as she joined forces with other parents who had similar educational and employment goals for their children with behavioral challenges and mental health needs. Anita's internship resulted in enhanced ties with other parents of children with vision and hearing loss in her city, and eventually, to similar associations and parent organizations in other states. As she described, the opportunity to meet with other parents was critical not only to her personal development, but to the very notion of parent leadership: "The bottom-line is that networking and attending meetings, activities and workshops provided by agencies, schools and other facilities is so necessary; parents need to attend every chance we get."

As parents expanded their networks and connections, they began to think more broadly about the collective needs of children with disabilities and their families. Moreover, a number of them were successful in contributing to change efforts occurring at state and national levels. Several stories are illustrative. Maria, who lived in a culturally and linguistically diverse section of a major U.S. city and whose internship involved encouraging members of her community to register to vote, commented on the ways in which the internship expanded her view of the power of grassroots community organizing. "I learned to think beyond the needs of my own family," she remarked," because the internship allowed me to get to know other residents in my community who share the same vision in creating a more equitable society." Gabriella, whose internship goals and activities included delivering testimony at legislative meetings, writing letters to congressmen, and developing a statewide committee designed to track services for families and individuals with autism, received recognition for her skills in facilitation and advocacy and was eventually hired by the state agency serving children and families with autism. As described by her mentor, Gabriella "has been hugely involved in legislative advocacy at the grassroots level and has modeled to people in her community how to do it." Lian and Carmella talked in great detail about the excitement they felt when, following the legislative breakfast that they organized, the eight attending legislators joined an Autism Caucus that went on to co-author important legislation benefitting families of children and youth with autism in their state.

Annie, Laurie, and Terry were all surprised to find that their internships took them well beyond their originally intended audiences. Laurie's initial role as a member of a non-profit board led to her becoming president of the organization. When she moved to another state, she quickly became involved in similar work and was able to use the knowledge she gained in her internship to establish herself as a leader in a new community. Annie's idea to create a support group for families of children with learning disabilities eventually expanded to include a broader range of topics of interest to families of children with a variety of disabilities and needs. She broadened her own education by attending national conferences and conventions on learning disabilities, and expressed surprise when she was selected to participate on a planning council for an international conference on learning disabilities that was held in her state.

During the orientation, Terry described her interest in helping members of her community to have a better understanding of disabilities and especially the needs of young adults with disabilities as they related to local opportunities for sports and recreation. A key part of her internship was the role she played in organizing and carrying out a large public disability awareness campaign. She planned a major community event centered around a minor league baseball game, arranged for publicity and newspaper coverage, and invited families to participate. Later, she created a national initiative that involved major and minor league baseball venues in supporting youth with disabilities, eventually publishing an article describing this initiative in *Exceptional Parent*. She described this broad-based outreach effort as "a much broader effort and a huge success that I hadn't really expected…It actually brought new resources to our state coordinating organization. I had been really interested in the recreation and sports aspect of things before the PCL project, but the self-esteem that I gained through the orientation and internship was really key to my work."

Finally, Helen's internship, which focused on connecting families whose children had a dual diagnosis, helped her to gain recognition as an expert on the topic within her state. She was asked to share her expertise with members of several state level committees related to children with co-occurring disorders. Helen produced reports, wrote articles for NADD publications and presented at a conference for all of the state mental health centers in her state. Her mentor noted "they expected to have the 13 directors at the training, but over 100 people attended. It was very gratifying and was part of a series of efforts that led to state level policy changes."

Additional Stories of Leadership

The experiences of parents participating in the PCL project suggest potential benefits of organized efforts to prepare and support parents in advocacy and leadership roles. Since its official conclusion as a grant-supported effort, the PCL curriculum, internship guide and general approach has been disseminated and incorporated into the offerings of parent centers, community resource centers, and projects supporting families of children who are visually impaired and deaf-blind. Each of these organizations has similar leadership initiatives, many of which predated the PCL project. As such, a growing network of parent organizations provides opportunities for leadership development and capacity building among families of children, youth, and adults with disabilities.

At the same time, we have encountered many parents who have developed leadership and advocacy skills on their own, without formal professional development opportunities. The stories of these parents substantiate the importance of leadership development and shows how it can occur in more informal ways. As was the case for PCL participants, parents who had found their own paths to leadership and advocacy did so at first out of necessity. Melissa and Georgia talked about finding their voices as they advocated within the IEP process; later on, they were able to extend their own emerging skills in advocacy to support other parents in similar circumstances. Jamie talked about a "mother's empowerment " group that she started in her school to help other parents obtain information and develop a sense of hope. B. B. started speaking up for her daughter during IEP meetings and quickly found herself engaged in advocating at the school level to ensure social inclusion for children with disabilities. Later, she played a key role in community advocacy effort to install an elevator in a old building lacking access for students with physical challenges.

These parents and others reflected on the value of transitioning from their personal experiences with advocacy to opportunities to advocate with and on behalf of other parents. Melissa, for example, was hired to support parents at her local school in a diverse neighborhood that included families who were refugees and families from low socioeconomic backgrounds. Almost immediately, she recognized the need to form relationships with family members who were the hardest to reach and/or who had had difficult times in their own school experiences. Having had her own challenges growing up and in the early years of parenting two children, she recognized the importance of expressing empathy through sharing her own struggles and being open to families with a range of strengths and challenges. She

149

told a powerful story in which she had succeeded in getting a parent of children with disabilities whom most professionals found to be "too difficult" to build a sense of trust with her, and later, with other school professionals. This parent was known for coming into the school building and speaking in a loud voice, often criticizing what was going on in school in a very direct manner. Melissa decided to "start small" by asking her to help her stuff envelopes for an upcoming parent event. Through this exchange, she was able to demonstrate to the parent that she valued her as a person and a parent. Melissa noted the following about this particular parent and others like her:

> I think the biggest thing is the acceptance. That's what we all want. We all want to feel smart. How do you make somebody, you know, a parent who has a fourth or fifth grade education feel smart? You have to create that opportunity, whether it be the language you use or something that you have picked up on about that person. We all want to feel that we have something to add. That we are growing leaders and a growing leader doesn't mean taking on being a PTO president. It's where are we at. Can you help another person? And acknowledging that if they did that.

B. B. focused on the ways in which her journey to leadership grew from her professional experiences as a social worker and her accompanying sense of social justice: "I know we're all connected and that sense of connection and solidarity as a movement is meaningful to me." She tended to employ a systems approach to problem-solving, so when she was concerned that her daughter was not being invited to birthday parties, she convinced the school principal to spearhead a school wide effort focused on creating a sense of belonging for all students, including those with disabilities. When her daughter moved to middle school, she took up other issues, including development of local policies for ensuring the continuation of services when special educators and related services providers had long-term absences, compliance with 504 standards for physical access to the middle school building, and supervision of teachers who were not properly implementing accommodations. She described this set of experiences as a "montage of experiences that I've had that have helped me to be actively involved, not only for my daughter, but for all kids." Many of these change efforts required her to organize other parents and local representatives of legal aid offices. Although she recognized that not all parents had the resources to engage in this level of advocacy and leadership, B. B. felt strongly that "for parents who are able – and you can define that any way you want to – we have the responsibility not only for our child, but every child, because there's many parents who can't do what I'm able to do. And the way that I'm able to do it – I owe that a lot to my own education."

B. B. also commented on the need for professionals to take on advocacy roles. She felt strongly that special educators needed to be better prepared to understand their role as advocates and how to leverage their advocacy within organizations that often marginalized their roles:

Number one, I think special educators need to be seriously educated in advocacy. Number two, they need to be educated and understand the impact of organizational culture on them, so they can understand the relationship between advocacy and culture. I think the third thing that would be really important is that we're still looking at special education as an appendage to education and so I think we have to move the education of all children to the center, of which that's a part. And I also think that special educators—because of these organizational and cultural issues – ought to have a year or two of post graduate supervision through a university, so the university hosts groups and they come and they talk about the challenges of working in a system that doesn't really support what they do.

Additionally, B. B. felt that principals needed to be educated about their roles as advocates for children with disabilities and to be held accountable for ensuring that special education services and accommodations were being properly implemented by teachers. She talked at length about the ways in which the advocacy and leadership efforts of parents and community members could achieve great things, but that in the end, the system would only change if evaluation and compensatory systems rewarded those who ensured that all students with disabilities and other challenges received an appropriate education.

The accomplishments of PCL participants and other parent leaders serve as testimony to the importance of ensuring that parents' voices are heard and honored throughout the system. Parents have a great deal to say about practices and policies at the individual, team, building, district, and state levels—and beyond. Parent leaders were at the heart of many of the early advocacy efforts leading to passage of IDEA, and their voices are still present and needed today. Melissa's point that not all parents have the resources to advocate beyond the level of planning for their child is important; still, the stories included in this chapter suggest that many more parents want to lead and can benefit from developing their skills in advocacy and leadership than is commonly assumed.

CHAPTER SUMMARY

The research, approaches and stories presented in this chapter point to the ways in which a focus on family engagement, advocacy, and parent leadership can serve to enhance and expand family and professional partnerships. There are many websites and state and national organizations that exist to support families in gaining information as well as sense of connection to other families, and these should be made available to families at the time when they learn of their child's disability as well as over time, when they may be ready for additional resources and networking opportunities. There are a number of tools available to educators and families— including MAPS, Essential Lifestyle Planning, PATH and COACH that can be used to promote family engagement and to develop formal education plans that reflect the hopes, dreams and needs of people with disabilities and their families. Families have spoken at length about the ways in which their roles as advocates—both within and beyond the formal planning process—have enhanced their engagement at all levels. Although we acknowledge that parents need to be supported in participating in the level of decision-making and advocacy that feels comfortable and "do-able" to them, our experiences suggest that many parents find that their levels of skill, confidence, hope and personal agency improve when their experiences with collaboration move beyond their own family experience. Similarly, school and other professionals may feel that efforts to promote family engagement, advocacy and leadership seem to go above and beyond the basic requirements of IDEA. This may in fact be the case— but we argue that in focusing attention and resources on increased opportunities for parents to become more engaged and to learn more nuanced skills in advocacy and leadership, both families and schools are likely to find increased benefits, including opportunities to improve family-school collaboration and to effect positive changes in practice and policy. Given these assumptions and the stories families have shared with us over the years, we suggest the following:

1. *Ensure that families are connected to existing community, state, and national resources.* The U.S. Department of Education, Office of Special Education Programs, invests considerable funding for local and regional Parent Information Centers, Community Parent Resource Centers, Deaf-Blind projects, and national technical assistance and professional development opportunities for families of children with disabilities. Together, these centers provide a rich set of resources, including accessible educational materials that support parents in learning how to navigate the special education process. Additionally, they provide ongoing training opportunities, including opportunities for parents to network with one another and to develop their skills in leadership and advocacy. All parents of children with disabilities should be provided with information about these invaluable (and free) resources, as well as the multitude of resources that exist to support families of all ages and disability types.

2. *Identify opportunities, tools and approaches that can promote family engagement and choice within educational decision-making processes, including IFSP, IEP and transition planning.* Processes such as Essential Lifestyle Planning, PATH, MAPS and COACH offer accessible family-centered approaches to engaging families in planning and decision-making. An emerging body of research suggests that these approaches have benefits for both school professionals and families, including opportunities for relationship building, empowerment, self-determination and improved collaboration. These processes require additional time for planning, but both professionals and families report that the long-term benefits of these enhanced planning meetings are well worth the initial investment. We have also encountered schools where the MAPS process has been used in some abbreviated forms that yield positive results with less investment of time. These include embedding "MAPS-like" questions into meeting agendas,

conducting group MAPS with parents of an incoming class (e.g., holding a "welcome night" for incoming parents of students with disabilities during which parents complete MAPS-related exercises), and using the five basic steps of MAPS to build a personalized learning plan for students that can in turn drive the IEP and transition planning processes.

3. *Focus on formal opportunities for parents to become engaged in more systemic advocacy and leadership opportunities.* Our experiences with PCL and related follow-up projects indicate the power of bringing families together to exchange ideas, develop skills in leadership and collaboration, and identify applied opportunities to exercise those skills. Parents participating in these projects have often talked about the ways in which their engagement in advocacy and leadership helped them to see beyond their own circumstances and to take strength from participating in a larger cause. Many attained a sense of personal growth and confidence that was somewhat unexpected and became the basis of continued strength and resilience. Although it may be difficult for schools to identify resources for these types of development opportunities, the federally funded parent centers, CPRCs, and projects serving families of children who are deaf-blind are charged with including leadership development opportunities for families as part of their work. Disability specific organizations (e.g., National Down Syndrome Congress, Learning Disabilities of America, National Alliance of Mental illness) also provide opportunities for leadership development. Hospitals and pediatric practices are becoming increasingly interested in this type of work, as are grass roots and other organizations devoted to disability law. Once again, collaboration and information sharing are key to connecting parents to these resources and to developing relationships between schools, parent centers, medical centers and community supports.

4. *Promote informal opportunities for parents to develop skills and experiences with systems-level advocacy and leadership.* We spoke in chapter six about the need to ensure that families have opportunities to attain the skills and opportunities they need to become effective collaborators, and we see the same to be true of the development of systems level advocacy and leadership skills. Skill development may come in the form of participation in formal training and development, but it may also come through smaller, less formal channels and opportunities. Melissa's story of engaging parents to become part of their school community offers key insights: start small, build from strengths and interests, and invite families to participate based on their level of comfort. These small steps sometimes lead to increased involvement and leadership and advocacy on a larger scale. Parents need to know that families before them were primary drivers of passage of Public Law 94-142, and that the need for their engagement and advocacy is as strong today as it was then.

5. *Encourage the development of advocacy and leadership among school and other professionals who work with families of children with disabilities.* Finally, we think it is important to focus on the many ways in which educators and other

professionals need to think of themselves as advocates and leaders. This includes advocacy on behalf of particular children and families, as well as advocacy and leadership on behalf of all students. As B.B. asserts, the overall education system will only improve when special education is seen as a fundamental and valued part of the overall system, and this vision is one that needs to be advocated for by special educators and other professionals. In its core function to provide specialized instruction and access to the general education curriculum, special education is by definition an act of advocacy at both the practice and policy levels. Special educators and other professionals are often short of time, but it is clear that school and family collaboration is enhanced when professionals are encouraged to use their own voices to carry forward the mission and purpose of special education.

SUGGESTED QUESTIONS FOR REFLECTION AND DISCUSSION

For parents and professionals:

1. Person-centered planning is often characterized as being a vehicle through which additional information about the family and child can be gathered outside the IEP meeting. How might person-centered planning and similar family-centered processes be used in your setting? If your school does not currently use these types of planning tools, what alternative strategies could be used to bring similar information and stories to light?
2. Melissa shared a story about how she reached out to a parent to engage her in the school community. What are ways that parents of children with disabilities are currently working as leaders in your school context? What additional approaches could be used to enlist more parents to become leaders?
3. What advocacy issues are of greatest interest to you personally? Which ones are most pressing within your school community? What action steps might parents and professionals make collectively to spearhead efforts to bring these issues to light?

SUGGESTED ACTIVITIES

For parents:

1. Consider the 5 steps of the MAPS process. Which question/step resonates the most with you? Write down your answer to the question and ask your special education case manager if you can start the next meeting by presenting your thoughts. Even better—talk with your child to identify her/his answers to the question.
2. Think about one aspect of your child's education that you think is in need of improvement. In what ways might this issue be of interest to other parents? How might you re-frame the issue and work together and/or with key school professionals to bring about change in your school or community?

3. Check out your local parent information center, CPRC, deaf-blind project or disability-specific organization to identify a training or leadership activity that you'd like to participate in. Invite another parent to go with you and take time afterwards to reflect on one action step you might take as a result of attending this activity.

4. Ask your child's special education case manager about the possibility of holding a MAPS meeting to assist in IEP or transition planning. If your special educator is not familiar with the process, reach out to your local parent information center to see if someone can help identify a person who is knowledgeable about MAPS.

5. Think about a contribution you might make – either individually, or in collaboration with other parents—that would improve some aspect of your child's life in school or the community. Research ways in which you might lead or assist with that change effort, and develop a plan for action.

6. Contact one or more of your state or national legislators. Find out more about their knowledge of disability policies and practices. Consider taking action to inform your representatives about successes or concerns you know of in your school or community. Take action by writing a letter to your representative, visiting one or more offices to speak with representatives or their education staff members, or attending a legislative breakfast or gathering. Practice delivering your message by stating clearly: who you are, what you want to talk about, and what your representative might do about the situation.

7. Identify a state or national organization that represents the needs of your child (see the list of resources earlier in this chapter). Browse the organization's website to see what kinds of opportunities they offer in the way of information and opportunities for leadership and advocacy.

For professionals:

8. Reflect on your role as a special educator/other professional. To what degree do you advocate for individual students? To what degree do you engage in advocacy for improved systems of service? How might you enlist parents in advocacy initiatives to bring about systemic changes?

9. Identify three to four colleagues from other schools in your community or state. Look for ways (face-to-face meetings, connections via list servs or Skype) that you can communicate on a regular basis to identify opportunities for advocacy, leadership and change within your schools.

10. Identify a family with whom you work who might benefit from participating in MAPS or one of the other planning tools described in this chapter. Read up on MAPS and/or consult with someone who is familiar with the process. Following completion of the MAP, transcribe results on to 81/2 × 11 inch paper or Google Doc so the family has it as a permanent record. Alternatively, conduct the MAP as an interview, framing key questions that relate to each of the five steps. Record the family's responses and share with them afterwards to be sure they represent what was shared.

11. Identify one to three activities in your school or community that need parent input and leadership in order to be successful. Reach out to a few parents who might be interested in leadership activities and support them as they enter into the process.

NOTE

¹ Portions of this chapter appeared in Shepherd, K. G., Kervick, C. T., & Salembier, G. (2015). Person-centered planning: Tools for promoting employment, self-direction and independence among persons with intellectual disabilities. In American Association on Intellectual and Developmental Disabilities (Ed.), *Way leads on to way: Employment of people with intellectual and developmental disabilities* (pp. 299–320). Washington, DC: American Association on Intellectual and Developmental Disabilities. Reprinted with permission.

REFERENCES

Brame, K. (1995, Summer). Strategies for recruiting family members from diverse backgrounds for roles in policy and program development. *Early Childhood Bulletin,* 1–4.

Callicott, K. J. (2003). Culturally sensitive collaboration within person-centered planning. *Focus on Autism and Other Developmental Disabilities, 18*(1), 60–68.

Childre, A., & Chambers, C. R. (2005). Family perceptions of student centered planning and IEP meetings. *Education and Training in Developmental Disabilities, 40,* 217–233.

Claes, C., Van Hove, G., Vandevelde, S., Van Loon, J., & Schalock, R. L. (2010). Person-centered planning: Analysis of research and effectiveness. *Intellectual and Developmental Disabilities, 48*(6), 432–453.

Flannery, K. B., Newton, S., Horner, R. H., Slovic, R., Blumberg, R., & Ard, W. R. (2000). The impact of person centered planning on the content and organization of individual supports. *Career Development of Exceptional Individuals, 23,* 123–137.

Forest, M., & Lusthaus, E. (1987). The kaleidoscope: Challenge to the cascade. In M. Forest (Ed.), *More education/integration* (pp. 1–16). Downsview, Ontario, CA: G. Allan Roeher Institute.

Forest, M., & O'Brien, J. (1993). *PATH: A workbook for planning positive possible futures: Planning alternative tomorrows with hope for schools, organizations, businesses, and families.* Toronto, Canada: Inclusion Press.

Friend, M., & Cook, L. (2013). *Interactions: Collaboration skills for school professionals* (7th ed.). Boston, MA: Pearson.

Furney, K. S., & Salembier, G. (2000). Rhetoric and reality: A review of the literature on parent and student participation in the IEP and transition planning process. *Issues influencing the future of transition programs and services in the United States* (pp. 111–126). Minneapolis, MN: National Transition Network at the Institute on Community Integration.

Furney, K. S., Carlson, N., Salembier, G., Cravedi-Cheng, L., & Blow, S. (1994). *Making dreams happen: How to facilitate the MAPS process.* Burlington, VT: University of Vermont, Vermont Transition Systems Change Project. Unpublished manual.

Garner, H., & Dietz, L. (1996). Person-centered planning: maps and paths to the future. *Four Runner, 11*(5).

Geenan, S., Powers, L. E., & Lopez-Vasquez, A. (2001). Multicultural aspects of parent involvement in transition planning. *Exceptional Children, 67,* 265–282.

Giangreco, M. F. (2002). Values, logical practices, and research: The three musketeers of effective education. In J. Downing (Ed.), *Including students with severe and multiple disabilities in typical classrooms* (2nd ed., pp. ix–xiii). Baltimore, MD: Paul H. Brookes.

Giangreco, M. F., Cloninger, C. J., & Iverson, V. S. (2011). *Choosing outcomes and accommodations for children (COACH): A guide to educational planning for students with disabilities* (3rd ed.). Baltimore, MD: Paul H. Brookes.

Jeppson, E. S., & Thomas, J. (1995). *Essential allies: Families as advisors.* Bethesda, MD: Institute for Family-Centered Care.

Koroloff, N., Hunter, R., & Gordon, L. (1995). *Family involvement in policy making: A final report on the families in action project.* Research and Training Center on Family Support and Children's Mental Health, Portland State University.

Meadan, H., Shelden, D. L., Appel, K., & DeGrazia, R. L. (2010). Developing a long-term vision: A road map for students' futures. *TEACHING Exceptional Children, 43*(2), 8–14.

Mueller, T. G. (2009). IEP Facilitation: A promising approach to resolving conflicts between families and schools. *TEACHING Exceptional Children, 41*(3), 60–67.

Miner, C. A., & Bates, P. E. (1997). The effect of person centered planning on the IEP/Transition Planning process. *Education and Training in Mental Retardation and Developmental Disabilities, 32*, 105–112.

Morris, D. A., & Shepherd, K. G. (2011). *Parent leadership institute.* Boston, MA: Unpublished curriculum.

Neece, C. L., Kraemer, B. R., & Blacher J. (2009). Transition satisfaction and family well-being among parents of young adults with severe intellectual disability. *Intellectual and Developmental Disabilities, 47*(1), 31–43.

O'Brien, C. L., & O'Brien, J. (2000). *The origins of person-centered planning: A community of practice perspective.* Atlanta, GA: Responsive Systems Associates. Retrieved from http://thechp.syr.edu/PCP_History.pdf

Parnes, S. J. (1992). *Source book for creative problem-solving: A fifty year digest of proven innovation processes.* Buffalo, NY: Creative Education Foundation Press.

Pearpoint, J., O'Brien, J., & Forest, M. (1993). *PATH: A workbook for planning positive possible futures.* Toronto, Canada: Inclusion Press.

Pipi, K. (2010). The PATH Planning Tool and its Potential for Whānau Research. *MAI Review, 2010.*

Rasheed, S. A., Fore, C., & Miller, S. (2006). Person-centered planning: Practices, promises, and provisos. *The Journal for Vocational Special Needs Education, 28*(3), 47–59.

Rudkin, A., & Rowe, D. (1999). A systematic review of the evidence base for lifestyle planning in adults with learning disabilities: Implications for other disabled populations. *Clinical Rehabilitation, 13*(5), 363–372.

Salembier, G., & Furney, K. S. (1994). Promoting self-advocacy and family participation in transition planning. *Journal for Vocational Special Needs Education, 17*(1), 12–17.

Salembier, G., & Furney, K. S. (1997). Facilitating participation: Parents' perceptions of their involvement in the IEP/transition planning process. *Career Development for Exceptional Individuals, 20*(l), 2942.

Sheehey, P., Ornelles, C., & Noonan, M. J. (2009). Biculturalization: Developing culturally appropriate responsive approaches to family participation. *Intervention in School and Clinic, 45*(132), 132–139.

Shepherd, K., Hasazi, S. B., Kucij, D., Brick, B., & Goldberg, P. (2007). *Parents as collaborative leaders: Improving outcomes for children with disabilities. Participant manual.* Minneapolis, MN: PACER Center.

Shepherd, K. G., & Kervick, C. T. (2016). Enhancing collaborative leadership among parents of children with disabilities: New directions for policy and practice. *Journal of Disability Policy Studies, 27*(1), 32–42. doi:10.1177/1044207315576081

Shepherd, K. G., Giangreco, M. F., & Cook, B. G. (2013). Parent participation in assessment and in development of Individualized Education Programs. In B. G. Cook & M. Tankersley (Eds.), *Research-based practices in special education* (pp. 260–271). Boston, MA: Pearson.

Shepherd, K. G., Kervick, C. T., & Salembier, G. (2015). Person-centered planning: Tools for promoting employment, self-direction and independence among persons with intellectual disabilities. In American Association on Intellectual and Developmental Disabilities (Ed.), *Way leads on to way: Employment of people with intellectual and developmental disabilities* (pp. 299–320). Washington, DC: American Association on Intellectual and Developmental Disabilities.

Smull, M. W., & Sanderson, H. (2005). *Essential lifestyle planning for everyone.* London: Helen Sanderson Associates.

Smull, M. W., Sanderson, H., Sweeney, C., Skelhorn, L., George, A., & Bourne, M. (2005). *Essential lifestyle planning for everyone.* Annapolis, MD: Learning Community: Essential Lifestyle Planning.

Thousand, J., & Villa, R. (1992). Collaborative teams: A powerful tool in school restructuring. In R. Villa, J. Thousand, W. Stainback, & S. Stainback (Eds.), *Restructuring for caring and effective education: An administrative guide to creating heterogeneous schools.* Baltimore, MD: Paul H. Brookes.

Trainor, A. A. (2007). Person-centered planning in two culturally distinct communities: Responding to divergent needs and preferences. *Career Development for Exceptional Individuals, 30,* 92–103.

Vandercook, T., York, J., & Forest, M. (1989). The McGill Action Planning System (MAPS): A strategy for building the vision. *Journal of the Association for Persons with Severe Handicaps, 14,* 205–215.

Wells, J. C., & Sheehey, P. H. (2012). Person-centered planning: Strategies to encourage participation and facilitate communication. *TEACHING Exceptional Children, 44*(3), 32–39.

Wehmeyer, M. L. (1996). Self-determination as an educational outcome: Why is it important to children, youth and adults with disabilities? In D. J. Sands & M. L. Wehmeyer (Eds.), *Self-determination across the lifespan: Independence and choice for people with disabilities* (pp. 15–34). Baltimore: Paul H. Brookes.

Wehmeyer, M. L., & Webb, K. W. (2011). *Handbook of adolescent transition education for youth with disabilities.* Florence, KY: Routledge, Taylor, & Francis Group.

Wolfensberger, W. (1972). *The principle of normalization in human services.* Downsview, Ontario, CA: National Institute on Mental Retardation.

BUILDING CAPACITY FOR COLLABORATION

Nurturing Self-Efficacy, Resiliency and Hope

I serve on a state committee representing the Deaf/Hard of Hearing community as both a parent and professional. During one of these meetings, we had a speaker who was introducing a new reading program for children who use ASL. About 10 minutes into the presentation, I found myself very emotional. Reading is something that our family has always valued and love to do, together and individually. It dawned on me that Malik will never read, at least not to the point I'd like him to. Frankly, not even close. The professional in me sat there trying my best to gather my wits and silently talk myself out of entertaining the internal meltdown that the parental side of me was now experiencing and having a hard time controlling this in a room full of governor appointed folks! I sat there frantically drying the tears that were welling up and pretending my sniffling was from a cold, praying no one would look my way. The red exit sign was calling my name but I was immobilized. "I can handle this," I repeated over and over to myself. But right then, I didn't want to be mature, be professional, let alone handle it. I wanted to allow the grief of knowing my son would never able to acquire even the skills that were being designed for kids like himself to overflow freely. I wanted to run screaming from the room and be comforted and like I do for the families I serve. For someone to tell me, it's okay to be sad, to acknowledge my surprisingly visceral reaction. But sat there, I did, collecting myself and counting my breaths until I ran out of tissues and tears.

(Djenne)

As will be revealed later, this story has a happy ending; however, the first part of Djenne's memory raises questions about what it takes for families to retain a sense of hope and to develop resiliency during difficult times and over time. In the previous chapter, we discussed approaches to creating positive and family-centered planning approaches and opportunities for advocacy and leadership that support parents of children with disabilities and promote collaboration. The MAPS process, as well as leadership opportunities such as the Parents as Collaborative Leaders project, are important tools that schools can provide and parents can request as they engage together in building collaborative partnerships. In this chapter, we focus on additional approaches that nurture self-efficacy, resiliency and hope in families. Our interviews with families suggest that these approaches serve to further enhance families' overall capacity to thrive and develop over time. In turn, they create conditions for increased capacity for collaboration between families and professionals.

We begin the chapter with a brief discussion of the concepts of resiliency and growth mindset, which we see as frameworks for thinking about capacity building. We then continue with parents' advice and perspectives on strategies and experiences that hold promise for promoting growth for both families and professionals. Some of these are specific to the issue of collaboration, while others point to broader factors that support families' ability to be resilient and to sustain hope and growth in challenging times. Throughout, we maintain that a focus on strengths-based and growth-oriented approaches holds the possibility for shifting our views and experiences within the family and professional collaboration and partnership. They call upon both families and professionals to move well beyond viewing barriers to collaboration to imagining the possibilities for growth and increased collaboration. Moreover, they focus on family members' own thoughts about what sustains their hope and resiliency during difficult times, providing additional windows into aspects of family life that professionals do not always have a chance to see.

RESILIENCY

Research on family resiliency has become more prevalent in recent years, with some researchers focusing on resiliency in general, and others on resiliency factors that appear to be related to particular stressful conditions (e.g., having a child with a disability) (Heiman, 2002). Although some argue that researchers and practitioners tend to use the term resilience in different ways (Patterson, 2002), most draw on Walsh's basic idea that resilience can be described as the ability to withstand hardship and rebound from adversity, resulting in greater strength for the family (Walsh, 1998, 2003). Key factors contributing to resiliency include: (1) making meaning of adversity, (2) affirming strength and keeping a positive outlook, and (3) employing spiritual or other beliefs that contribute to positive perspectives on difficult circumstances (Bayat, 2007; Walsh, 1998). Resiliency is also associated with certain family characteristics, including flexibility, connectedness, communication and the ability to utilize resources (Walsh, 2003), and the presence of social supports that assist families in coping with and adapting to chronic stressors (McCubbin & Patterson, 1983). Patterson (2002) asserts that the focus on resiliency is part of a movement in positive psychology (Seligman & Csikszentmihali, 2000) towards identifying factors of health as opposed to factors of pathology (Antonovsky, 1987; Antonovsky & Sourani, 1988) that have been the focus of more traditional approaches in developmental and clinical psychology. She notes that although researchers tend to distinguish between resiliency as a trait or characteristic exhibited by particular families as opposed to a process that may be experienced by all families, practitioners tend to focus less on the origins of resiliency than its positive benefits (Patterson, 2002).

Studies focused on factors contributing to resiliency within families of children with disabilities (Bayat, 2007; Heiman, 2002; Patterson, 2002; Patterson & Garwick, 1994) suggest that the ways in which families make meaning of their child's disability tend to be associated with the degree to which resiliency is present in the family. That is, families who maintain more positive perceptions of disability tend to exhibit more characteristics associated with resiliency. This is true whether or not these perceptions are assumed at the outset of a child's birth or disability diagnosis or whether they are developed over time. Parents with a more positive view of their child tend to be in a better position to arrange the family's structure and balance the family's resources against the stressors of having a child with a disability (Bayat, 2007; Patterson, 1993).

If one takes the view that there is a process by which families can become resilient (Patterson, 2002) it follows that a positive collaborative partnership with school professionals could contribute to growth and resiliency within a family. In fact, many of the families we have interviewed note that when they experience collaborative relationships, outcomes for their children tend to improve, thereby contributing to reduced stress and a more positive view of the school as a resource. Conversely, when relationships with school professionals are difficult, many families experience increased levels of stress and a more negative view of school. As such, it is our belief that one of the important roles that professionals can play is to listen to family members' stories about what contributes to their sense of resiliency and to reinforce positive aspects of the child with a disability, their experiences in school, and the family's role in developing and supporting these positive attributes and outcomes.

GROWTH MINDSET

A second framework that may be helpful for both families and school professionals is that of the growth mindset, developed by psychologist Carol Dweck and her colleagues (Blackwell, Trzesniewski, & Dweck, 2007; Dweck, 2006, 2015). As Dweck notes, theories of mindset assert that there are two distinct ways in which individuals view intelligence and learning: fixed mindset and growth mindset. Individuals who operate with a fixed mindset view intelligence and other attributes as inborn traits that determine what they will and will not be able to do. In contrast, individuals with a growth mindset believe that intelligence can be developed over time. People with a growth mindset view humans as malleable and having the capacity for change in their intelligence, personality, and individual pursuits (e.g., music, art, sports), while those with a fixed mindset tend to see similar traits as being static or fixed (Mercer & Ryan, 2010). The concept of mindset may also vary within individuals, such that one could have a growth mindset about some domains (e.g., the ability to improve in athletics) and a fixed mindset in others (e.g., the ability to succeed in mathematics). In fact, some of Dweck's more recent work suggests that it is probably inaccurate to portray mindset as an "either/or" concept, since most

161

people move back and forth between mindsets depending on the situation in which they find themselves (2015).

Educators in many schools have applied the growth mindset in their classrooms, focusing on the ways in which children can be taught to develop skills and habits related to empathy, flexibility, persistence, resilience and optimism in order to develop and sustain growth mindset (Dweck, 2006; Mraz & Hertz, 2015). Similarly, the literature suggests that professional development opportunities are increasingly focused on fostering a growth mindset among teachers, not only in relation to their students, but in relation to their practice as professionals (Heggart, 2015). That is, teachers are being asked to consider their self-beliefs in relation to their teaching practice and to consider how they might adopt a growth mindset by becoming more open to feedback, risk-taking, and persistence in their practice in the classroom. Parents, too, have been writing about mindset in relation to parenting strategies that foster a growth mindset in children (see, for example, Taylor, 2014).

Although peer-reviewed literature in some of these areas is still emerging, we see the idea of growth mindset as a useful framework that could be extended to the context of family and professional collaboration. Teachers who convey to parents that their child with a disability has the capacity to grow and learn are modeling a belief in growth mindset that can in turn support those parents who may initially be more focused on their child's learning challenges. Conversely, parents who see their children in a more positive light than do educators can help teachers understand their child's strength and opportunities for growth. The notion of applying a growth mindset to parent and professional partnerships seems universally important, but may be even more important when the child in question has a disability. Teachers – and sometimes parents – who are less acquainted with what it means for a child to have a disability may at first assume that disability is a fixed characteristic, when in fact we know this not to be the case. Teachers and other school professionals who ascribe to and apply practices associated with a growth mindset may in fact be more likely to promote positive academic, behavioral and/or social-emotional outcomes for children with disabilities, including those with the most intensive needs.

The concept may also be useful for thinking more specifically about the nature of collaborative partnerships. As described in Chapter 6, the process of collaboration is often thought of as a developmental process that moves through certain stages. Relationships among professionals and families are likely to encounter both challenges and opportunities for growth and if both parties maintain a belief that collaboration can grow and improve, the likelihood of working through difficult times seems to be increased. If all parties in a collaborative partnership believe that growth is possible for both the child with a disability *and* the adults who support that child, it follows that we might expect more growth in the collaborative relationship and process.

Taken together, theories of resiliency and growth mindset offer frameworks and approaches that may support capacity building in families and collaborative relationships. We turn now to some examples from parents about their own growth and the factors that have contributed to it. Some of these examples come from parents who have looked retroactively at their own journeys to talk about growth and give advice to others, including families and professionals. Other examples come from parents' direct conversations about how they have developed and sustained a sense of hope over time. For many, the presence of a sense of hope and belief in the possibilities for growth in their child contribute to feelings of resiliency and empowerment that are sustaining over time and have great benefits for them and their children.

ADVICE FOR THE JOURNEY TO COLLABORATION:
FROM PARENTS, FOR PARENTS

Many of the parents we have interviewed and worked with have talked about the ways in which they have developed their skills in collaboration, advocacy and leadership over time. As part of these conversations, they have given advice to others. Although advice differs, much of it falls under three categories of "becoming" (a.k.a. growing): becoming informed, becoming an advocate and becoming engaged. *Becoming informed* acknowledges the value of networking, asking questions and seeking information. *Becoming an advocate* involves developing sense of one's goals and expectations and learning not to be afraid to push back if the school or system does not share a similar view. *Becoming engaged* refers to the importance of forming collaborative relationships with professionals so as to establish a "seat at the table." In reflecting on their stories of becoming informed, becoming an advocate, and becoming engaged, parents observed their personal growth, the growth (in some cases) of their teams, and the strength and resiliency that came from what they learned along the way.

Becoming Informed

In reflecting on the process of becoming informed, Will and Katie emphasized the importance of "knowing your rights" and "knowing the system." Lindsay built upon this idea, encouraging parents to "Reach out to any connections you have who are in education or organizations like the ones that were offered to us to help represent families or help with the navigation process, because I really wish we had known about that earlier. I wish we had known about that when our son was in kindergarten." Will noted that he learned how important it was to "find other families who get that same service or who get that and talk with other parents that have a child with a similar disability, similar circumstance and find out what services they're receiving." Our interviewees also talked about the need for parents to not be afraid to ask questions. Jane reminded parents to "Ask for information, keep asking questions, and search for information until you feel like you understand everything and don't be afraid to do that." For Kelly, asking questions and probing professionals about their roles served a broader purpose. Asking clarifying and probing questions increased the degree to which she was informed about her daughter's program and became a tool for advocacy. She urged parents to use questioning as a strategy to reach a desired outcome, explaining:

> My advice is to approach your child's needs by asking a lot of questions. I don't think professionals tend to respond well to being told what to do or how to do it, but it also isn't helpful to just not say anything and I found that if I ask, if I ask enough questions, then it will usually lead … to the right outcome if I ask enough questions about what's happening and how that's affecting [my child] or how it's affecting the class or the teacher.

Andrew made a similar point, commenting on the need to ask not only for information, but for answers to bigger questions from professionals about their rationale for providing—or not providing—certain interventions. As he advised, "Don't give up your right to be the professional parent, but be clear about what you don't know by understanding what you need to know. And let the professionals tell you what that is and convince you that it's true." In each instance, parents saw the value of gathering information, asking clarifying and probing questions, and being transparent about what they knew and did not know. They acknowledged that their entry into the world of special education did not come quickly or easily; rather, becoming informed meant reaching out and taking the time and effort to develop their knowledge base.

Becoming an Advocate

The process of becoming an advocate was also described as a journey that involved risk-taking, effort and growth. Although they rarely used the term, parents who saw themselves as advocates were demonstrating the presence of a growth mindset. Many acknowledged that in developing a sense of advocacy, they sometimes made mistakes and were not always heard; regardless, the process of developing effective skills was critical to their personal growth and the growth of their child.

Holly found her voice through years of practice in navigating challenging interpersonal dynamics among team members. Her advice for other parents reflected this journey:

> Speak up. Schools have their own agenda sometimes and the LEAs have their own agendas and usually it's finances and they tell you we're going to do this and then tell you, "well we'll home school [your son]. We'll come into your house." That's ridiculous. And I mean really just speaking up and going to somebody if you don't know. And not to be embarrassed that you don't know the system either.

Lulu echoed this sentiment, urging parents to be confident in their knowledge of their children and their presentation of ideas to school professionals. She acknowledged the importance of "having the confidence to say you've made a decision and then having the confidence to come in and say 'this is the decision I've made, let's work on a way to work with the rest of everything around it.'" Jane echoed this idea, noting, "Be confident in what you have to offer the process, no matter what. Don't let anything sway you from feeling confident about that." This included using the tools available in the system to advocate for the child's needs.

Will encouraged parents not to be afraid to utilize legal mechanisms to access services or accommodations for children. As he put it:

> Know that – if it's something that you really think is going to benefit your child – don't just stop if they tell you no. I mean there's a process for it. Know about due process and how to access that. And if you think it's something that can help your child, really fight for it.

Katie concurred, noting that the child's needs should drive the process and parents should not feel limited by school's expectations for their children. She encouraged parents to be clear in communicating their own expectations of their children to professionals. She offered:

> I think it's important not to buy into their expectations of what your child should achieve. I think that's a key. It's to have your own expectations of what your child should achieve, what your child should be able to do between you and your child. And if there are special educators and teachers along the way that you can trust, have your child's best interests at heart, then ask them "what do you think?"

Katie's comments about expectations demonstrated her own understanding of a growth mindset, even if she did not explicitly refer to that framework. In reflecting on her conversations with special educators, she identified an important aspect of collaboration: the ability to develop a relationship over time that is based in trust and a shared understanding of a child's potential. In arriving at this stage, parents can come to feel that both parents and professionals are becoming advocates by focusing on what is best for the child.

Becoming Engaged

The sense of becoming engaged further emphasized the reciprocal nature of collaboration, especially for parents who had come to understand it over time as a two-way street characterized by equal participation by all team members. Parents who had become successful advocates *and* gone a step further to foster collaborative partnerships with professionals expressed a greater sense of satisfaction with the collaborative process than those who chose or did not have the opportunity to engage in this way. Parents who spoke more specifically about the idea of engagement described it as being involved, forming positive partnerships and making contributions to others.

165

For example, She' Ra Monroe used her frequent presence in the school as a strategy for demonstrating her commitment to her team and her son's education. Her advice for parents was to "Be present." She explained her rationale:

> There's that really wonderful quote that, how much more improved student learning is when parents are present. It's like 35% more, I can't think of the number but it's pretty significant. When a parent is involved in their child's learning whether it's directly or indirectly, the child learns better, so – be involved.

Maggie described the multiple ways in which she tried to partner with her daughter's team, whether it was reinforcing concepts at home, sharing strategies with the school or seeking supplemental services to enhance her daughter's learning. She advised parents to actively seek opportunities to form a true partnership with professionals. She coined this approach as having "skin in the game." She attributed her positive experience collaborating with her daughter's elementary school to the efforts she made to form a partnership:

> I think it's because I'm willing to meet them part way, that I'm going back to that, I'm willing to be a partner. I really felt like that gave a positive response back to me. That I'm not expecting you to be a miracle worker and all of a sudden make my daughter's learning disability disappear.

Maggie emphasized the importance of maximizing ways to address a child's needs through avenues both at school and home. As she advised, "Try not to expect the school to do everything." Lina concurred, noting that parents needed to be open to what is happening:

> With schools, I think we all need to be a little flexible. The school is trying to provide a best service also but sometimes you have to just be flexible with them and understand things from their standpoint. At the same time, get the best for your kid. Everyone has to work together.

The spirit of cooperation and reciprocity was reflected through final pieces of advice shared by Maggie and Bethany. In their minds, parents can exhibit a willingness to be a good partner through the ways they give back to the school, to each other and to the broader field. In their minds, making a contribution reflected the spirit of partnership. Bethany acknowledged both the challenge and importance of balancing acknowledgement of the stress of parenting with the desire to contribute to others. She reflected on her experiences serving as a spokesperson for herself and other parents:

> We are the busiest and most stressed people. So I feel like it's a challenge and a good thing that we get called in all the time to talk at [the university] or to help another parent or to do whatever. I like doing that and I get fed in some ways by that, but I also have more on my plate than the average person. But I

think it helps that we're seen as people contributing and not just always asking for stuff.

In a similar vein Maggie expressed the importance of being "helpful" and acknowledging that there are times in the year when special educators are very busy attending to the needs of multiple children. She felt at those times, "maybe you as a parent can pick the ball up for those two/three weeks that the special educators are meeting every second of their life to get, to make sure all kids are set." Still, Maggie noted that although parents should be willing to be partners, their kids' needs are their priority so "if they [the professionals] keep dropping balls, you need to really step in and if you're not going to be heard, you need to find a way to be heard."

Each of these pieces of advice regarding engagement reflects the importance of trust and growth within collaborative processes. Parents who were able to see their relationships with professionals develop over time and in a positive direction also saw their own growth as a developmental process. They began by becoming informed and developing skills as advocates, eventually seeing themselves as partners in the process. As collaboration moved in this direction, parents affirmed the need to be seen as deeply engaged in the process, in spite of their busy and stressful lives. These stories, we believe, show the possibility for collaborative relationships to be growth-oriented and a contributor to resiliency—perhaps for *both* parents and professionals.

ADVICE FOR PROFESSIONALS

In asking parents to give advice to professionals, we see further evidence of possibilities for growth and reciprocity in collaborative partnerships. In general, parents' advice to professionals can be summarized through three themes: providing resources, prioritizing the child, and employing family-centered practices. *Providing resources* speaks to the need for professionals to share information, communicate clearly, and remain transparent about the special education process. *Prioritizing the child* includes the need for professionals to be child-centered and to advocate for the child's individual needs. Lastly, *employing family-centered practices* means establishing personal connections with families, expressing empathy, and honoring the expertise of parents. Interestingly, these three pieces of advice corresponded strongly to parents' thoughts and advice about their own development. Parents saw their first role as becoming critical consumers of information; similarly, they wanted professionals to identify and share resources. Over time, parents saw themselves as advocates, and they wanted professionals to be advocates as well. Beyond advocacy, family members saw themselves as engaged partners in the collaborative process and they wanted professionals to engage in family-centered practices that would reinforce this sense of partnership. In conveying this advice to professionals, parents suggested ways in which enhanced collaborative partnerships could contribute to a family's sense of well-being and capacity—with the potential benefit of supporting growth and resiliency for family members.

Providing Resources

The term "resource" is often used to describe the financial resources and services that students with disabilities and their families need to access a free and appropriate public education for the student. In the context of advice to professionals, however, parents used the term resource more broadly. Andrew, for example, talked at length about data as being one of the most important resources that professionals could give to him and his family. He believed that an essential activity of special educators was to create systems to collect and share data on his son's progress for the purpose of evaluating the effectiveness of interventions. Andrew's advice to professionals was built upon his desire to see data sharing as an essential element of communication and decision-making. He advised professionals to be sure that they were using data to make "a convincing argument for the services they provide." He believed strongly that professionals needed to demonstrate to parents that the research-based interventions they selected worked for individual children, "because it is a very individual case by case situation and I know that more clearly today than I've every known that in my life. And I know that's what makes special education a daunting task but it's what keeps it appropriate."

Maggie's advice to professionals centered on supporting parents in accessing information that would help them better understand their child's learning needs. That said, she advised professionals to be cognizant of the amount and type of information they shared. She suggested that professionals "give parents books or even just a couple of pages because sometimes parents don't have time to read a whole book. Just say, 'you know this might give you some insight into why we are doing this program' or 'maybe this would work for you at home.'" Maggie acknowledged that at times parents might find it overwhelming to receive additional information; at the same time, she felt that professionals should be skilled in understanding appropriate times to share materials. Additionally, she hoped that professionals would find themselves open to looking at resources brought to them by families.

Kelly added a third dimension to what it means for professionals to serve as a resource to parents. Her advice was for professionals to pay particular attention to helping parents—and especially parents who were new to special education—to understand the special education process and its interaction with general education. As she noted "I think that professionals forget about how much parents don't know about what all this stuff in and the special ed process, about what does it mean to have an IEP meeting or to have an evaluation planning meeting or any of the pieces that just have to happen." She explained that over time, she learned how to ask questions in the "right way" to be sure that issues she was concerned about were covered, but realized that "what professionals take for granted as an obvious system is not at all obvious to parents."

Earlier discussions about parent and professional knowledge in chapters three and four highlight both the benefits and challenges associated in knowledge acquisition and use. Here, we see that the degree to which professionals can help parents navigate information and resources serves as a key to developing positive and reciprocal family and professional partnerships. Clearly, it takes efforts on both sides to promote growth within these relationships and to foster a sense of hope and resiliency among families.

Prioritizing the Child

Parents who have been given the opportunity to provide advice to professionals nearly always talk about how important it is to them to feel that professionals know, value and prioritize their children as teams select interventions, identify needed services and engage in decision-making. Holly advised professionals to "leave their personal feelings inside" and to recognize that success for a child is based on individual needs. Regardless of personal biases about programs, she wanted professionals to recognize when a program is working and let that be the driver in determining funding and placements.

Will had had relatively positive experiences collaborating with his daughter's team, and as a special educator himself, he was able to participate actively in planning and decision-making. Still, he stressed the importance of having professionals "rise to the challenge" through their advocacy and transparency about what may work for a child. He advised professionals to "be open about what's available," noting that he appreciated it when they stepped forward: "They need to come out and say, 'hey I think we should provide this service'."

Employing Family-Centered Practices

A third piece of advice that we heard regularly focused on the importance of employing family-centered practices. Parents defined several key elements including honoring parents' expertise, being empathetic to the stressors families experience and forming personal connections with families. As described in Chapter 7, some parents have participated in specific family-centered practices (e.g., MAPS) and viewed those as helpful. Others used the term more broadly to describe a more fundamental aspect of the family and professional relationship.

Both Georgia and Lulu, for example, talked about frequent check-ins as a form of family-centered practice that professionals could easily implement. Lulu described how "there's easy ways to communicate about little blips as they come up rather than saving them for the meetings and having them become big problems by then."

Lina came to understand the importance of empathy intimately after her daughter was born with severe disabilities. A professional nurse by training, Lina found herself re-examining her own practices after becoming a parent of a child with a disability. She suggested that professionals

…think from the family's standpoint, or step into somebody else's shoes. Yeah. Because I found before I had a child with a disability as a nurse, I did not understand much of special needs kids. I work in pediatric units in hospital and I didn't know much about these kids. I was kinda not able to be sympathetic with them. Now I do because I have a kid like this of my own. I provide extra love to those special needs kids...

Bethany echoed the importance of empathy, acknowledging how much effort parents of children with severe disabilities exert and how stressful it can be:

So I think for professionals to just think about that family system and how tired we are, how stressed we are, how we have to advocate all the time for every blessed thing and meanwhile we're just like you. We're trying to be good parents. We're trying to have a good marriage. We're trying to get eight hours of sleep. We're trying to put dinner on the table. We're trying to do our paid work or whatever, and we didn't, this is going to sound weird, but we didn't ask for this challenge and we ask for him to have x, y, and z, we just think "this is what he needs to learn best".... So just kinda having that empathy and that compassion for that big picture that we're juggling.

Georgia gave examples of things that teachers might do in their classrooms to demonstrate their belief in a growth mindset and use of family-centered practices. She reflected first on what new teachers should be thinking about in the classroom:

Provide an environment where the parents feel like they can come to you. Show that your disposition and your attitude about learning about their child is positive. Even if the kid has had a hard day, you don't show that on your face. You say "I'm so glad they made it to school today and you're doing a great job." ... It's a hard job. I guess you just have to decide how important it is to you to develop relationships with parents and to be the best you can be for kids with needs. ...You have to commit to doing it. It's just that simple.

Georgia also offered advice for experienced teachers. She acknowledged that the culture of school can be difficult and that it takes courage for teachers to remain true to their commitments to families. Still, she felt that teachers should be committed to improving their practice, demonstrating their belief in a growth mindset:

What I say is, I mean I don't think it's ever too late to change course. To be more self- reflective. To say "wow, I don't know if I handled that okay," or "if I look back on my teaching career, have I gotten better at this or does it stay the same? Is there something I can do differently? Is there a class I could take, a workshop? Should I start a workshop? A book group?"

Lastly, Andrew spoke to the importance of hope and resiliency when he asserted "All parents have is their knowledge of their child and their hope for their child. Everything else is out of their control." Andrew's point reinforces the simplicity of describing family-centered practices: they begin with who the family is, what parents know, and what they hope and expect to achieve with respect to their child.

Using family-centered practices, professionals can build upon a family's hopes and dreams to create positive collaborative relationships that in turn reinforce resiliency and capacity building for children and families.

LOOKING WITHIN AND BEYOND

The examples provided above and in previous chapters speak to ways in which parents and professionals can maximize collaborative relationships to support and strengthen families of children with disabilities. In the following sections, we discuss possibilities for building hope and resiliency that are largely outside of the collaborative process as it occurs in the school setting. Rather, they occur through parents' personal growth and development through increased self-efficacy and self-confidence; connections to the larger community, including other parents of children with disabilities; and more personal connections to faith, spirituality or some other sense of a larger purpose. Although these kinds of experiences are generally outside of the domain of school professionals, we feel it is important to acknowledge them and to consider ways that professionals might acknowledge, encourage or even foster them in the larger effort to contribute to a family's capacity to mange what can be a complex and challenging set of circumstances.

Self-Knowledge, Self-Efficacy and Self-Confidence

Many of the parents we spoke with talked about the ways in which their sense of resiliency grew over time in conjunction with an increase in their sense of confidence and self-efficacy. As they gained knowledge, skills, and opportunities, parents felt better about who they were, how they could support their children, and how they could interact with school professionals. Greta described how her initial sense of fear about how to care for her newborn child with sensory and health issues was replaced over time with a strong sense of her own competence as a mother. She gave this advice to other parents:

> You really have to step back and take a deep breath and believe you have the ability to figure it out. I didn't believe I had the brainpower and stamina to carry it out at first, but I believe I was carried through the process. As we had more incremental success, my confidence grew. I started from ground zero and build from there. After working so hard to keep my kid alive, I started to believe that I could raise her and it would be OK.

Greta went on to talk about the importance of problem-solving and perseverance, noting that in "staying the course" parents can become stronger:

> You've got to hang in there. This is your child. You can't run away, it's not an option. When you hit a wall, brainstorm and keep moving. Do something for yourself. The positive talk you give yourself is better than anything. Telling yourself "You can do this with a lot of help" is key.

171

Over and over again, parents have told us stories about how their "small successes" gradually built upon one another in a way that contributed to their belief in themselves and their children. Success was defined in different ways for different parents: sometimes it meant feeling good about asking questions and getting results at an IEP meeting, and other times it meant watching their child achieve something that professionals told them would not happen. Either way, it was clear that parents' beliefs in themselves and their skills as a parent and advocate were built over time, with one success leading to another and contributing to the family's growth and resiliency.

Drawing on the past. Several parents talked about a form of resiliency that was drawn from their own childhood memories and lived experiences. In reflecting on previous challenges, these parents found strength in remembering what they had already been through as children and young adults growing up in families facing different kinds of challenges. Georgia noted:

> I think I've developed resiliency over the years, even before having children. I think my own upbringing was pretty challenging. We didn't have a lot growing up and my parents expected us to pull our own weight and find our own way. So just to make it through college on my own and living on my own was a lot. I didn't have kids then, but well, you know, I've done worse. I've gone through harder things. This isn't the hardest thing I've ever had to do.

Djenne told a similar story, noting that her ability to deal with Malik's diagnosis and the conflict and decision-making that accompanied his early life and education could be traced back to her own upbringing:

> It all goes back to my childhood. I lived in the Bronx with my mother, grandparents and sister, and because my mother advocated for me to go to a better school, I was bussed to New York City every day. This school was far from my neighborhood and family, and it wasn't always easy to go there. I've always had to navigate my way, and I learned the art of negotiation through that.

Melissa talked about how the difficulties she encountered as a child and a young woman gave her a role model and a sense of strength that she drew upon during challenging times. She told this story:

> I think some of that comes from my life growing up. I have a father who is Italian, mobster looking (and acting sometimes when we were younger); a very strong man. And then I have my mother who was a single mother, my parents split up because my father was abusive and they split up and I had this incredible role model of what a strong woman looks like and who had drive and so I had this foundation of strength.

Melissa also talked about the ways in which she drew on her past when working as a school and family liaison. She reflected on the fact that her ability to share her memories often helped families of children with disabilities who faced additional challenges such as poverty and the aftermath of childhood trauma. She reflected that:

Partly because of my own past, I feel I was able to give people a sense of belonging and acceptance and leadership opportunities. And the respect was given and they just gave it back freely. I was not judgmental of how they lived, what their house looked like. I complimented them for the things that I saw in their children and in themselves. And so I'm very proud to have had the opportunity to engage and have the relationships that I shared. I think it was easier for me than some of the other folks that were parent coordinators who didn't have their own struggles.

Connecting to the community. Parents also talked about the importance of having people and activities in their lives that offered a sense of identity, support and hope. Georgia talked about a range of people in her support system, noting:

I think we have pretty good support system with our friends. My husband's family has been really, really supportive. They've helped us out financially like a lot when it's gotten tough. I think being in the arts has helped me a lot. Keeping that something that's active in my life has been a really helpful outlet, so I get to talk to other adults about something other than my children or school. I picked up the guitar along the way. …That's all been important. I think also my husband and I have a sense of humor about all of it. It's like okay, we can either laugh or cry in this situation.

She went on to note the importance of telling her story, both as a means to make meaning from stressful situations and to build a sense of community with parents facing similar challenges:

My husband actually started a blog for us, like maybe five years ago or so. I actually wrote a new one yesterday about a bad interaction with a Social Security guy and that's a great outlet. I mean we have, I don't know if we have any followers but quite a few people have viewed our page before – so okay, so out in the web-verse somebody might be having the same experience and get some relief reading about this.

Similarly, Djenne talks often about being part of a "village." "Malik's life sent us on a unique journey," she notes. "We have become a 'village family.' If not for Malik, we wouldn't know three quarters of the people we know."

For some parents, connecting to others and gaining a sense of hope meant becoming part of a larger societal purpose. B.B. noted "since I was a kid (and my other daughter has this too), I've had a fierce sense of justice and my whole life has been animated by that. But it's justice with love. Not just bang the table kind of justice." As described earlier, B.B. became engaged in a range of advocacy activities, some of which connected directly to her daughter's needs and some that benefitted other children who experienced a disability and/or other forms of marginalization. She described working with children, teachers, the principal and parents in her daughter's elementary school to bring about a focus on inclusion:

> We were not just talking about inclusion of kids with disabilities, but all kids that come from other countries, refugee children. We said that if we're going to be a school community, they need to be invited to birthdays and play dates... It's gone now, but for a long time the school had on its welcome page a page and a half story about all the different people here, single parents, married parents, grandparents, gay and lesbian families, and so on.

B.B. recognized that her level of advocacy was not one that would be possible for all families; still she spoke passionately about the degree to which she felt called to do this work and the ways in which it contributed to her sense of hope for the future:

> You do it because it needs to be done, and you don't have the option of not doing it. Because if you take that option, your child is not gonna have the chance to develop as fully as they can and that's my goal for Marjorie. Whatever it is, I want her to be as full a person as she wants to be and she's capable of, in whatever areas those are in and she has a human right to that. I also take great solace in the fact that I am standing on the shoulders and many generations that came before me that have fought for the human rights of people with disabilities and while I'm doing my little thing here, I also take great solace in the fact that there are people everywhere who are doing the same thing. Just 'cuz I don't know them all, I know we're all connected and that sense of connection and solidarity as a movement is meaningful to me.

B.B. spoke eloquently about another aspect of creating hope and resiliency through connecting to the community: creating a sense of belonging for children with disabilities and their families. In B.B.'s view "there's still not a real understanding of or commitment to the fact that everybody's a human being and I've come to understand that I'm not really looking for inclusion. I'm looking for belonging. There's huge difference between those two concepts." Her words serve as a reminder that in order for parents to experience hope and resiliency, they need to feel that they and their children belong somewhere.

Connecting through shared understanding. Along with advocacy and community connections, many parents talked about the power of connecting with others—whether they were professionals, other parents, family or friends—to arrive at a common understanding of what it meant to have a child with a disability. These connections occurred at a more conceptual or emotional level in which parents found others who shared their experiences and thoughts about moving away from a focus on challenges and towards a sense of growth, happiness or fulfillment. Melissa was particularly concerned about reaching out to families of children with disabilities whose own past and present lives had included difficult circumstances. In her parent support role, she found it important to think about how "Everyone has something to offer. It's really finding what they're comfortable with…You have to gain their trust." She noted that her own experiences with challenging situations helped her to connect with those families:

> Even though I could dress nice and look different from some parents, sometimes my tone says something different. The swear words fly out—and so then there are just the stories that connect me to them.… And connecting with them so that they don't feel that you're better than them. …And I wonder though, if I didn't have my own baggage and struggles, would I be able to do that? My gift came out of the struggles.

Although she acknowledged that her personal background made it easier for her to connect with certain families, Melissa still believed that professionals who had not personally experienced significant challenges could be more intentional in understanding the processes that led families toward hope and resilience. She imagined a process of reflection that would help in this regard:

> I think some of that would go back to thinking about your own life—what are your own struggles? So I think happiness can come out of sadness because the knowledge and the strength comes from a lot of trials and tribulations. And so thinking about that as if I were a special educator and I had all that stuff on my plate, I think I would want to reflect on myself and an obstacle I've overcome or something that's personal to me. Whether it be a loved one that's passed or something else—but a reflection that the strength is ultimately going to come out of the trials and tribulations.

Her comments point to the need for all of us to look inward, to accept others' lives without judgment, and to think about the universal nature of how we become stronger through adversity.

Hope and faith.   "Hope," says Djenne. "From hoping Malik will live to hoping for the best education possible to hoping in general. Other families don't have hope; we were lucky to find it." Many of the parents we spoke to talked about the idea of hope as a key to their ability to experience growth and resilience. In speaking about her daughter, one mother noted, "Taylor has given me hope. I look at her and remember the tears I cried in the beginning when I didn't know what to do. Now I cry tears of joy when I see her dance or do well in sports." Some made direct reference to the link between hope and faith in God or "something larger than me." Greta commented:

> Hope and belief is what had kept me strong. I've learned to step back, take a deep breath and believe you can figure it out. From the beginning, there were so many people in my home. I knew God gave me the right people to work with him at every level in his development. Having people who are compassionate in our lives has made us less isolated. I know that God has got this and He will

give me the wisdom to know what to do next. Things fall into place. I know I'm led every step of the way.

Jamie expressed a similar thought and advised other parents to "Love your kid. God gives special kids to special parents. My faith has grown and helped me get through the hard times." Melissa talked about the faith she gained as a result of an abusive relationship in her late teenage years and how, following one particularly harrowing time, she experienced a "sense of peace that came over me and I really felt that strength came from within that peace to get up and continue." She described this event as one that had renewed her faith and stayed with her as she negotiated other challenges in life, including having a son with a disability. As she described:

> It's like, when you don't know or you think you don't have any more, it comes out of nowhere. For me some of that comes from my faith…. Faith is a huge part of what gets me through and what I have told my kids is, sometimes when you say, when you think you can't handle it, you say to God "I can't handle this one. I need you to do it." And you give it to him and you'll have that peace. It's definitely helped me tremendously, many times.

Djenne tells a story about the evolution of her faith in the context of Malik's life:

> Faith makes all the difference. My husband and I were in the Christian ministry when Malik was born. The circumstances of his birth broke our faith at first; we saw the ministry as not working for us and some other families. We made some mistakes in ignorance—then we *made* our faith. We became the voice of families with kids like Malik. It opened us up to other people of faith, including those not of the Christian faith. There was a Creole woman who prayed with Malik, a Jewish lawyer who became very important to our family, my mother who has a more universal faith. Malik brought all of these people together.

The beginning of this chapter includes a story from a time when Djenne's sense of hope was challenged. She reminds us that moving towards resiliency is a journey that moves back and forth between hope and fear, faith and disappointment. At the same time, her story over time is one that reminds us of how an orientation towards hope and growth and faith in something larger can lead to a sense of resiliency and a reminder of the power of love for one's child and family. The story ends happily:

> Earlier, I wrote about the worst part of identifying Malik's disability was never hearing him say "I love you." I also shared a story about controlling a meltdown in a professional setting due the realization of my son's limitations. Now not every story has a happy ending. Life is what it is, the joys and challenges. But, this one did. As I spent the meeting lamenting over my son's inability to gain a specific skill set, I arrived home with mixed feelings about seeing him. As I do every week when he comes home from his residential program, I greeted Malik signing, "Hi Malik, Mommy loves you." As if he intuitively knew I

needed something more to hold on to that day, Malik, as usual responded signing, 'Mommy loves, Malik', and gave me the biggest kiss! This turned into the most wonderful reciprocal 3 word conversation, "Mommy loves Malik", "Malik loves Mommy," followed by several rounds of kisses from Malik. This for me is the source of my hope and resilience. Though I may occasionally grieve for what may not be according to my own desires as a mother and expectations as a professional in the field of deafness and hard of hearing, what I do have the blessing of seeing what really is before me. This is the thing that matters to me most, the love between a child and parent. The ability to communicate the most important concept, LOVE.

CHAPTER SUMMARY

In this chapter, we have focused on the concepts of resiliency and growth mindset, positing that if families and school professionals view teaching, parenting, and collaboration as developmental processes, families are more likely to develop their capacity to deal with the challenges they may encounter in raising a child with a disability. The concept of resiliency contributes to the idea of collaboration by offering a strengths-based approach to thinking about family systems and their potential for growth over time. Similarly, the concept of a growth mindset as it applies to teaching and parenting children with disabilities and the development of family-school partnerships offers a positive view of the potential for even the most difficult school-family relationships to improve over time. In the spirit of fostering a growth mindset and the possibility for resiliency, we have included advice on improving collaboration from parents to parents as well as parents to professionals. We have also included thoughts from parents regarding the ways in which they have drawn upon their inner strength and faith in things larger than their child and family to develop and maintain a sense of hope and to grow in their capacity to be resilient. We offer the following suggestions to parents and school professionals as they consider how these strengths-based frameworks and experiences can be emphasized within and outside of the collaborative process.

1. *As parents, build capacity for you and your family by becoming informed, becoming an advocate, and becoming engaged with your child's school and educational process.* The majority of the parents we have spoken to stress that no matter how difficult, it is always better to move towards engagement and collaboration than away from it. In assuming an active stance in your child's education, there are more opportunities for you to make your voice heard and to be present for key decisions in your child's life. For most parents, engagement with the process contributes to a sense of growth and resiliency. That said, there are also times when the idea of more engagement will feel difficult or even impossible – and this needs to be honored as a part of the experience.

2. *As professionals, provide resources, prioritize the child, and employ family-centered practices.* The literature on family systems and resiliency makes it clear that the context of the whole family is always relevant to what is going on in school. Think about families as a system with the capacity for growth by recognizing their complexity, honoring strengths, maintaining empathy, and acting on parents' expertise and knowledge of their child. The term "family centered practices" can be applied broadly to include formal processes such as person-centered planning as well as less formal but equally important practices such as open communication, listening and being cognizant of the realities of families. These practices signal positive beliefs to families they may in turn resonate with them in the form of more positive beliefs about their situation and their capacity to see it in a more positive light.

3. *Promote hope and resiliency by looking beyond the realm of education.* For school professionals, this means recognizing, acknowledging and honoring parents' growth in self-knowledge, self-efficacy, and self-confidence. It also means eliciting and listening to parents' stories of their own education and upbringing to identify stories of resiliency that may contribute to their experience as a parent of a child with a disability. It may mean encouraging parents to connect to the larger community by developing relationships, participating in activities that develop their happiness and sense of self, and/or connecting to broader advocacy efforts. For parents, the journey to hope and resiliency may occur through reflection and conversations with others that reveal shared understandings and experiences. Similarly, professionals who reflect on their own lives are more likely to develop a broader appreciation of and connection to the challenges that face many of the families with whom they work.

4. *Hold conversations about hope and resiliency.* In sharing the stories of family members who have drawn strength from their inner life, from others, and from a larger sense of faith, we are reminded of the personal and somewhat intimate nature of these kinds of journeys. They are matters that are specific to families and family culture; as such, they may not often surface in appear the typical discourse between families and professionals. Still, there may be times when school-based conversations can include questions about or statements of support for the activities, beliefs, and people who surround and give strength to families of children with disabilities. We have discussed elsewhere the critical importance of getting to know children and families in ways that build trust and collaboration. In developing an understanding of what brings about a sense of hope and capacity building for parents, school professionals can come to know families at a deeper level and can nurture their growth as a family system. Listening to stories of growth, hope, faith and resiliency may contribute to family-centered practice and the possibility for a deeper sense of collaboration among school professionals and families. Believing in the strengths that children and families bring to the table—regardless of their circumstances—helps to promote a re-framing of difficult situations and a sense of possibility and growth.

SUGGESTED QUESTIONS FOR REFLECTION AND DISCUSSION

For parents:

1. What aspects of your life contribute to a sense of hope, faith and resiliency for you? What are some of the activities and beliefs you engage with that help get you through the more difficult times for you and your family? Where might you turn to if you find that you need more opportunities to develop your sense of hope and resiliency?
2. Where do you see yourself on the "growth mindset" continuum? Do you have a sense that you, your child, and your team can continue to grow and develop or do you have a more fixed mindset about some of these issues? How might you foster a growth mindset?

For professionals:

3. In what ways do you apply a growth mindset in your teaching practice? Your collaborative practice? Are there ways you might expand your mindset so as to model it for students and families?
4. Think about the families with whom you work. What examples do you see of hope and resiliency? How might you learn more or talk about those aspects of resiliency during your interactions with families?

SUGGESTED ACTIVITIES

For parents:

5. Make a circle with you in the middle, followed by a surrounding circle representing your family, and additional concentric circles showing the people, places, ideas and activities that are most important to you. Which ones bring you the greatest sense of hope and resilience? Which circles could be expanded to provide more support to you? Share your drawing with someone who is close to you to talk about the strengths and opportunities for hope and growth within your support system.

For professionals:

6. Make a list of the things that bring you a sense of growth or hope in your professional practice. Who supports you in your work? What activities, ideas and beliefs bring you strength when your work or personal life feels difficult? Identify one or more areas where you might need more support and talk to a colleague about how you might strengthen your support network.
7. Identify three questions that you might ask of family members to learn more about what supports are in their lives and how they maintain a sense of hope when things are difficult. During your next meeting with a family, try to ask at least one related question.

REFERENCES

Antonovsky, A. (1987). *Unraveling the mystery of health.* San Francisco, CA: Jossey-Bass.

Antonovsky, A., & Sourant, T. (1988). Family sense of coherence and family adaptation. *Journal of Marriage and the Family, 50,* 79–92.

Bayat, M. (2007). Evidence of resilience in families of children with autism. *Journal of Intellectual Disability Research, 51*(9), 702–714.

Blackwell, L. S., Trzeniewski, K. H., & Dweck, C. S. (2007). Implicit theories of intelligence predict achievement across an adolescent transition: A longitudinal study and an intervention. *Child Development, 78*(1), 246–263.

Dweck, C. (2015). Growth mindset, revisited. *Education Week.* Retrieved from http://www.edweek.org/ew/articles/2015/09/23/carol-dweck-revisits-the-growth-mindset.html?r=234782000&preview=1

Dweck, C. S. (2006). *Mindset: The new psychology of success.* New York, NY: Random House.

Heggart, K. (2015). Developing a growth mindset in teachers and staff. *Edutopia.* Retrieved from http://www.edutopia.org/discussion/developing-growth-mindset-teachers-and-staff

Heiman, T. (2002). Parents of children with disabilities: Resilience, coping, and future expectations. *Journal of Developmental and Physical Disabilities, 14*(2), 159–171.

McCubbin, H., & Patterson, J. (1983). The family stress process: The double ABCX model of family adjustment and adaptation. *Marriage and Family Review, 6,* 7–37.

Mercer, S., & Ryan, S. (2010). A mindset for EFL: Learners' beliefs about the role of natural talent. *ELT Journal, 64,* 436–444.

Mraz, K., & Hertz, C. (2015). *A mindset for learning: Teaching the traits of joyful, independent growth.* Portsmouth, NH: Heinemann.

Patterson, J. (1993). The role of family means in adaptation to chronic illness and disability. In A. P. Turnbull, J. M. Patterson, S. K. Behr, D. L. Murphy, J. G. Marquis, & M. J. Blue-Banning (Eds.), *Cognitive coping research and developmental disabilities* (pp. 221–238). Baltimore, MD: Paul H. Brookes.

Patterson, J. (2002). Understanding family resilience. *Journal of Clinical Psychology, 58*(3), 233–246.

Patterson, J., & Garwick, A. W. (1994). Levels of family meaning in family stress theory. *Family Process, 33,* 287–304.

Seligman, M. E. P., & Csikszentmihali, M. (2000). Positive psychology: An introduction. *American Psychologist, 55,* 5–14.

Taylor, M. (2014). 5 parenting strategies to develop a growth mindset. *Imagination Soup.* Retrieved from http://imaginationsoup.net/2014/09/17/help-child-unmotivated-growth-fixed-mindset/

Walsh, F. (1998). *Strengthening family resilience.* New York, NY: Guilford Press.

Walsh, F. (2003). Changing families in a changing world: Reconstructing family normality. In F. Walsh (Ed.), *Normal family processes: Growing diversity and complexity* (pp. 3–26). New York, NY: Guildford.

Yuan, S. (2003). Seeing with new eyes: Metaphors of family experience. *Mental Retardation, 41*(3), 207–211.

CHAPTER 9

CONCLUSION

Where do we go Next?
Alone we can do so little; together we can do so much.

(Helen Keller)

Throughout this book, we have heard powerful stories from families of children with disabilities that remind us of why collaboration is so important. We have witnessed how it can work, and how and why it sometimes breaks down. These stories also suggest possibilities for expanded roles for parents (e.g., parents as experts, advocates and leaders). We have also explored strategies that parents have used to improve collaboration and to make change, family-centered practices and tools that may be helpful to both families and professionals as they look to build strong and collaborative partnerships, and beliefs, experiences and conditions that may promote hope and resiliency. Throughout, we have come to see the importance of understanding collaboration as a developmental process that requires attention and support in order to grow over time. We have acknowledged that collaboration requires equal effort on the part of both families and professionals and that it may at times appear challenging; still, we believe it to be a worthy goal.

In this final chapter, we continue to build on parents' stories to reflect their enhanced definition and views of collaboration and the approaches that might be used to accomplish it. In suggesting the concepts and strategies that follow, we acknowledge the importance of the research base behind family and school collaboration, and the many "how to" books and articles that currently exist on the topic. We offer the idea that in the next generation of collaboration, we will need to move beyond some of our current conceptions to consider how we can better address increased diversity in our families, school, and communities; changes in technology and knowledge generation and dissemination; and new thinking about growth mindset and development over the life span, We assert that increased opportunities for parents to connect with each other to make change will continue to push our thinking on what collaboration means in today's world. To that end, we propose six ways of re-defining and re-envisioning collaboration, all moving in the direction of understanding and practicing—as our participant Andrew calls it—the "*art*" of collaboration. The first two—clarifying the purpose of collaboration and focusing on its human and relational dimensions—speak to our basic beliefs and assumptions about collaboration and the possibility of those beliefs to inform a more positive collaborative partnership between professionals and families. In contrast, the remaining four – recognizing formal and informal knowledge, advocating for improved conditions for collaboration, incorporating strategies for the growth and development of collaboration, and encouraging families to connect with others—focus on changes in practice that might be made to promote enhanced opportunities for collaboration and a more positive future for children and families. We also acknowledge the degree to which efforts to enhance parent and professional collaboration and partnerships go well beyond the realm of school to include broader societal changes.

CLARIFYING THE PURPOSE OF COLLABORATION

As we look to the future, we find it important to re-think the purpose of collaboration. Given that it is so hard to find "true collaboration," why do we continue to believe that it is so important? How might we do a better job of cultivating collaborative relationships and partnerships than we are doing at this time? And to what end do we engage in it?

As we re-focus on the purpose of collaboration, it is important to remember its connection to the increasing diversity in our schools and communities. We need collaborative approaches that will enable us to navigate an increasingly diverse world and to make sense of the many options facing children, youth, and adults with disabilities and their families. The stories families tell remind us that school is only one part of the fabric of their lives and that parents are deeply concerned about and engaged with a complex web of issues and life experiences. As schools are held more accountable to ensuring that students meet rigorous content standards, it is imperative that professionals work with families to understand their composition and cultural backgrounds, their hopes and dreams, and the full nature of their lives. Likewise, families need to have opportunities to understand the ever-changing demands of schooling and education and thus, the changing responsibilities of school professionals. We have talked a great deal in this book about the importance of collaboration as a means to solve problems together, to resolve conflicts, and to make the best possible decisions for students with disabilities and their families. Each of these processes requires that all parties learn to listen to and understand one another in ways that allow them to move beyond preconceived notions and false assumptions. As such, it seems important for both professionals and parents to realize that the central purpose of collaboration is to develop a sense of shared understanding that enhances the ability of all individuals in a collaborative partnership to respect one another and to be open to potentially differing perspectives. In a world that is changing rapidly, we need to develop collaborative practices that help both professionals and families negotiate situations that can be complex and challenging. We need to remember that our beliefs about collaboration are powerful, and that if we understand its purpose as being related to listening, understanding others, and moving to mutually acceptable solutions, we will be better prepared to engage in true collaboration. It is in this space of shared understanding that we may discover the art of collaboration and a third space that no individual could have arrived at on their own.

FOCUSING ON HUMAN DIMENSIONS AND RELATIONSHIPS

Throughout the stories told in this book, we see the importance of focusing on the "human-ness" of families and school professionals, from both vantage points. As humans, we are complex beings; thus our individual complexities exist within the relationships we have with one another. It is clear that professionals need to have empathy for parents and to understand their context and full set of obligations within and outside of their family constellation. The lives of most families are multi-faceted; school is not the epicenter. Similarly, families can contribute by attempting to understand the ways in which the school context can be challenging for special educators and other school professionals, and work with them to overcome the institutional barriers to collaboration. We propose that parents and professionals alike adopt the "least dangerous assumption" (Jorgenson, 2005) with respect to one another, imagining that in most cases, the person "on the other side of the table" is doing their best to work to a similar end—to what is best for the child. If we can be open to each other's points of views, assume good intentions, focus on strengths and search for common goals, we are much more likely to find creative approaches to supporting students and families. There is no doubt that professionals and families face real barriers in terms of time, resources, opportunities, and the beliefs of others about what is or is not possible, but by focusing on relationships and remembering the need to come together to solve human problems, we are in a better position to practice the art of collaboration.

RECOGNIZING THE POWER OF FORMAL AND INFORMAL KNOWLEDGE

Many of the lessons learned through our research come back to the idea that collaboration occurs through shared and co-created knowledge that draws on established research as well as knowledge of individual children and families. Although we tend to think of families as the ones who draw on more informal knowledge and professionals as the ones drawing from an established research base, this is not always the case. It seems that a more reciprocal approach to knowledge generation and sharing is appropriate and necessary, especially given the digital and information-rich world in which we live. Technology has moved us well beyond the days when school professionals served as the keepers and disseminators of formal knowledge; now parents access information on a regular basis and may be better informed of cutting edge research than professionals. We propose a more reciprocal and layered approach to thinking about knowledge that recognizes the importance of valuing multiple forms of knowledge (e.g., parents' knowledge of their children at home, parents' knowledge of the research related to their child's specific needs, professionals' knowledge of established research on effective practices, and professionals' knowledge of how children learn and behave in the school settings) and gathering multiple forms of data (e.g., data addressing academic achievement, social-emotional well-being, behavior, and health and mental health, etc.) so as to have thoughtful and balanced discussions about important educational decisions. Both parents and professionals need to acknowledge that information is everywhere and that there will be times when one party has a better grasp on the knowledge base than the other. We need to move away from thinking of "parent expertise" vs. "professional expertise" in a dichotomous sense, and think differently about knowledge as a shared and iterative process in which diverse forms of knowledge and data can serve to inform decisions about what we will pursue with respect to the education of a child with a disability. Figure 2 illustrates this new conception of knowledge, viewing it as a more dynamic and shared process that links the expertise and wisdom of parents and professionals with what is known through research.

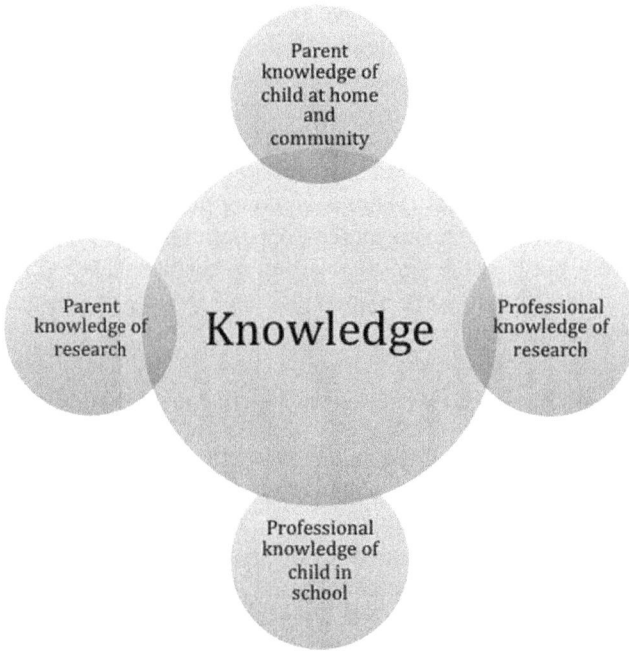

Figure 2. A new conception of parent and professional knowledge

ADVOCATING FOR IMPROVED CONDITIONS FOR COLLABORATION

In acknowledging the complexity of collaboration, we also acknowledge the inter-related set of conditions that appear to promote or inhibit it, as well as the ways in which parents and professionals can advocate for improved collaborative practices. Professionals need to think more deeply about family-centered practices and opportunities for family advocacy and leadership that can lead to a more positive culture of collaboration. Schools need to re-think how special educators and other professionals spend their time, and create more intentional spaces and opportunities for special educators to approach the development of collaborative relationships. We need to acknowledge that collaboration does not just occur in annual, semi-annual, or even monthly meetings; rather, schools need to allow time for special educators to collaborate with families and colleagues and to address the different types of needs that families have over time. Parents need to recognize that many schools do not fully support special educators in this regard and that special educators often feel marginalized.

There is a need for professional development and stronger communities of practice that will support professionals in learning how to advocate for families and in maintaining their support for families with varying levels of need. Programs that prepare special educators need to commit to more extensive approaches to ensuring that future teachers and leaders understand family-school partnerships and have the capacity and will to advocate for improved systems. Similarly, there is a need to support the development of collaborative relationships for families who are in various stages of engagement with special education processes. The supports needed by families of very young children or families who are new to the special education process are quite different from the supports needed by families who have been involved with special education for multiple years, but school systems are not generally equipped to differentiate support based on a family's needs. Family leaders may play a role in identifying the resources and time needed for collaboration in school settings; likewise, we hope that special educators will see their roles as advocates and agents of systems change as central to their identities as special educators, especially as they progress from the early to later stages of their careers.

INCORPORATING STRATEGIES AND TOOLS FOCUSED ON COLLABORATION AS A DEVELOPMENTAL AND GROWTH-ORIENTED PROCESS

It is clear from the stories included in this book that many parents experience collaboration not as an event that occurs within specific meetings, but as a process and a relational experience that develops over time. Professionals can do a great deal to nurture and support parents as they enter the special education system, gain knowledge, learn how to express their choices and advocate for their child, and engage in effective conversations and conflict resolution. Parents' stories about the power of the process of diagnosis suggest that its early phases can set either a positive or negative tone that may carry forward into all future parent-professional relationships. Professionals can assist in ensuring that the early experiences of parents with the special education system (whenever they may occur) include sincere attempts to build trust and to convey information in transparent and accessible ways. Parents may need to be supported in understanding that although their entrance into the world of disability can be scary, it does not need to be negative. We need to do much more to ensure that the early experiences of parents include opportunities for them to connect with others and to access information. Once

185

initial relationships have been formed, professionals need to pay close attention to understanding the particular kinds of support parents may need in understanding and accessing information, becoming acquainted with expectations for meeting structures and collaborative processes, and developing skills in communication and conflict resolution that help to create a sense of equal footing for parents and professionals. At some point (and the time may come earlier for some parents than others) professionals should pay attention for opportunities for families to engage in advocacy and leadership. Clearly, many of the parents interviewed in our studies benefitted greatly from connecting with other parents and engaging in systems change efforts that helped them to see special education and disability policy as a larger effort. It can be helpful for professionals to recognize and help parents identify the kinds of roles they would like to play in their child's education or in the field in general.

As children and families move along in the education system, it is important to think about how the transition to adult life will occur. Many books and articles on collaboration focus primarily on collaboration as it relates to the PK-12 process, but most families understand this as a process occurring over the lifespan and within many contexts. It is imperative that school personnel work alongside parents to give them access to the necessary tools that will guide them through the transition process and beyond.

Along with understanding collaboration as a developmental process, it is critical for both parents and professionals to operate within a growth mindset that remains open to many possibilities. The notion of growth mindset applies both to how professionals and parents view the potential of a child as well as to how they view the possibilities for the development of a collaborative parent-professional relationship. There are too many stories of parents being identified as the "difficult parent," the "squeaky wheel" or the parent who "just doesn't care." These types of labels are damaging to collaboration and represent a fixed view of a parent's relationship with professionals. In looking to a more expanded view of collaboration, we see the need for parents and professionals to be open to the possibility for growth within the partnership, no matter how difficult some parts of the past have been.

In reflecting on the journey that Malik, his family, and school professionals have been on over time, Djenne recalls this process of growth and change. She recounts this final story:

Who would have known? As Malik has grown and matured as a young man, his ability to access and navigate the community has definitely increased! We have had to learn to collaborate in a new and different way with Malik's school and home personnel. We both have had to make adjustments in his educational and personal world to broaden his access to the community as he has become increasingly familiar with his surroundings. The boy knows his way around town! We had to educate his team to understand the breadth of his ability to know where things are and sense of recall. For example, a recent goal on his IEP was the appropriate use of money. The team debated the best way to help him to learn these skills, since he is unable to read or count money in the conventional manner (or so we thought!) We have provided him with a wallet, in his favorite color, red. Malik is now able to communicate that he wants to go to the store and shop and use his own money from his wallet. By working as a team to brainstorm ideas to assist him in learning skills needed in his transition process, Malik has a newfound sense of independence and decision making ability. Now, a new challenge…to keep it stocked full of cash!

ENCOURAGING FAMILIES TO PARTICIPATE IN ACTIVITIES THAT LINK THEM TO OTHERS

In the end, professionals and families need to understand and support whatever it is that helps parents to experience a sense of hope and resiliency. For professionals, this requires getting to know families well, listening to their stories of life outside of school, and recognizing that multiple factors may lead to resiliency, even for families experiencing the most intense challenges. For some families, the journey to hope and resiliency may be experienced in a more inward fashion through a re-framing of their beliefs about disability and diversity, experiences of personal growth and increased confidence, and spiritual or faith connections, however they may be defined. For other families, resiliency emerges in in a more outward journey through connections with others through sports, the arts, faith communities, and other aspects of life in the community.

Many of the families we interviewed told stories of the ways in which their inner and outer journeys contributed to their sense of belonging—both for their child and for the family as a whole. In addition, family members who had opportunities to participate in leadership activities found that as they connected with other families involved in the world of disability, they found a sense of caring and connection that contributed to their own sense of hope. The notion of leadership was defined broadly, occurring within schools and communities, as well as through participation in local, regional and national opportunities for advocacy and leadership. The lesson learned here is that the majority of families seek to find ways to make their lives more positive and whole, and that in connecting with others—at whatever level seems possible or interesting—they may find a sense of community, growth and possibility that helps them to move forward on behalf of their own child, as well as other children, youth and adults with disabilities. Throughout, we see a need to stay focused on the place where the disability movement began—as a space in which parents and others could come together to be allies in the world, envisioning and working towards a new and better future for their children and themselves. Both parties have so much to gain by recognizing and embracing the unique perspectives and skills brought to the table.

ACKNOWLEDGING THE NEED FOR BROADER SOCIAL CHANGE

Clearly, there is a great deal that schools and families can do to strengthen their partnerships and collaborative processes so as to bring about better outcomes for all children with disabilities. At the same time, we acknowledge that there are many families whose lives are so complex that the answers need to be more systemic and broad. Disability is often associated with poverty, trauma, and other challenges that may cross generations. Some families of children with disabilities come from backgrounds that included negative experiences with the education system and it may be hard for them to shed that past. We need to partner with policy makers and change agents to create a world that better supports those who are in the most need. Schools can make a difference, but efforts to make significant changes in the lives of all families will require broader social changes, beginning before children are born, continuing throughout school, and expanding across the lifespan. As parents and professionals, we need to work together to convey a broader message of change that will support families with children with disabilities as well as all families who face the most difficult circumstances.

FINAL THOUGHTS

Parent-professional collaboration can, has, and will work. It takes flexibility, compromise, mutual respect and a belief that working together brings better results than any one of us can achieve alone. It requires us to listen to and care about the well-being of others in search of a shared understanding about what is possible for educators and families to accomplish in school, at home and in the community. Most of all it takes letting go of our biases as parents and professionals—and perhaps our titles and egos – to reach a common goal: a goal that all parents want for their children, a goal that every professional desires for their students. That goal is to see our children learn, grow and become happy and productive members of society. The key is this: within the child lies the REAL teacher and the lessons parents and professionals can all learn as we work collectively and collaboratively for the best of our children. Achieving the art of collaboration is not an easy task, but belief in the process and its benefits seem well worth the effort.

REFERENCE

Jorgenson, C. (2005). The least dangerous assumption: A challenge to create a new paradigm. *Disability Solutions, 6*(3), 1–15.

ABOUT THE AUTHORS

Katharine G. Shepherd, Ed.D., is a professor in the College of Education and Social Services at the University of Vermont. Her teaching and research activities focus on collaboration and leadership development for families of children with disabilities, person-centered approaches in educational planning, and preparation of teachers and leaders for collaborative and inclusive schools. Dr. Shepherd served as co-Principal Investigator of a five- year research study known as *Parents as Collaborative Leaders* funded by the U.S. Department of Education, and is a current co-PI on a federal grant supporting special education leaders who are committed to culturally responsive and family-centered practices that promote the success of all children and youth.

Colby T. Kervick, Ed.D., is an assistant professor in the College of Education and Social Services at the University of Vermont. Dr. Kervick's teaching and research activities focus on effective practices for collaborating with families of children with disabilities, inclusive teaching practices, special education policy, and dual certification teacher preparation. Dr. Kervick teaches undergraduate and graduate courses and supervises pre-service teacher candidates in the field, emphasizing the role that parent and professional collaboration plays in creating inclusive schools. Dr. Kervick also provides consultation and professional development on IEP development, collaboration, inclusive approaches and other topics to selected VT schools.

Djenne-amal N. Morris, B.A., is a national parent/professional trainer, facilitator and motivational speaker whose is most interested in sharing her view of the world not as it is, but as it could be. As a mother of an amazing son with CHARGE Syndrome, she strives to build an atmosphere of support and empowerment for families of children with special needs and the professionals who serve them. Her work with families with children with special needs includes roles as Family Specialist for the New England and North Carolina Deaf-Blind Projects, Parent Educator/Training Coordinator at BEGINNINGS for Parents of Children Who Are Deaf or Hard of Hearing, and member of the Board of Directors for Hands & Voices. Djenne and her husband oversee a consulting business that provides trainings, workshops and personal coaching to families and professionals in the area of family dynamics and special needs (www.todaywithdjenne.com). She lives in Knightdale, N.C., with her husband, Michael, son Malik, 20, and daughters Imani, 21 and Zakiya, 15.

CPSIA information can be obtained
at www.ICGtesting.com
Printed in the USA
LVOW13s1547160618
580974LV00003B/63/P

9 789463 008228